Casio Moonlander

SmokeStack

An Android Echo Server Application

Personal Chat Server Communication

Open Source Technical Website Reference
Documentation 2020-11-15

Volume II: SmokeStack

[Volume I: Smoke]

Impressum

Moonlander, Casio: SmokeStack
    - An Android Echo Server Application:
    Personal Chat Server Communication /
    Open Source Technical Website Reference Documentation 2020-11-15,
    Volume II: SmokeStack,
    Norderstedt 2020, ISBN 9783752692006.

[Volume I: Smoke – ISBN 9783752691993],

Manufacturing & Publisher:
BoD - Books on Demand, Norderstedt.
Further bibliographic Information under: https://portal.dnb.de

This book is also available as ePDF.

Welcome to SmokeStack!

SmokeStack provides mobile server services to the companion application: Smoke.

Smoke is an open source communications project. The purpose of Smoke is to introduce and investigate the Echo protocol on mobile technologies.

Some of the characteristics of Smoke are summarized below.

- Aliases. Preserve your contacts.
- Almost zero-dependency software.
- Argon2id key-derivation function.
- Automatic, oscillatory public-key exchange protocol, EPKS, via SipHash.
- BSD 3-clause license.
- Decentralized. TCP, and UDP multicast and unicast.
- Does not require Internet connectivity.
- Does not require registration. Telephone numbers are not required.
- Fiasco forward secrecy.
- Introduces Cryptographic Discovery. Cryptographic Discovery is a practical protocol which creates coordinated data paths.
- Juggling Juggernaut Protocol!
- McEliece Fujisaka and Pointcheval.
- Message structures do not explicitly expose contents. Header-less protocols!
- Mobile servers via SmokeStack.
- Optional foreground services.
- Post offices for messages of the past.
- Private servers.
- Public and private public-key servers.
- SSL/TLS through SmokeStack.
- Semi-compatible with Spot-On via Fire.
- Share files with TCP utilities such as Netcat.
- Software congestion control.
- Steam file sharing.

Summary of SmokeStack:

- BouncyCastle.
- Client and server functionality.
- Congestion control via SipHash.
- Cryptographic discovery.
- Eventful tasks. Limited polling.
- F-Droid.

- ➢ Infinite participants.
- ➢ Local data recorded in SQLite via authenticated encryption.
- ➢ McEliece support.
- ➢ Private and public post offices via Ozone addresses.
- ➢ Private and public servers.
- ➢ Public-key server.
- ➢ Reliable distribution of messages.
- ➢ SSL, TLS 1.0, 1.1, 1.2, 1.3.
- ➢ SipHash-128.
- ➢ UDP multicast and unicast client services.

This Open Source Technical Website Reference Documentation on paper addresses to students, teachers, and developers to create a Personal Communication Software based on Java for learning and teaching purposes.

Casio Moonlander, 2020-11-15.

Content

About

SmokeStack provides mobile server services to the companion application: Smoke. Smoke is an Android communications project. The software is composed of a single multitasking application.

Application descriptions and the references to the content of this book are available at https://github.com/textbrowser/smoke and https://github.com/textbrowser/smokestack.

https://textbrowser.github.io/smoke/

Activity Authenticate

After launching a prepared Smoke instance, the Authenticate activity is displayed. The original password must be provided. If the correct password is provided, essential containers are populated and the kernel is activated. The previously-accessed activity is also activated.

Smoke may be reset within the Authenticate activity.

Activity Chat

The Chat activity is one of three messaging activities. From this activity, one may message one or more defined participants. The Send button is enabled if at least one participant is selected and a writable neighbor (not necessarily network-ready) is available.

Before a messaging session may begin between two participants, the participants must exchange private key material. Exchanging private key material may be achieved via the Call and Custom Session mechanisms.

A context menu may be activated by pressing and holding on the right-hand Participants widget. Context-menu items are described below.

Custom Session

> Private key material may be generated per the selected participant. The generated material is not transferred over the network. Please note the following conversion of the input string: if the input string's length is less than or equal to 64, the input string is converted to Base64(SHA512(string)).

New Window

> Display a new Member Chat activity with the selected participant.

Optional Signatures

> Messaging and status messages are digitally signed. Signatures may be disabled per participant. Please note that if one party requires digital signatures and digital signatures are not provided by the other party, messages will be ignored by the receiving party. Juggernaut messages and read-acknowledgments are always signed.

Purge Session

> Discard the session's private key material for the specified participant.

Refresh Participants Table

> Refresh the Participants widget.

Retrieve Messages

> Retrieve messages from SmokeStack instances. An Ozone and an active network must be present for this option to be enabled.

Show Details

Disable or enable various Participants details.

Show Icons

Disable or enable Participants status icons.

Activity Fire

The Fire activity is one of three messaging activities. From this activity, one may communicate with one or more groups of anonymous participants. Fire is compatible with Spot-On's Buzz. 256-bit AES-CBC along with SHA-384 HMAC provide encryption and authentication.

The Send button is enabled if at least one network-ready neighbor is available.

Activity Member Chat

The Member Chat activity is one of three messaging activities. From this activity, one may message one participant.

Before a messaging session may begin between two participants, the parties must exchange private key material. Exchanging private key material may be achieved via the Call and Custom Session mechanisms. The Send button is enabled if a session is established and if a writable neighbor (not necessarily network-ready) is available.

Context menus may be activated by pressing and holding various widgets. Context-menu items are described below.

Call via McEliece

Exchange private key material via an ephemeral McEliece ($m = 11$, $t = 50$) public-key pair.

Call via RSA

Exchange private key material via an ephemeral RSA (2048-bit) public-key pair.

Copy Text

Place the selected message's text into the clipboard buffer.

Custom Session

Private key material may be generated. The generated material is not transferred over the network.

Delete All Messages

If confirmed, all messages associated with the specified participant are deleted.

Delete Message

If confirmed, the selected message is deleted.

JuggerKnot Credentials

Display an input dialog. If the dialog is confirmed, the Juggernaut Protocol is initiated with the specified participant. If the protocol completes successfully, authentication and encryption credentials are created.

Juggernaut

Display an input dialog. If the dialog is confirmed, the Juggernaut Protocol is initiated with the specified participant.

Optional Signatures

Messaging and status messages are digitally signed. Signatures may be disabled per participant. Please note that if one party requires digital signatures and digital signatures are not provided by the other party, messages will be ignored by the receiving party. Juggernaut messages and read-acknowledgments are always signed.

Retrieve Messages

Retrieve messages from SmokeStack instances. An Ozone and an active network must be present for this option to be enabled.

Save Attachment

If the selected message contains an image, this option is enabled. Once activated, the attached bitmap is saved.

Activity Settings

The Settings activity contains various configuration items. Smoke may also be reset from this activity. This page will describe miscellaneous portions.

About

Describes software information, including the Android version of the device. Log clearing may also be performed in this section. The Foreground Service option disables or enables a Smoke foreground service. The Prefer Active CPU option, if enabled, ensures that the CPU remains active if the screen is turned off.

Ozone

One Ozone address may be defined in this section. Please refer to the Ozone page for more details.

Participants

A list of participants. A context menu is available.

Password

Generate new local authentication and encryption keys. If confirmed, all existing data will be purged. A new public and private key pair may also be generated.

Public Data

Contains the Smoke Alias and Smoke Chat ID. A Smoke Alias is synonymous to an e-mail address. The Smoke Alias is optional. If provided, it must contain at least eight characters. Preferably, it should be a unique value. A Smoke Identity is synonymous to a telephone number. Basic public-key data are also displayed in this section.

Share Smoke ID

Share the Smoke ID with a SmokeStack instance via the defined Ozone. Please note that the Smoke Alias, if one is defined, is transformed into a Smoke ID.

Activity Smokescreen

Lock or unlock the Smoke application.

Activity Steam

The Steam activity allows for the transferring of files to Steam participants and/or anonymous destinations. Received files are stored in the Downloads folder.

Please note that Simple Steams (files transferred to anonymous destinations) will be streamed sequentially in the order in which they were registered for transfer.

Android

Smoke has been successfully tested on Android versions 7.x, 8.x, and 9.x. Versions older than 7.x are not supported.

Congestion Control

Smoke implements a software-based congestion control mechanism. The SipHash algorithm is used for computing digests. Computed digests are stored in an SQLite database table.

Congestion-control items are inspected every 5 seconds. Items older than 60 seconds are discarded.

Corrupted Database Values

Encrypted database values pose an interesting design problem. How should an application depict a faulty database value to the user if the application is unable to properly decipher an encrypted value? Some software packages ignore the potential problem altogether. Others delete or hide the corrupted entries; logging the failures in squandered logs. Smoke offers an exceptionally-transparent solution. Damaged database entries are depicted in various widgets. These depictions offer insight into potential system failures.

Custom Session Credentials

Credentials are generated as follows (stretch the first key stream):

```
keystream1 := pbkdf2(sha512(string), // Salt
                     string,
                     4096,          // Iteration Count
                     160)           // Bits (20 Bytes)
keystream2 := pbkdf2(sha512(string), // Salt
                     base64(keystream1),
                     1,             // Iteration Count
                     768)           // Bits (96 Bytes)
```

Database Containers

Most of the database fields contain authentically-encrypted values. Some fields contain keyed digests, including keyed digests of binary (false / true) values. Values are stored as $E(Data, K_e)$ || $HMAC(E(Data, K_e), K_a)$ and $HMAC(Data, K_a)$. 256-bit AES-CBC is used for encrypting data. SHA-512 HMAC is used for data authentication.

Developers

Android Studio is required for development. Please download the application from https://developer.android.com/studio/index.html. Building Smoke may be performed via Studio or a terminal. Please refer to the included Makefile and Makefile.linux files for guidance.

Discovery via Cryptography

Cryptographic Discovery is a novel mechanism which allows servers to lighten the computational and data responsibilities of mobile devices.

Shortly after a Smoke instance connects to a SmokeStack service, the Smoke instance shares some non-private material. The material allows a SmokeStack server to transfer messages to their correct destinations.

To mitigate replay attacks, Smoke instances offer SmokeStack instances random identity streams during message-retrieval requests. The identity streams self-expire.

Exchanging Private Credentials

The Calling feature allows two parties to exchange private key material. The process of exchanging private credentials is as follows:

1. A participant issues a Call via a selected participant. A new ephemeral McEliece or RSA public-key pair is generated. A signature binding the two participants is computed. The bundle is then transferred to the recipient.

2. A participant receives the bundle, verifies the included signature, and generates private authentication and encryption keys. The private key material is bundled via the included public McEliece or RSA key. The participant transfers the signed private key material bundle to the initial participant.

3. The initiating participant receives the private key material, verifies the included signature, and unpacks the private key material via the ephemeral private key. The two participants are now paired.

Exporting / Importing Participant Personalities

Smoke provides an elegant, yet tedious, process for exporting and importing participant credentials. Available in the Settings activity, participant credentials may be shared with SmokeStack instances. Simply select individual participants and share the identifiers followed by the public-key personalities. The important process is similarly simple. After participant identifiers have been recorded, request public-key personalities via selected identifiers.

Fiasco Keys

Authentication and encryption key data which are established via the so-called calling mechanism are recorded within the participants_keys database table. Whenever a message from a SmokeStack instance is received, the message's digest is verified using each of the recorded authentication keys. Smoke iterates through the set of Fiasco authentication keys until a correct authentication key is discovered or the search is exhausted. If an authentication key is recovered, the message is deciphered and delivered locally. Newer authentication keys are tested first.

A key pair has a lifetime of 864,000 seconds.

Fire

Fire introduces communication channels between Smoke and Spot-On. Key generation is described below.

```
authentication_key = pbkdf2(sha512(Digest || "sha384"), // Salt
```

```
                  Digest,
                  10000,
                  896)                          // Bits (112 Bytes)
authentication_key, destination_key := authentication_key[0 … 48],
authentication_key[48 … ]
encryption_key := pbkdf2(Salt,
                  Channel || "aes256" || "sha384",
                  10000,         // Iteration Count
                  2304)          // Bits (288 Bytes)
encryption_key := encryption_key[0 … 31]
```

Forward Secrecy and SmokeStack

Smoke includes a mechanism for establishing session-based authentication and encryption keys. The key material is exchanged via ephemeral and permanent public keys. Forward secrecy is constituted by the use of ephemeral public keys.

The Forward Fiasco release provides a mechanism for storing secret key pairs for some period of time. After a message-retrieval request has been initiated, a Smoke instance will attempt to uncover the received content using previously-established secret keys.

Inflate

Smoke expands text-messaging data to 8192 bytes. If the provided data exceeds 8192 bytes, Smoke expands the provided data by 1024 + mod(data length, 2) bytes. Inflation does not apply to Fire as Fire must remain compatible with Spot-On.

Juggernaut Protocol

Smoke implements the Password Authenticated Key Exchange by Juggling protocol. The data are exchanged within a messaging session. Please note the following conversion of the input string: if the input string's length is less than or equal to 64, the input string is converted to Base64(SHA512(string)). JuggerKnot credentials are generated as follows (stretch the first key stream):

```
keystream1 := pbkdf2(sha512(key material), // Salt
                  base64(key material),
                  4096,          // Iteration Count
                  160)           // Bits (20 Bytes)
keystream2 := pbkdf2(sha512(key material), // Salt
                  base64(keystream1),
                  1,             // Iteration Count
                  768)           // Bits (96 Bytes)
```

Please read https://en.wikipedia.org/wiki/Password_Authenticated_Key_Exchange_by_Juggling for more information.

Local Broadcast Manager

Communications between the Kernel and the user interface utilize a Local Broadcast Manager instance.

McEliece CCA2

Smoke supports McEliece-Fujisaki and McEliece-Pointcheval via BouncyCastle. Parameters are SHA-256, m = 11, m = 12 (Fujisaki only), t = 50, t = 68 (Fujisaki only). Some discussions:

- Authentication process may require several minutes to complete.

- Communications between McEliece and RSA are fully functional.

- Degraded performance is expected during key sharing.

- During the key-sharing process, McEliece signatures are not provided and therefore are not verified.

- Initialization processes may require several minutes to complete.

Message Structures

This section will detail the various message structures.

AUTHENTICATE
```
[PK Signature] (1)
{
      Random Bytes (1)                                        Variable
}
```

CALL-HALF-AND-HALF-A
```
[PK] (1)
{
      AES-256 Key (1)
      SHA-512 Key (2)
}


[AES-256] (2)
{
      0x00 (1)                                                1 Byte
      A Timestamp (2)                                         8 Bytes (Base-64)
      \n
      Ephemeral Public Key (3)                               Variable (Base-64)
      \n
      Ephemeral Public Key Type (4)                          1 Byte (Base-64)
      \n
      Sender's Identity (5)                                  8 Bytes (Base-64)
      \n
      Sender's Public Encryption Key SHA-512 Digest (6)    64 Bytes (Base-64)
      \n
      [PK Signature] (7)                                     Variable (Base-64)
      {
            [PK] (1 ... 2) || [AES-256] (1 ... 6) ||
            Recipient's Public Encryption Key SHA-512 Digest (1)
      }
}


[SHA-512 HMAC] (3)                                           64 Bytes
{
      [PK] || [AES-256] (1)
}


/*
** The destination is created via the recipient's Smoke Identity.
*/


[Destination SHA-512 HMAC] (4)                               64 Bytes
{
      [PK] || [AES-256] || [SHA-512] (1)
}
```

CALL-HALF-AND-HALF-B

```
[PK] (1)
{
     AES-256 Key (1)
     SHA-512 Key (2)
}


[AES-256] (2)
{
     0x01 (1)                                              1 Byte
     A Timestamp (2)                                       8 Bytes (Base-64)
     \n
     Ephemeral Public Key (3)                             Variable (Base-64)
     {
          AES-256 Key (1)
          SHA-512 Key (2)
     }
     \n
     Ephemeral Public Key Type (Ignored) (4)              1 Byte (Base-64)
     \n
     Sender's Identity (5)                                8 Bytes (Base-64)
     \n
     Sender's Public Encryption Key SHA-512 Digest (6)    64 Bytes (Base-64)
     \n
     [PK Signature] (7)                                   Variable (Base-64)
     {
          [PK] (1 ... 2) || [AES-256] (1 ... 6) ||
          Recipient's Public Encryption Key SHA-512 Digest (1)
     }
}


[SHA-512 HMAC] (3)                                        64 Bytes
{
     [PK] || [AES-256] (1)
}


/*
** The destination is created via the recipient's Smoke Identity.
*/

[Destination SHA-512 HMAC] (4)                            64 Bytes
{
     [PK] || [AES-256] || [SHA-512] (1)
}
```

CHAT

```
[PK] (1)
{
     Sender's Public Encryption Key SHA-512 Digest (1)    64 Bytes
}


[AES-256] (2)
{
     0x00 (1)                                             1 Byte
     A Timestamp (2)                                      8 Bytes (Base-64)
     \n
     Message (3)                                          Variable (Base-64)
     \n
     Sequence (4)                                         8 Bytes (Base-64)
     \n
     Attachment (5)                                       Variable (Base-64)
     \n
     Message Identity (6)                                 64 Bytes (Base-64)
     \n
     [PK Signature] (7)                                   Variable (Base-64)
     {
```

```
                [PK] (1) || [AES-256] (1 ... 6) ||
                Recipient's Public Encryption Key SHA-512 Digest (1)
        }
}

[SHA-512 HMAC] (3)                                          64 Bytes
{
        [PK] || [AES-256] (1)
}

/*
** The destination is created via the recipient's Smoke Identity.
*/

[Destination SHA-512 HMAC] (4)                              64 Bytes
{
        [PK] || [AES-256] || [SHA-512 HMAC] (1)
}
```

CHAT-RETRIEVAL (Via Ozone)

```
[AES-256] (1)
{
        0x00 (1)                                            1 Byte
        A Timestamp (2)                                     8 Bytes
        An Identity (3)                                     64 Bytes
        Sender's Public Encryption Key SHA-512 Digest (4)  64 Bytes
        [PK Signature] (5)                                  Variable
        {
                [AES-256] (1 ... 4) (1)
        }
}

[SHA-512 HMAC] (2)                                          64 Bytes
{
        [AES-256] (1)
}
```

CHAT-STATUS

```
[PK] (1)
{
        Sender's Public Encryption Key SHA-512 Digest (1)   64 Bytes
}

[AES-256] (2)
{
        0x01 (1)                                            1 Byte
        A Timestamp (2)                                     8 Bytes
        Status (3)                                          1 Byte (Ignored)
        [PK Signature] (4)                                  Variable
        {
                [PK] (1) || [AES-256] (1 ... 3) ||
                Recipient's Public Encryption Key SHA-512 Digest (1)
        }
}

[SHA-512 HMAC] (3)                                          64 Bytes
{
        [PK] || [AES-256] (1)
}

/*
** The destination is created via the recipient's Smoke Identity.
*/

[Destination SHA-512 HMAC] (4)                              64 Bytes
```

```
{
      [PK] || [AES-256] || [SHA-512 HMAC] (1)
}
```

EPKS
```
[AES-256] (1)
{
      A Timestamp (1)                                         8 Bytes (Base-64)
      \n
      Key Type (2)                                            1 Byte (Base-64)
      \n
      Sender's Smoke Identity (3)                             Variable (Base-64)
      \n
      Public Key (4)                                          Variable (Base-64)
      \n
      Public Key Signature ((3) || (4) || (6)) (5)            Variable (Base-64)
      \n
      Signature Public Key (6)                                Variable (Base-64)
      \n
      Signature Public Key Signature ((3) || (4) || (6)) (7)
                                                              Variable (Base-64)
}

[SHA-512 HMAC] (2)                                            64 Bytes
{
      [AES-256] (1)
}

/*
** The destination is created via the recipient's Smoke Identity.
*/

[Destination SHA-512 HMAC] (3)                                64 Bytes
{
      [AES-256] || [SHA-512 HMAC] (1)
}
```

FIRE-CHAT
```
[AES-256] (1)
{
      0040b (1)                                               Base-64
      \n
      Name (2)                                                Base-64
      \n
      ID (3)                                                  Base-64
      \n
      Message (4)                                             Base-64
      \n
      UTC Date (5)                                            Base-64
}

[SHA-384 HMAC] (2)                                            Base-64
{
      [AES-256] (1)
}

[Destination SHA-512 HMAC] (3)                                Base-64
{
      [AES-256] || [SHA-384 HMAC] (1)
}
```

FIRE-STATUS
```
[AES-256] (1)
{
      0040a (1)                                               Base-64
```

```
        \n
        Name (2)                                                     Base-64
        \n
        ID (3)                                                       Base-64
        \n
        UTC Date (4)                                                 Base-64
}


[SHA-384 HMAC] (2)                                                   Base-64
{
        [AES-256] (1)
}


[Destination SHA-512 HMAC] (3)                                       Base-64
{
        [AES-256] || [SHA-384 HMAC] (1)
}
```

JUGGERNAUT

```
[PK] (1)
{
        Sender's Public Encryption Key SHA-512 Digest (1)    64 Bytes
}


[AES-256] (2)
{
        0x03 (1)                                             1 Byte
        A Timestamp (2)                                      8 Bytes (Base-64)
        \n
        Payload (3)                                          Variable (Base-64)
        \n
        [PK Signature] (4)                                   Variable (Base-64)
        {
                [PK] (1) || [AES-256] (1 ... 3) ||
                Recipient's Public Encryption Key SHA-512 Digest (1)
        }
}


[SHA-512 HMAC] (3)                                           64 Bytes
{
        [PK] || [AES-256] (1)
}


/*
** The destination is created via the recipient's Smoke Identity.
*/


[Destination SHA-512 HMAC] (4)                               64 Bytes
{
        [PK] || [AES-256] || [SHA-512 HMAC] (1)
}
```

MESSAGE-READ

```
[PK] (1)
{
        Sender's Public Encryption Key SHA-512 Digest (1)    64 Bytes
}


[AES-256] (2)
{
        0x02 (1)                                             1 Byte
        Message Identity (2)                                 64 Bytes
        [PK Signature] (3)                                   Variable
        {
                [PK] (1) || [AES-256] (1 ... 2) ||
```

```
                  Recipient's Public Encryption Key SHA-512 Digest (1)
      }
}


[SHA-512 HMAC] (3)                                              64 Bytes
{
      [PK] || [AES-256] (1)
}


/*
** The destination is created via the recipient's Smoke Identity.
*/


[Destination SHA-512 HMAC] (4)                                  64 Bytes
{
      [PK] || [AES-256] || [SHA-512] (1)
}
```

MESSAGE-READ (Via Ozone)

```
[AES-256] (1)
{
      0x04 (1)                                                  1 Byte
      A Timestamp (2)                                           8 Bytes
      Message Identity SHA-512 Digest (3)                       64 Bytes
      Sender's Public Encryption Key SHA-512 Digest (4)         64 Bytes
      [PK Signature] (5)                                        Variable
      {
            [AES-256] (1 ... 4) (1)
      }
}


[SHA-512 HMAC] (2)                                              64 Bytes
{
      [AES-256] (1)
}
```

PKP-REQUEST (Via Ozone)

```
[AES-256] (1)
{
      0x01 (1)                                                  1 Byte
      A Timestamp (2)                                           8 Bytes
      Destination Smoke Identity (3)                            Variable
      Requested Smoke Identity (4)                              Variable
}


[SHA-512 HMAC] (2)                                              64 Bytes
{
      [AES-256] (1)
}
```

SHARE-SMOKE-ID (Via Ozone)

```
[AES-256] (1)
{
      0x02 (1)                                                  1 Byte
      A Timestamp (2)                                           8 Bytes
      Smoke Identity (3)                                        Variable
      Temporary Identity (4)                                    8 Bytes
}


[SHA-512 HMAC] (2)                                              64 Bytes
{
      [AES-256] (1)
}
```

SHARE-SMOKE-ID-CONFIRMATION (Via Ozone)

```
[AES-256] (1)
{
     0x03 (1)                                         1 Byte
     A Timestamp (2)                                  8 Bytes
     Smoke Identity (3)                               Variable
     Temporary Identity (4)                           8 Bytes
}

[SHA-512 HMAC] (2)                                    64 Bytes
{
     [AES-256] (1)
}


/*
** The destination is created via the recipient's Smoke Identity.
*/

[Destination SHA-512 HMAC] (3)                        64 Bytes
{
     [AES-256] || [SHA-512] (1)
}
```

STEAM-KEY-EXCHANGE-A

```
[PK] (1)
{
     AES-256 Key (1)
     SHA-512 Key (2)
}

[AES-256] (2)
{
     0x04 (1)                                         1 Byte
     A Timestamp (2)                                  8 Bytes (Base-64)
     \n
     Ephemeral Public Key (3)                         Variable (Base-64)
     \n
     Ephemeral Public Key Type (4)                    1 Byte (Base-64)
     \n
     File Digest (5)                                  32 Bytes (Base-64)
     \n
     File Identity (6)                                48 Bytes (Base-64)
     \n
     File Name (7)                                    Variable (Base-64)
     \n
     File Size (8)                                    8 Bytes (Base-64)
     \n
     Sender's Public Encryption Key SHA-512 Digest (9)   64 Bytes (Base-64)
     \n
     [PK Signature] (10)                              Variable (Base-64)
     {
          [PK] (1 ... 2) || [AES-256] (1 ... 9) ||
          Recipient's Public Encryption Key SHA-512 Digest (1)
     }
}

[SHA-512 HMAC] (3)                                    64 Bytes
{
     [PK] || [AES-256] (1)
}


/*
** The destination is created via the recipient's Smoke Identity.
*/

[Destination SHA-512 HMAC] (4)                        64 Bytes
{
```

```
        [PK] || [AES-256] || [SHA-512] (1)
}
```

STEAM-KEY-EXCHANGE-B

```
[PK] (1)
{
      AES-256 Key (1)
      SHA-512 Key (2)
}


[AES-256] (2)
{
      0x05 (1)                                              1 Byte
      A Timestamp (2)                                       8 Bytes (Base-64)
      \n
      Ephemeral Public Key (3)                             Variable (Base-64)
      {
            AES-256 Key (1)
            SHA-512 Key (2)
      }
      \n
      Ephemeral Public Key Type (4)                        1 Byte (Base-64)
      \n
      File Digest (5)                                       32 Bytes (Base-64)
      \n
      File Identity (6)                                     48 Bytes (Base-64)
      \n
      File Name (Empty) (7)                                 Variable (Base-64)
      \n
      File Size (8)                                         8 Bytes (Base-64)
      \n
      Sender's Public Encryption Key SHA-512 Digest (9)    64 Bytes (Base-64)
      \n
      [PK Signature] (10)                                  Variable (Base-64)
      {
            [PK] (1 ... 2) || [AES-256] (1 ... 9) ||
            Recipient's Public Encryption Key SHA-512 Digest (1)
      }
}

[SHA-512 HMAC] (3)                                         64 Bytes
{
      [PK] || [AES-256] (1)
}

/*
** The destination is created via the recipient's Smoke Identity.
*/

[Destination SHA-512 HMAC] (4)                             64 Bytes
{
      [PK] || [AES-256] || [SHA-512] (1)
}
```

STEAM-SHARE-A

```
[PK] (1)
{
      File Identity (1)                                     48 Bytes
}


[AES-256] (2)
{
      0x06 (1)                                              1 Byte
      A Timestamp (2)                                       8 Bytes
      File Offset (3)                                       8 Bytes
```

```
        File Packet (4)                                         Variable
}

[SHA-512 HMAC] (3)                                          64 Bytes
{
     [PK] || [AES-256] (1)
}

/*
** The destination is created via the recipient's Smoke Identity.
*/

[Destination SHA-512 HMAC] (4)                              64 Bytes
{
     [PK] || [AES-256] || [SHA-512] (1)
}
```

STEAM-SHARE-B
```
[PK] (1)
{
     File Identity (1)                                      48 Bytes
}

[AES-256] (2)
{
     0x07 (1)                                               1 Byte
     A Timestamp (2)                                        8 Bytes
     File Offset (3)                                        8 Bytes
}

[SHA-512 HMAC] (3)                                          64 Bytes
{
     [PK] || [AES-256] (1)
}

/*
** The destination is created via the recipient's Smoke Identity.
*/

[Destination SHA-512 HMAC] (4)                              64 Bytes
{
     [PK] || [AES-256] || [SHA-512] (1)
}
```

Neighbors

Neighbors may be defined via the Settings activity. This page will describe the various nuances of network peers.

Smoke offers infinitely-many IPv4 and IPv6 TCP and UDP client definitions. Each network peer includes dedicated and independent data-parsing, socket-reading, and socket-writing tasks. TCP neighbors support HTTP and SOCKS proxies. Please note that host translations are not performed via assigned proxies.

Initialize Ozone

If enabled, the Ozone credentials will be generated from the specified neighbor values. For example, let's suppose that a SmokeStack is attached to the service bee.service.org:4710. When preparing the neighbor information in Smoke using the aforementioned SmokeStack destination, the Ozone will be initialized to bee.service.org:4710:TCP. In SmokeStack, the Ozone bee.service.org:4710:TCP should also be defined. When completed, the Smoke and SmokeStack instances are artificially paired.

Non-TLS

Allows the neighbor to observe traditional socket operations.

Passthrough

Passthrough neighbors are special full-duplex connections which Smoke utilizes for distributing data to non-Smoke destinations. Data which is received on passthrough connections is echoed directly to other non-passthrough neighbors if echoing is enabled.

A menu accompanies each defined neighbor.

Connect

> Instruct Smoke to place the specified neighbor in a connect status. Connection attempts are performed every 2.5 seconds. A TCP socket is required to connect within 10 seconds. After a connection is established, the SSL/TLS handshake must complete within 10 seconds.

Delete

> Display a confirmation prompt. If confirmed, the specified neighbor is scheduled for deletion.

Disconnect

> Instruct Smoke to place the specified neighbor in a disconnected status.

Purge Queue

> Purge the outbound queue of the specified neighbor.

Reset SSL/TLS Credentials

> Reset the locally-stored SSL/TLS credentials of a TCP neighbor.

A connected neighbor attempts to read 1 MiB of data from its socket every 100 milliseconds. The read request blocks indefinitely. Data are appended to an internal buffer. The internal buffer may accumulate at most 8 MiB of data, with the potential of overflow. Parsing of data occurs every 100 milliseconds. Because the parsing and read tasks are independent, it's possible that the internal buffer may temporarily overflow by $1024^2 - 1$ bytes.

Each neighbor object includes two internal queues, Echo and real-time queues. Echo queues allow Smoke to echo internal data from local neighbor to local neighbor. This mechanism must be enabled via the Echo option. Each Echo queue may contain at most 256 messages. Please note that the Echo mechanism may burden a device. A neighbor will echo data if it discovers that the data are not intended for it. Calling, Chat statuses, Fire statuses, and SmokeStack message-retrieval requests utilize real-time queues. Real-time queues are not limited.

Various per-neighbor statistics are included in the Settings activity. Also included are per-neighbor descriptive errors.

New Installation

After launching a new installation of Smoke, some initial settings are required.

Encryption

> Public-key algorithm. McEliece-Fujisaki, McEliece-Pointcheval, and 3072-bit RSA are supported.

Iteration Count

> Local authentication and encryption keys are generated via Argon2id or PBKDF2. The functions require an iteration count. If the selected value exceeds 10 for Argon2id or 7500 for PBKDF2, a confirmation prompt is displayed.

Password

> At least one character is required.

Signature

> Public-key digital signatures. 384-bit ECDSA and 3072-bit RSA are supported.

Outbound Queues

Smoke offers near-real-time communications. As network services may be unreliable, certain outbound messages are enqueued in an SQLite database table. Each network peer is assigned a separate queue. Messages are dequeued in a timely manner and placed onto the network. Calling messages, retrieval of offline messages, and status messages are considered disposable and are therefore written to network sockets regardless of network availability.

Please note that peers which are in disconnected status-control states are ignored during the enqueue processes.

Ozone Address

An Ozone address may be assigned via the Settings activity. An Ozone address is a pseudo-private string which identifies a virtual entity. Smoke and SmokeStack utilize Ozones as a means of retrieving and storing offline messages and public-key pairs. Smoke supports one Ozone while SmokeStack supports infinitely many. Ozone addresses must be exchanged separately. It is possible for multiple Smoke parties to house distinct Ozones if common SmokeStack instances are aware of the distinct Ozone addresses.

If an Ozone address is defined and the network is available, Smoke will request external messages once per minute.

Please note that public Ozone addresses will introduce denial of service vulnerabilities.

Participants

Smoke Identities may be defined within the Participants section of the Settings activity. After defining a participant, local public-key pairs may be shared manually. An automatic process distributes key pairs to participants which have not been paired. A context menu may be activated by pressing and holding on the Participants widget. The contents of the context menu are described below.

Delete (Smoke Identity)

> Delete the selected participant. A confirmation dialog is displayed.

Delete Fiasco Keys (Smoke Identity)

> Delete all of the recorded Fiasco keys. The current session keys of the selected participant are not deleted. A confirmation dialog is displayed.

Delete Public Keys (Smoke Identity)

> Delete the Fiasco and public keys of the specified participant. A confirmation dialog is displayed.

New Name (Smoke Identity)

> Assign a new name to the selected participant.

Request Keys via Ozone (Smoke Identity)

> Submit a public-key request to SmokeStack instances via the selected Smoke Identity. An Ozone address must be defined for this option to be enabled.

Share Keys Of (Smoke Identity)

The selected participant's public-key pair is distributed using the specified Smoke Identity. If a public-key pair does not exist for the specified participant, the option is disabled.

Share Smoke ID Of (Smoke Identity)

The selected participant's Smoke Identity is distributed using the defined Ozone address. An Ozone address must be defined for this option to be enabled.

View Details (Smoke Identity)

View details of the selected participant.

Performance Considerations

Smoke is a multi-tasking process and several of its internal operations are performed in separate tasks, thus allowing the main thread to remain as responsive as possible.

- A single Steam writer records packets to respective files. The writer contains a separate task for storing status information.

- A special database cursor is maintained for rapid access to data for the Member Chat activity. The cursor is synchronized in various logical regions.

- Automatic requesting of SmokeStack messages is performed in a separate task.

- Neighbor data are written in a separate task.

- Neighbor objects are prepared in a separate task.

- Neighbor statistics and statuses are prepared in a separate task.

- Network data are read in a separate task. Accumulated data are also parsed in a separate task.

- Network status information is gathered in a separate task and reported to the main thread.

- Outbound messages (Chat, Fire, Juggernaut, Message Retrieval Request, Share Smoke Identity) are prepared in a separate task.

- Participant calling keys are generated in a separate task.

- Participant elements for various interface widgets are gathered in a separate task.

- Public-key publications are performed in a separate task.

- Purging of expired Juggernaut credentials, congestion control data, and participant key streams is performed in a separate task.

- Purging of expired temporary identifiers is performed in a separate task.

- Purging of malformed outbound data and participants is performed in a separate task.

- Purging of neighbor queues is performed in a separate task.

- Status message broadcasting is performed in a separate task.

- Steam files are distributed on separate tasks. A separate task prepares Steam tasks.

- Steam files are read in separate tasks.

Private Public-Key Server

In addition to housing messages, SmokeStack also serves as a private public-key server. A SmokeStack administrator is responsible for coordinating the storage of public-key pairs of participants. Participants may request public-key pairs of specific participants via Ozone addresses.

Private Servers

SmokeStack supports the concept of private servers for TCP clients. A private server will disregard non-authentication data until a remote peer has been authenticated. The authentication process is as follows:

1. A private server generates a 64-byte stream of random data and concatenates the data with the current system time.

2. The server submits the SHA-512 hash of the information generated in the previous step to the remote peer after the SSL/TLS handshake has been completed. The server will repeatedly submit unique information every 10 seconds until the peer has authenticated itself.

3. The remote peer retrieves a stream of 64 random bytes as well as its signature key digest. It digitally signs the 64 random bytes, the signature key digest, and the original stream of random data and submits the 64 random bytes, the signature key digest, and the digital signature to the remote server. Please note that SmokeStack servers are conceptually indistinguishable from one another. Therefore, remote peers do not provide SmokeStack identifiers during this step.

4. The server reviews the two random-byte streams for uniqueness. If the two byte streams are dissimilar, it validates the digital signature. If the digital signature is valid and the two random-byte streams are dissimilar, the remote peer is authenticated.

Please define private servers after the desired participants have been completely defined in SmokeStack. This is required because SmokeStack instances must be in possession of public-key pairs.

Please note that multiple devices may contain identical Smoke instances. Thus, several identical Smoke instances may authenticate themselves with a given SmokeStack instance.

Smoke Aliases

A Smoke Alias is a unique stream of characters. The minimum length of a Smoke Alias is eight. Similar to e-mail addresses and telephone numbers, Smoke Aliases allow simple pairing of participants. Internally, a Smoke Alias is transformed into a Smoke Identity via the SipHash algorithm. Let's consider a simple pairing scenario:

1. Participant vanya@nasa.gov assigns the Smoke Alias in the Public Data section of the Settings activity. Once assigned, the participant notifies other participants via e-mail or another form of communication.
2. Notified participants define vanya@nasa.gov within the Participants section of the Settings activity. The Smoke Alias option must be enabled.
3. Participants notify vanya@nasa.gov of their aliases.
4. Within new instances, the pairing process is automatically initiated once the participants are online. Pairing may also be performed via the Share Keys mechanism.

Please note that a Smoke instance must synchronize itself with a remote server after a new Smoke Alias is assigned within Public Data. Synchronization generally completes in approximately 15 seconds.

A Smoke identity is generated as follows:

```
id := siphash(alias,
           pbkdf2(sha512(alias), // Salt
                     alias,
                     4096, // Iteration Count
                     128)) // Bits (16 Bytes)
```

Smoke Identities

Exchanging public-key pairs is often an involved process. Smoke implements the pseudo-random function SipHash to simplify the process. The SipHash function generates outputs of 128 bits (16 bytes). A Smoke identity is generated as follows:

```
id := siphash(public-encryption-key || public-signature-key,
            pbkdf2(sha512(public-encryption-key || public-signature-key), // Salt
                    public-encryption-key || public-signature-key,
                    4096, // Iteration Count
                    128)) // Bits (16 Bytes)
```

Non-confidential authentication and encryption key streams from a Smoke identity are generated as follows (elongate the first key stream):

```
keystream1 := pbkdf2(sha512(id), // Salt
                    id,
                    4096,         // Iteration Count
                    160)          // Bits (20 Bytes)
keystream2 := pbkdf2(sha512(id), // Salt
                    base64(keystream1),
                    1,            // Iteration Count
                    768)          // Bits (96 Bytes)
```

The transport keys which are generated from Smoke identities may be used for exchanging public-key data via the Echo Public-Key Share (EPKS) protocol.

It is impossible to avoid SipHash collisions as there are infinitely-many inputs and a limited number of outputs.

Smoke Pipes (Simple Steams)

Piping through Smoke allows for the transfer of data from Smoke devices to network-capable, non-Smoke devices. The process is as follows:

1. Define a passthrough network interface in the Settings activity. Optionally, disable or enable TLS. If TLS is enabled, it is expected that the defined endpoint supports TLS.

2. Prepare the endpoint service on the destination device. In this example: nc -l 192.168.178.15 4710 > output.

3. In the Steam activity, select a single file and specify the destination as Other (Non-Smoke). Tag the file for transfer. Repeat as often as desired.

4. Resume each file.

5. The first file to be tagged is the first file to be transferred.

Using commands such as head and tail, it's possible to partition the output file into separate files. Data may also be piped to multiple endpoints.

A concrete example follows.

1. In a console: "nc -k -l 192.168.178.15 4710 > output". If necessary, disable the firewall or prepare specific firewall rules on the destination device.

2. Define the non-TLS passthrough 192.168.178.15:4710 in Smoke's Settings activity.

3. Prepare 3 image files for distribution in Smoke.

4. Activate the Rewind & Resume All Steams context-menu option in the Steam activity.

5. Once the 3 files have been transferred, observe the file sizes of each Steam.

6. In a console: "head -c sizeof(file a) output > file1".

7. In a console: "sha256 file1". The digest must match the digest provided by Smoke.

8. In a console: "tail -c "$((sizeof(file a) + sizeof(file b)))" output | head -c sizeof(file a) > file2".

9. In a console: "sha256 file2". The digest must match the digest provided by Smoke.

10. In a console: "tail -c sizeof(file c) output > file3".

11. Finally: "sha256 file3". The digest must match the digest provided by Smoke.

The Scripts directory contains a program for partitioning a received aggregate into individual components.

Software Distribution

Smoke is distributed in debug (smoke-debug.apk) form. Sometimes, a release (smoke.apk) form is also distributed. The release bundle is signed and may include the source.

Steam Ephemeral Key Exchange

Please note that this protocol is a partial forward secrecy key exchange as the generator of the ephemeral public-key pair temporarily records the pair in an SQLite database. The ephemeral key-pair is removed from the database after a response is received from the destination participant. The destination participant removes the ephemeral public key after the first packet is recorded.

1. Generate an ephemeral public-key pair. A public-key pair is generated per file. Do not generate a public-key pair if one already exists or if private keys (4) have been recorded.

2. Locally record the ephemeral public-key pair.

3. Transfer the ephemeral public key to the destination participant.

4. Destination receives the ephemeral public key and generates private keys. Do not generate private keys if private keys already exist.

5. Locally record the private keys, unless the private keys exist.

6. Destination encrypts the private keys via the ephemeral public key and submits the results to the source participant.

7. Source participant receives the bundle and deciphers the private keys via the ephemeral private key.

8. Source participant records the private keys (4).

9. Source participant deletes the ephemeral public-key pair from the local SQLite database.

10. Destination participant the deletes ephemeral public key after the first packet of the Steam is recorded.

TCP, UDP Protocols

Smoke supports both the TCP and UDP network protocols. Multicast and unicast UDP varieties are provided. Multiple clients may be defined via the Settings activity. A limit on the number of clients is not imposed. When defining neighbors, one may define SmokeStack and/or Spot-On neighbors. SmokeStack, the companion application of Smoke, offers mobile server services as well as message and public-key storage.

Example UDP multicast address: 239.255.43.21.

Task Utilization

Smoke is an extremely task-oriented application. For example, the Kernel object utilizes 10 tasks while a single Neighbor object spawns 4 tasks. Various tasks are also defined in the activities.

Time

Time references are included in various message structures. Therefore, it is important that a device's local clock is correct. Smoke also performs numerous internal processes which are time-sensitive.

Smoke shall notify the operator if the device's Unix time differs from the Unix time of an external source by approximately five seconds. Notifications, if enabled, will occur every thirty seconds.

UDP Datagrams

Outbound UDP messages are partitioned into 576-byte datagrams. For example, a 15000-byte message will be partitioned into 27 datagrams.

Verifying Public-Key Ownership

Before initiating an exchange of public-key pairs, Smoke generates digital signatures using the private keys of the encryption and signature public keys. The digital signatures are composed of the concatenation of the public encryption and signature keys. The signatures are included in the EPKS bundle. A recipient verifies the signatures and accepts the public-key pairs if the signatures are valid. McEliece signatures are not included and are therefore not verified. Summary:

1. Concatenate the encoded forms of the encryption and the signature public keys.
2. Digitally sign the concatenated product using the private encryption key.
3. Digitally sign the concatenated product using the private signature key.
4. Bundle the two digital signatures.

dir /s >directory.txt

```
Directory of C:\

05.12.2020  11:52    <DIR>          .
05.12.2020  11:52    <DIR>          ..
12.11.2020  14:09    <DIR>          smokestack-2020.11.15
05.12.2020  11:54                47 directory.txt
              1 File(s),           47 Bytes

 Directory of C:\smokestack-2020.11.15

12.11.2020  14:09    <DIR>          .
12.11.2020  14:09    <DIR>          ..
12.11.2020  14:09               284 Android
12.11.2020  14:09    <DIR>          Documentation
12.11.2020  14:09    <DIR>          Images
12.11.2020  14:09             1.025 Makefile
12.11.2020  14:09             3.358 Makefile.linux
12.11.2020  14:09               605 README.md
12.11.2020  14:09    <DIR>          Scripts
12.11.2020  14:09    <DIR>          SmokeStack
12.11.2020  14:09             1.294 TO-DO
12.11.2020  14:09               203 adb.bash
12.11.2020  14:09             1.179 smokestack-download-dependencies.bash
              7 File(s),        7.948 Bytes

 Directory of C:\smokestack-2020.11.15\Documentation

12.11.2020  14:09    <DIR>          .
12.11.2020  14:09    <DIR>          ..
12.11.2020  14:09               124 BouncyCastle
12.11.2020  14:09               214 DESTINATION-ORIGIN-IDENTITY
12.11.2020  14:09               279 MESSAGES-CHAT-RETRIEVAL
12.11.2020  14:09               554 MESSAGES-EPKS
12.11.2020  14:09               283 MESSAGES-MESSAGE-READ
12.11.2020  14:09               212 MESSAGES-PKP-REQUEST
12.11.2020  14:09               194 MESSAGES-SHARE-SIPHASHID
12.11.2020  14:09               351 MESSAGES-SHARE-SIPHASHID-CONFIRMATION
12.11.2020  14:09             6.549 RELEASE-NOTES.html
12.11.2020  14:09               793 SIPHASH.README
12.11.2020  14:09           365.541 SipHash.pdf
             11 File(s),      375.094 Bytes

 Directory of C:\smokestack-2020.11.15\Images

12.11.2020  14:09    <DIR>          .
12.11.2020  14:09    <DIR>          ..
12.11.2020  14:09            83.512 smokestack_1.png
              1 File(s),       83.512 Bytes

 Directory of C:\smokestack-2020.11.15\Scripts

12.11.2020  14:09    <DIR>          .
12.11.2020  14:09    <DIR>          ..
12.11.2020  14:09               119 openssl-connection-test.bash
              1 File(s),          119 Bytes

 Directory of C:\smokestack-2020.11.15\SmokeStack

12.11.2020  14:09    <DIR>          .
```

```
12.11.2020  14:09    <DIR>                    ..
12.11.2020  14:09                     118 .gitignore
12.11.2020  14:09    <DIR>                    app
12.11.2020  14:09                     518 build.gradle
12.11.2020  14:09                     702 gradle.properties
12.11.2020  14:09    <DIR>                    gradle
12.11.2020  14:09                   4.971 gradlew
12.11.2020  14:09                   2.404 gradlew.bat
12.11.2020  14:09                      15 settings.gradle
                   6 File(s),          8.728 Bytes

 Directory of C:\smokestack-2020.11.15\SmokeStack\app

12.11.2020  14:09    <DIR>                    .
12.11.2020  14:09    <DIR>                    ..
12.11.2020  14:09                       7 .gitignore
12.11.2020  14:09                   1.582 build.gradle
12.11.2020  14:09    <DIR>                    libs
12.11.2020  14:09                     654 proguard-rules.pro
12.11.2020  14:09    <DIR>                    src
                   3 File(s),          2.243 Bytes

 Directory of C:\smokestack-2020.11.15\SmokeStack\app\libs

12.11.2020  14:09    <DIR>                    .
12.11.2020  14:09    <DIR>                    ..
12.11.2020  14:09                 887.810 bcpkix-jdk15on-167.jar
12.11.2020  14:09               1.616.435 bcpkix-jdk15on-167.tar.gz
12.11.2020  14:09               6.031.520 bcprov-ext-jdk15on-167.jar
12.11.2020  14:09               9.715.254 bcprov-jdk15on-167.tar.gz
                   4 File(s),       18.251.019 Bytes

 Directory of C:\smokestack-2020.11.15\SmokeStack\app\src

12.11.2020  14:09    <DIR>                    .
12.11.2020  14:09    <DIR>                    ..
12.11.2020  14:09    <DIR>                    main
                   0 File(s),              0 Bytes

 Directory of C:\smokestack-2020.11.15\SmokeStack\app\src\main

12.11.2020  14:09    <DIR>                    .
12.11.2020  14:09    <DIR>                    ..
12.11.2020  14:09                   1.433 AndroidManifest.xml
12.11.2020  14:09    <DIR>                    java
12.11.2020  14:09    <DIR>                    res
                   1 File(s),          1.433 Bytes

 Directory of C:\smokestack-2020.11.15\SmokeStack\app\src\main\java

12.11.2020  14:09    <DIR>                    .
12.11.2020  14:09    <DIR>                    ..
12.11.2020  14:09    <DIR>                    org
                   0 File(s),              0 Bytes

 Directory of C:\smokestack-2020.11.15\SmokeStack\app\src\main\java\org

12.11.2020  14:09    <DIR>                    .
12.11.2020  14:09    <DIR>                    ..
12.11.2020  14:09    <DIR>                    purple
                   0 File(s),              0 Bytes

 Directory of C:\smokestack-2020.11.15\SmokeStack\app\src\main\java\org\purple
```

```
12.11.2020  14:09    <DIR>              .
12.11.2020  14:09    <DIR>              ..
12.11.2020  14:09    <DIR>              smokestack
               0 File(s),              0 Bytes

 Directory of C:\smokestack-
2020.11.15\SmokeStack\app\src\main\java\org\purple\smokestack

12.11.2020  14:09    <DIR>              .
12.11.2020  14:09    <DIR>              ..
12.11.2020  14:09              2.695 About.java
12.11.2020  14:09              9.712 Authenticate.java
12.11.2020  14:09              2.224 ClientBubble.java
12.11.2020  14:09              1.592 ClientElement.java
12.11.2020  14:09             16.979 Cryptography.java
12.11.2020  14:09            103.323 Database.java
12.11.2020  14:09             32.549 Kernel.java
12.11.2020  14:09              2.071 ListenerElement.java
12.11.2020  14:09              3.344 ListenersAdapter.java
12.11.2020  14:09              1.667 MessageTotals.java
12.11.2020  14:09              9.509 Messages.java
12.11.2020  14:09             11.657 Miscellaneous.java
12.11.2020  14:09             17.048 Neighbor.java
12.11.2020  14:09              2.427 NeighborElement.java
12.11.2020  14:09              1.659 OzoneElement.java
12.11.2020  14:09             81.183 Settings.java
12.11.2020  14:09              7.564 SipHash.java
12.11.2020  14:09              2.029 SipHashIdElement.java
12.11.2020  14:09              2.451 SmokeStack.java
12.11.2020  14:09              4.056 SmokeStackService.java
12.11.2020  14:09              3.607 State.java
12.11.2020  14:09             16.392 TcpListener.java
12.11.2020  14:09             17.437 TcpNeighbor.java
12.11.2020  14:09              6.791 UdpMulticastNeighbor.java
12.11.2020  14:09              6.906 UdpNeighbor.java
              25 File(s),        366.872 Bytes

 Directory of C:\smokestack-2020.11.15\SmokeStack\app\src\main\res

12.11.2020  14:09    <DIR>              .
12.11.2020  14:09    <DIR>              ..
12.11.2020  14:09    <DIR>              drawable
12.11.2020  14:09    <DIR>              layout
12.11.2020  14:09    <DIR>              menu
12.11.2020  14:09    <DIR>              values
               0 File(s),              0 Bytes

 Directory of C:\smokestack-2020.11.15\SmokeStack\app\src\main\res\drawable

12.11.2020  14:09    <DIR>              .
12.11.2020  14:09    <DIR>              ..
12.11.2020  14:09              1.100 help.png
12.11.2020  14:09                832 keys_not_signed.png
12.11.2020  14:09                933 keys_signed.png
12.11.2020  14:09                295 sectiongradient.xml
12.11.2020  14:09              4.174 smokestack.png
12.11.2020  14:09                937 warning.png
               6 File(s),          8.271 Bytes

 Directory of C:\smokestack-2020.11.15\SmokeStack\app\src\main\res\layout

12.11.2020  14:09    <DIR>              .
```

```
12.11.2020  14:09    <DIR>                 ..
12.11.2020  14:09                 2.226 activity_authenticate.xml
12.11.2020  14:09                32.764 activity_settings.xml
12.11.2020  14:09                   424 client_bubble.xml
               3 File(s),           35.414 Bytes

 Directory of C:\smokestack-2020.11.15\SmokeStack\app\src\main\res\menu

12.11.2020  14:09    <DIR>                 .
12.11.2020  14:09    <DIR>                 ..
12.11.2020  14:09                   341 authenticate_menu.xml
12.11.2020  14:09                   342 settings_menu.xml
               2 File(s),              683 Bytes

 Directory of C:\smokestack-2020.11.15\SmokeStack\app\src\main\res\values

12.11.2020  14:09    <DIR>                 .
12.11.2020  14:09    <DIR>                 ..
12.11.2020  14:09                   205 colors.xml
12.11.2020  14:09                   211 dimens.xml
12.11.2020  14:09                 2.448 strings.xml
12.11.2020  14:09                   380 styles.xml
               4 File(s),            3.244 Bytes

 Directory of C:\smokestack-2020.11.15\SmokeStack\gradle

12.11.2020  14:09    <DIR>                 .
12.11.2020  14:09    <DIR>                 ..
12.11.2020  14:09    <DIR>                 wrapper
               0 File(s),                0 Bytes

 Directory of C:\smokestack-2020.11.15\SmokeStack\gradle\wrapper

12.11.2020  14:09    <DIR>                 .
12.11.2020  14:09    <DIR>                 ..
12.11.2020  14:09                53.636 gradle-wrapper.jar
12.11.2020  14:09                   230 gradle-wrapper.properties
               2 File(s),           53.866 Bytes

              77 File(s),      19.198.493 Bytes
              62 Directory(s)
```

Android

https://raw.githubusercontent.com/textbrowser/smokestack/master/Android
SmokeStack has been successfully tested on Android versions
4.4, 5.0, 5.1, 6.0, 7.0, and 7.1.

Android versions 4.4, 5.0, and 5.1 are not officially supported.

According to https://developer.android.com/about/dashboards/index.html,
SmokeStack supports 92.7% of all Android versions.

Makefile

https://raw.githubusercontent.com/textbrowser/smokestack/master/Makefile
```
UNAME := $(shell uname)

ifeq ($(UNAME), Linux)
        MAKEFILE=Makefile.linux
else
        MAKEFILE=Makefile.windows
endif

all:
        $(MAKE) -f $(MAKEFILE)

clean:
        $(MAKE) -f $(MAKEFILE) clean

clear-smokestack:
        $(MAKE) -f $(MAKEFILE) clear-smokestack

copy-apk:
        $(MAKE) -f $(MAKEFILE) copy-apk

debug-with-source:
        $(MAKE) -f $(MAKEFILE) debug-with-source

distclean:
        $(MAKE) -f $(MAKEFILE) distclean

kill-adb-server:
        $(MAKE) -f $(MAKEFILE) kill-adb-server

kill-gradle-daemon:
        $(MAKE) -f $(MAKEFILE) kill-gradle-daemon

launch-emulator:
        $(MAKE) -f $(MAKEFILE) launch-emulator

list-devices:
        $(MAKE) -f $(MAKEFILE) list-devices

list-files:
        $(MAKE) -f $(MAKEFILE) list-files

load-apk:
        $(MAKE) -f $(MAKEFILE) load-apk

load-apk-release:
        $(MAKE) -f $(MAKEFILE) load-apk-release
```

```
pull-database:
        $(MAKE) -f $(MAKEFILE) pull-database

purge:
        $(MAKE) -f $(MAKEFILE) purge

release:
        $(MAKE) -f $(MAKEFILE) release

remove-database:
        $(MAKE) -f $(MAKEFILE) remove-database

stop-smokestack:
        $(MAKE) -f $(MAKEFILE) stop-smokestack
```


Makefile.linux

https://raw.githubusercontent.com/textbrowser/smokestack/master/Makefile.linux

```
# You must have at least one AVD defined.


ADB = ~/Android/Sdk/platform-tools/adb
EMULATOR = ~/Android/Sdk/tools/emulator
GRADLEW = ./SmokeStack/gradlew
JARSIGNER = "/snap/android-studio/current/android-studio/jre/bin/jarsigner"
JDK = "/snap/android-studio/current/android-studio/jre"
export JAVA_HOME = /snap/android-studio/current/android-studio/jre

all:
        $(GRADLEW) -Dorg.gradle.java.home=$(JDK) \
        -Dorg.gradle.warning.mode=all \
        --build-file SmokeStack/build.gradle assembleDebug \
        --configure-on-demand --daemon --parallel

clean:
        rm -f SmokeStack/app/src/main/assets/smokestack.src.d.zip
        rm -f smokestack.src.d.zip
        $(GRADLEW) --build-file SmokeStack/build.gradle clean

clear-smokestack:
        ./adb.bash shell pm clear org.purple.smokestack

copy-apk: all
        cp ./SmokeStack/app/build/outputs/apk/debug/apk/smokestack.apk \
        ~/Desktop/.

debug-with-source: clean all
        rm -rf SmokeStack/build SmokeStack/captures
        mkdir -p SmokeStack/app/src/main/assets
        zip -r smokestack.src.d.zip \
        Android \
        Documentation \
        Makefile \
        Makefile.linux \
        README.md \
        Scripts \
        SmokeStack \
        TO-DO \
        adb.bash \
        fastlane \
        smokestack-download-dependencies.bash \
        -x *.git* -x *.gradle* -x *.idea* \
```

```makefile
	&& mv smokestack.src.d.zip SmokeStack/app/src/main/assets/.
	$(GRADLEW) -Dorg.gradle.java.home=$(JDK) \
	--build-file SmokeStack/build.gradle assembleDebug \
	--configure-on-demand --daemon --parallel
	rm -f SmokeStack/app/src/main/assets/smokestack.src.d.zip

distclean: clean kill-adb-server kill-gradle-daemon
	rm -f smokestack.db

kill-adb-server:
	$(ADB) kill-server

kill-gradle-daemon:
	$(GRADLEW) --stop

launch-emulator:
	$(EMULATOR) -netdelay none -netspeed full -avd \
	`$(EMULATOR) -list-avds | sort | sed "1q;d"` &

list-devices:
	$(ADB) devices -l

list-files:
	./adb.bash shell run-as org.purple.smokestack \
	ls -l /data/data/org.purple.smokestack/databases

load-apk: all
	./adb.bash install -r \
	./SmokeStack/app/build/outputs/apk/debug/apk/smokestack.apk
	./adb.bash shell am start -S -W \
	-n org.purple.smokestack/org.purple.smokestack.Settings \
	-a android.intent.action.MAIN -c android.intent.category.LAUNCHER

load-apk-release: release
	$(JARSIGNER) -verbose -keystore \
	~/Android-Keys/smokestack-release.keystore \
	./SmokeStack/app/build/outputs/apk/release/apk/smokestack.apk \
	smokestack
	$(JARSIGNER) -verify \
	./SmokeStack/app/build/outputs/apk/release/apk/smokestack.apk
	./adb.bash install -r \
	./SmokeStack/app/build/outputs/apk/release/apk/smokestack.apk
	./adb.bash shell am start -S -W \
	-n org.purple.smokestack/org.purple.smokestack.Settings \
	-a android.intent.action.MAIN -c android.intent.category.LAUNCHER

pull-database:
	./adb.bash exec-out run-as org.purple.smokestack cat \
	/data/data/org.purple.smokestack/databases/smokestack.db > smokestack.db

purge:
	find . -name '*~*' -exec rm -f {} \;

release: clean
	rm -rf SmokeStack/build SmokeStack/captures
	$(GRADLEW) -Dorg.gradle.java.home=$(JDK) \
	--build-file SmokeStack/build.gradle assembleRelease \
	--configure-on-demand --daemon --parallel
	rm -f SmokeStack/app/src/main/assets/smokestack.src.d.zip

remove-database:
	./adb.bash shell run-as org.purple.smokestack \
	rm -f /data/data/org.purple.smokestack/databases/smokestack.db
```

```
    ./adb.bash shell run-as org.purple.smokestack \
    rm -f /data/data/org.purple.smokestack/databases/smokestack.db-journal

stop-smokestack:
    ./adb.bash shell am force-stop org.purple.smokestack
```

README.md

https://raw.githubusercontent.com/textbrowser/smokestack/master/README.md
Summary of SmokeStack

```
<ul>
<li>BouncyCastle.</li>
<li>Client and server functionality.</li>
<li>Congestion control via SipHash.</li>
<li>Cryptographic discovery.</li>
<li>Eventful tasks. Limited polling.</li>
<li>F-Droid.</li>
<li>Infinite participants.</li>
<li>Local data recorded in SQLite via authenticated encryption.</li>
<li>McEliece support.</li>
<li>Private and public post offices via Ozone addresses.</li>
<li>Private and public servers.</li>
<li>Public-key server.</li>
<li>Reliable distribution of messages.</li>
<li>SSL, TLS 1.0, 1.1, 1.2, 1.3.</li>
<li>SipHash-128.</li>
<li>UDP multicast and unicast client services.</li>
</ul>
```

TO-DO

https://raw.githubusercontent.com/textbrowser/smokestack/master/TO-DO
Completed Items

- Allow removal of messages per participant.
- Create a single statement in purgeReleasedMessages() to delete specific
OIDs.
- Decrease the lock area of m_stringBuilder in Neighbor.java.
- Discovery via cryptography.
- Dialogs are not dismissed correctly on rotation changes. Unable to
  reproduce.
- Display the number of internal Neighbors.
- Echo shared Smoke identities.
- Enable android:largeHeap=true.
- Entries in routing_identities expire.
- Fire compatibility.
- Integrate EOM in Messages.java.
- Listeners.
- Message accounting.
- Optional signatures on shared key pairs.
- Per-participant message retrieval schedulers.
- Populate containers in the kernel as required.
- Private servers are susceptible to replay attacks.
- Private servers. SHA-512 (Random || Time).
- Purge expired messages.
- Refresh Ozones.
- Rename participant in Participants section.
- Replace SipHash ID with Smoke ID.

- Share-identity confirmation.
- Signed release.
- TLS 1.3 and Android 10.
- Verify status of requested messages. Smoke also.
- m_isValidCertificate should be an AtomicBoolean.

Remaining Items

- Abnormal native termination on Android 8.x. SSL/TLS and/or libc.
- Distribute routing identity algorithms.
- Future-proof.
- The Settings activity has many views (ANDROID_LINT_MAX_VIEW_COUNT).

adb.bash

https://raw.githubusercontent.com/textbrowser/smokestack/master/adb.bash

```bash
#!/bin/bash

adb="${HOME}/Android/Sdk/platform-tools/adb"

$adb devices | sort -u | grep 'device$' | while read line
do
    device=$(echo $line | awk '{print $1}')
    $adb -s $device $@ &
    wait
done
```


smokestack-download-dependencies.bash

https://raw.githubusercontent.com/textbrowser/smokestack/master/smokestack-download-dependencies.bash

```bash
#!/bin/bash

# Must be executed in the top-level source directory.

# Bouncy Castle

bouncycastle1=bcpkix-jdk15on-167.jar
bouncycastle2=bcprov-ext-jdk15on-167.jar

rm -f $bouncycastle1
rm -f $bouncycastle2
wget --progress=bar https://bouncycastle.org/download/$bouncycastle1
wget --progress=bar https://bouncycastle.org/download/$bouncycastle2

if [ -r "$bouncycastle1" ]; then
    mv $bouncycastle1 SmokeStack/app/libs/.
else
    echo "Cannot read $bouncycastle1."
fi

if [ -r "$bouncycastle2" ]; then
    mv $bouncycastle2 SmokeStack/app/libs/.
else
    echo "Cannot read $bouncycastle2."
fi

echo "Please review SmokeStack/app/build.gradle and SmokeStack/app/libs!"
```

Documentation

https://github.com/textbrowser/smokestack/tree/master/Documentation

```
Directory of C:\smokestack-2020.11.15\Documentation
12.11.2020  14:09    <DIR>              .
12.11.2020  14:09    <DIR>              ..
12.11.2020  14:09                124 BouncyCastle
12.11.2020  14:09                214 DESTINATION-ORIGIN-IDENTITY
12.11.2020  14:09                279 MESSAGES-CHAT-RETRIEVAL
12.11.2020  14:09                554 MESSAGES-EPKS
12.11.2020  14:09                283 MESSAGES-MESSAGE-READ
12.11.2020  14:09                212 MESSAGES-PKP-REQUEST
12.11.2020  14:09                194 MESSAGES-SHARE-SIPHASHID
12.11.2020  14:09                351 MESSAGES-SHARE-SIPHASHID-CONFIRMATION
12.11.2020  14:09              6.549 RELEASE-NOTES.html
12.11.2020  14:09                793 SIPHASH.README
12.11.2020  14:09            365.541 SipHash.pdf
               11 File(s),        375.094 Bytes

124 BouncyCastle
Please keep SmokeStack/app/build.gradle and SmokeStack/app/libs current.
https://www.bouncycastle.org/latest_releases.html

214 DESTINATION-ORIGIN-IDENTITY
Various message constructs require destination tags. A destination
tag may be created, for example, as SHA-512(Data, Destination-Identity). An
identity should be unique. Identities are not considered confidential.

279 MESSAGES-CHAT-RETRIEVAL
[AES-256] (1)
{
     0x00 (1)                                   1 Byte
     A Timestamp (2)                              8 Bytes
     An Identity (3)                             64 Bytes
     Sender's Public Encryption Key SHA-512 Digest (4)  64 Bytes
     [PK Signature] (5)                         Variable
     {
          [AES-256] (1 ... 4) (1)
     }
}

[SHA-512 HMAC] (2)                                64 Bytes
{
     [AES-256] (1)
}


554 MESSAGES-EPKS
[AES-256] (1)
{
     A Timestamp (1)                  8 Bytes (Base-64)
     \n
     Key Type (2)                     1 Byte (Base-64)
     \n
     Sender's Smoke Identity (3)      Variable (Base-64)
     \n
     Public Key (4)                   Variable (Base-64)
     \n
     Public Key Signature (5)         Variable (Base-64)
     \n
     Signature Public Key (6)         Variable (Base-64)
     \n
```

```
    Signature Public Key Signature (7)      Variable (Base-64)
}

[SHA-512 HMAC] (2)                          64 Bytes
{
    [AES-256] (1)
}

/*
** The destination is created via the recipient's SipHash identity.
*/

[Destination SHA-512 HMAC] (3)              64 Bytes
{
    [AES-256] || [SHA-512 HMAC] (1)
}


283 MESSAGES-MESSAGE-READ
[AES-256] (1)
{
    0x04 (1)                                1 Byte
    A Timestamp (2)                            8 Bytes
    Message Identity (3)                       64 Bytes
    Sender's Public Encryption Key SHA-512 Digest (4)  64 Bytes
    [PK Signature] (5)                         Variable
    {
        [AES-256] (1 ... 4) (1)
    }
}

[SHA-512 HMAC] (2)                          64 Bytes
{
    [AES-256] (1)
}

212 MESSAGES-PKP-REQUEST
[AES-256] (1)
{
    0x01 (1)                                1 Byte
    A Timestamp (2)                            8 Bytes
    Destination SipHash Identity (3)        Variable
    Requested SipHash Identity (4)              Variable
}

[SHA-512 HMAC] (2)                          64 Bytes
{
    [AES-256] (1)
}


194 MESSAGES-SHARE-SIPHASHID
[AES-256] (1)
{
    0x02 (1)                                1 Byte
    A Timestamp (2)                            8 Bytes
    SipHash Identity (3)                     Variable
    Temporary Identity (4)                   8 Bytes
}

[SHA-512 HMAC] (2)                          64 Bytes
{
    [AES-256] (1)
```

```
}


351 MESSAGES-SHARE-SIPHASHID-CONFIRMATION
[AES-256] (1)
{
    0x03 (1)                                   1 Byte
    A Timestamp (2)                               8 Bytes
    SipHash Identity (3)                          Variable
    Temporary Identity (4)                        8 Bytes
}

[SHA-512 HMAC] (2)                            64 Bytes
{
    [AES-256] (1)
}

/*
** The destination is created via the recipient's SipHash identity.
*/

[Destination SHA-512 HMAC] (3)                      64 Bytes
{
    [AES-256] || [SHA-512 HMAC] (1)
}


793 SIPHASH.README
SipHash identities are generated as follows:

id := siphash(public-encryption-key || public-signature-key,
         pbkdf2(sha512(public-encryption-key || public-signature-key), //
Salt
               public-encryption-key || public-signature-key,
               4096,       // Iteration Count
               128))       // Bits (16 Bytes)

Generating of non-confidential authentication and encryption key streams from
SipHash identities:

keystream1 := pbkdf2(sha512(id), // Salt
              id,
              4096,       // Iteration Count
              160)        // Bits (20 Bytes)
keystream2 := pbkdf2(sha512(id), // Salt
              keystream1,
              1,          // Iteration Count
              768)        // Bits (96 Bytes)

The contents of keystream2 may be used to distribute public key pairs
as well as other non-confidential material.
```

RELEASE-NOTES.html

https://github.com/textbrowser/smokestack/tree/master/Documentation


```
2020.11.15
<br>
<ol>
  <li>Bouncy Castle 1.67.</li>
```

```
  <li>SipHash-128.</li>
</ol>
2020.08.30
<br>
<ol>
  <li>Modified primary key on stack database table. SmokeStack must be
reinstalled.</li>
  <li>Reliable message distribution.</li>
  <li>Removed SecureRandom.getInstance("SHA1PRNG").</li>
</ol>
2020.08.10
<br>
<ol>
  <li>Brief pause after message-retrieval request. Allows for distribution of
random identities.</li>
</ol>
2020.08.08
<br>
<ol>
  <li>Configure SO_RCVBUF and SO_SNDBUF to 32 KiB.</li>
  <li>Deregister broadcast manager within onPause().</li>
  <li>Enabled large heap size.</li>
  <li>Improved removal of released messages.</li>
  <li>Manual garbage collection.</li>
</ol>
2020.07.11
<br>
<ol>
  <li>Pause if necessary.</li>
</ol>
2020.07.07
<br>
<ol>
  <li>Bouncy Castle 1.66!</li>
  <li>Eventful tasks.</li>
  <li>TLS 1.3.</li>
</ol>
2020.06.10
<br>
<ol>
  <li>Toggle listener privacy. New context menu item.</li>
</ol>
2020.05.15
<br>
<ol>
  <li>TLS 1.3 on Android 10. Android 10 or newer is required.</li>
</ol>
2020.04.22
<br>
<ol>
  <li>Bouncy Castle 1.65!</li>
  <li>Increased TLS public key sizes to 3048 bits. May not be supported by
legacy Android versions.</li>
  <li>WakeLock and WifiLock Kernel members.</li>
</ol>
2020.04.04
<br>
<ol>
  <li>Create Ozone on Listener creation.</li>
</ol>
2020.02.25
<br>
<ol>
```

```
  <li>Depict remote peers.</li>
</ol>
2020.02.02
<br>
<ol>
  <li>Legacy devices. Replaced Integer.BYTES, Long.BYTES.</li>
</ol>
2019.12.10
<br>
<ol>
  <li>Bouncy Castle version 1.64.</li>
  <li>Corrected the private server authentication protocol.</li>
</ol>
2019.09.30
<br>
<ol>
  <li>Allocate resources in onStart().</li>
  <li>Bouncy Castle version 1.63.</li>
  <li>Corrected recording of shared public keys via EPKS. The previous
implementation recorded keys within incorrect participants.</li>
  <li>Exit option. May be incomplete on some devices.</li>
  <li>New icons.</li>
  <li>Protect buffers against overflow.</li>
</ol>
2019.04.14
<br>
<ol>
  <li>Properly create strings from bytes.</li>
</ol>
2019.04.04
<br>
<ol>
  <li>Close Java streams.</li>
  <li>Release resources.</li>
  <li>Removed deepCopy().</li>
</ol>
2019.03.03
<br>
<ol>
  <li>Decreased buffer size from 32 MiB to 8 MiB.</li>
  <li>Purge buffer contents via delete() instead of setLength(0).</li>
</ol>
2019.02.25
<br>
<ol>
  <li>Bouncy Castle version 1.61.</li>
  <li>Foreground service.</li>
</ol>
2019.02.04
<br>
<ol>
  <li>Gather statistics in a timely manner.</li>
</ol>
2019.02.02
<br>
<ol>
  <li>Array lengths are positive or zero.</li>
  <li>Automatic removal of incorrect network data.</li>
  <li>Corrected conditional in UdpMulticastNeighbor::send().</li>
  <li>Replaced Spongy Castle with Bouncy Castle. Please replace existing
listeners.</li>
  <li>Smaller lock regions.</li>
  <li>StringBuilder over StringBuffer, if possible.</li>
```

</ol>
2018.10.10

<ol>
  <li>Compute SHA-512 display digest of PEM(certificate).</li>
  <li>Initialize widgets within onResume().</li>
  <li>Inspect String::substring() parameters.</li>
  <li>New server (tulip-ipv4.tilaa.cloud).</li>
</ol>
2018.09.01

<ol>
  <li>Corrected echoing of data of remote peers.</li>
  <li>New message_digest field in the outbound_queue database table.
SmokeStack must be reset.</li>
  <li>New statistics.</li>
</ol>
2018.08.29

<ol>
  <li>Lock SipHash::hmac().</li>
  <li>Removed the Echo Queue container from the Neighbor class. The database
table outbound_queue has been modified. Please reset SmokeStack.</li>
</ol>
2018.08.26

<ol>
  <li>More socket writes per second.</li>
  <li>New statistics. SmokeStack must be reset.</li>
  <li>Notify Android system of software version.</li>
</ol>
2018.08.22

<ol>
  <li>Exceptions and optimizations.</li>
</ol>
2018.08.21

<ol>
  <li>Corrected password entry on new instances.</li>
  <li>Corrected widget states on new instances.</li>
</ol>
2018.08.19

<ol>
  <li>Blocking socket reads.</li>
  <li>Bouncy Castle has been upgraded to version 1.60.</li>
  <li>Broadcasting of device identities has been removed. Lighter
cryptographic discovery.</li>
  <li>Fire is now compatible with SmokeStack.</li>
  <li>Material Design-compliant colors.</li>
  <li>New Smoke identity format.</li>
  <li>Private servers.</li>
  <li>Some member variables in the Neighbor class were incorrectly defined as
static.</li>
</ol>
2018.04.04

<ol>
  <li>Display the first discovered IP address of the device in the Listeners
IP Address field.</li>
  <li>Limit the number of identities to 512.</li>
  <li>LocalBroadcastManager instances.</li>

```
</ol>
2018.03.20
<br>
<ol>
  <li>Replaced some insert() statements with insertOrThrow().</li>
</ol>
2018.03.03
<br>
<ol>
  <li>Corrected local echo behavior.</li>
  <li>Host translation must be performed before every socket connection
attempt.</li>
  <li>Large-area congestion-control mutex.</li>
  <li>Partition data over UDP links into 576-byte datagrams.</li>
</ol>
2018.02.20
<br>
<ol>
  <li>Corrected abortive socket releases.</li>
  <li>Disconnect listeners on loss of WiFi.</li>
</ol>
2018.02.10
<br>
<ol>
  <li>Denote corrupted database values.</li>
  <li>McEliece support.</li>
</ol>
2018.01.01
<br>
<ol>
  <li>Spongy Castle archives prov and core have been upgraded to version
1.58.0.0.</li>
</ol>
2017.08.19
<br>
<ol>
  <li>Purge neighbor statistics shortly after launch.</li>
  <li>Set a non-zero SO_TIMEOUT as some devices do not unblock socket reads
after sockets are closed.</li>
</ol>
2017.07.20
<br>
<ol>
  <li>Do not attempt to send duplicate data.</li>
  <li>Do not linger on server socket close.</li>
  <li>Do not specify timeouts in socket reads as separate threads are
responsible for socket reads.</li>
  <li>Per-participant message retrieval is fine.</li>
  <li>Removed non-necessary Thread.sleep() instances.</li>
  <li>Replaced StringBuilder Neighbor member with StringBuffer. StringBuffer
is thread-safe.</li>
  <li>Signed release.</li>
  <li>Some server socket operations must be performed before the sockets are
bound.</li>
  <li>WiFi lock.</li>
</ol>
2017.07.16
<br>
<ol>
  <li>Corrected outbound-queued statistic.</li>
  <li>Less computations on disconnected neighbors.</li>
  <li>Per-participant message retrieval is too expensive. Replaced with single
thread.</li>
```

```
</ol>
2017.07.09
<br>
<ol>
  <li>Allow renaming of existing participants.</li>
  <li>Discard duplicate public keys on arrival.</li>
  <li>Smaller database transaction areas.</li>
</ol>
2017.07.07
<br>
<ol>
  <li>SmokeStack as a private public key repository.</li>
</ol>
```

openssl-connection-test.bash

https://raw.githubusercontent.com/textbrowser/smokestack/master/Scripts/openss
l-connection-test.bash

```bash
#!/bin/bash
# A test script.

for i in {1 .. 10};
do
    openssl s_client -connect 192.168.178.30:4710 &
done
sleep 10
```

.gitignore

https://raw.githubusercontent.com/textbrowser/smokestack/master/SmokeStack/.gi
tignore

```
*.iml
.gradle
/local.properties
/.idea/workspace.xml
/.idea/libraries
.DS_Store
/build
/captures
.externalNativeBuild
```

build.gradle

https://raw.githubusercontent.com/textbrowser/smokestack/master/SmokeStack/bui
ld.gradle

```gradle
// Top-level build file where you can add configuration options common to all
sub-projects/modules.

buildscript {
    repositories {
      google()
      jcenter()
    }
    dependencies {
        classpath 'com.android.tools.build:gradle:4.1.0'

        // NOTE: Do not place your application dependencies here; they belong
```

```
        // in the individual module build.gradle files
    }
}

allprojects {
    repositories {
        jcenter()
        google()
    }
}

task clean(type: Delete) {
    delete rootProject.buildDir
}
```


gradle.properties

https://raw.githubusercontent.com/textbrowser/smokestack/master/SmokeStack/gra
dle.properties
```
# Project-wide Gradle settings.

# IDE (e.g. Android Studio) users:
# Gradle settings configured through the IDE *will override*
# any settings specified in this file.

# For more details on how to configure your build environment visit
# http://www.gradle.org/docs/current/userguide/build_environment.html

# Specifies the JVM arguments used for the daemon process.
# The setting is particularly useful for tweaking memory settings.


# When configured, Gradle will run in incubating parallel mode.
# This option should only be used with decoupled projects. More details, visit
#
http://www.gradle.org/docs/current/userguide/multi_project_builds.html#sec:dec
oupled_projects
# org.gradle.parallel=true
```


gradlew

https://raw.githubusercontent.com/textbrowser/smokestack/master/SmokeStack/gra
dlew
```
#!/usr/bin/env bash

##############################################################################
##
##  Gradle start up script for UN*X
##
##############################################################################

# Add default JVM options here. You can also use JAVA_OPTS and GRADLE_OPTS to
pass JVM options to this script.
DEFAULT_JVM_OPTS=""

APP_NAME="Gradle"
APP_BASE_NAME=`basename "$0"`

# Use the maximum available, or set MAX_FD != -1 to use that value.
```

```bash
MAX_FD="maximum"

warn ( ) {
    echo "$*"
}

die ( ) {
    echo
    echo "$*"
    echo
    exit 1
}

# OS specific support (must be 'true' or 'false').
cygwin=false
msys=false
darwin=false
case "`uname`" in
  CYGWIN* )
    cygwin=true
    ;;
  Darwin* )
    darwin=true
    ;;
  MINGW* )
    msys=true
    ;;
esac

# Attempt to set APP_HOME
# Resolve links: $0 may be a link
PRG="$0"
# Need this for relative symlinks.
while [ -h "$PRG" ] ; do
    ls=`ls -ld "$PRG"`
    link=`expr "$ls" : '.*-> \(.*\)$'`
    if expr "$link" : '/.*' > /dev/null; then
        PRG="$link"
    else
        PRG=`dirname "$PRG"`"/$link"
    fi
done
SAVED="`pwd`"
cd "`dirname \"$PRG\"`/" >/dev/null
APP_HOME="`pwd -P`"
cd "$SAVED" >/dev/null

CLASSPATH=$APP_HOME/gradle/wrapper/gradle-wrapper.jar

# Determine the Java command to use to start the JVM.
if [ -n "$JAVA_HOME" ] ; then
    if [ -x "$JAVA_HOME/jre/sh/java" ] ; then
        # IBM's JDK on AIX uses strange locations for the executables
        JAVACMD="$JAVA_HOME/jre/sh/java"
    else
        JAVACMD="$JAVA_HOME/bin/java"
    fi
    if [ ! -x "$JAVACMD" ] ; then
        die "ERROR: JAVA_HOME is set to an invalid directory: $JAVA_HOME

Please set the JAVA_HOME variable in your environment to match the
location of your Java installation."
    fi
```

```bash
else
    JAVACMD="java"
    which java >/dev/null 2>&1 || die "ERROR: JAVA_HOME is not set and no
'java' command could be found in your PATH.

Please set the JAVA_HOME variable in your environment to match the
location of your Java installation."
fi

# Increase the maximum file descriptors if we can.
if [ "$cygwin" = "false" -a "$darwin" = "false" ] ; then
    MAX_FD_LIMIT=`ulimit -H -n`
    if [ $? -eq 0 ] ; then
        if [ "$MAX_FD" = "maximum" -o "$MAX_FD" = "max" ] ; then
            MAX_FD="$MAX_FD_LIMIT"
        fi
        ulimit -n $MAX_FD
        if [ $? -ne 0 ] ; then
            warn "Could not set maximum file descriptor limit: $MAX_FD"
        fi
    else
        warn "Could not query maximum file descriptor limit: $MAX_FD_LIMIT"
    fi
fi

# For Darwin, add options to specify how the application appears in the dock
if $darwin; then
    GRADLE_OPTS="$GRADLE_OPTS \"-Xdock:name=$APP_NAME\" \"-
Xdock:icon=$APP_HOME/media/gradle.icns\""
fi

# For Cygwin, switch paths to Windows format before running java
if $cygwin ; then
    APP_HOME=`cygpath --path --mixed "$APP_HOME"`
    CLASSPATH=`cygpath --path --mixed "$CLASSPATH"`
    JAVACMD=`cygpath --unix "$JAVACMD"`

    # We build the pattern for arguments to be converted via cygpath
    ROOTDIRSRAW=`find -L / -maxdepth 1 -mindepth 1 -type d 2>/dev/null`
    SEP=""
    for dir in $ROOTDIRSRAW ; do
        ROOTDIRS="$ROOTDIRS$SEP$dir"
        SEP="|"
    done
    OURCYGPATTERN="(^($ROOTDIRS))"
    # Add a user-defined pattern to the cygpath arguments
    if [ "$GRADLE_CYGPATTERN" != "" ] ; then
        OURCYGPATTERN="$OURCYGPATTERN|($GRADLE_CYGPATTERN)"
    fi
    # Now convert the arguments - kludge to limit ourselves to /bin/sh
    i=0
    for arg in "$@" ; do
        CHECK=`echo "$arg"|egrep -c "$OURCYGPATTERN" -`
        CHECK2=`echo "$arg"|egrep -c "^-"`                              ###
Determine if an option

        if [ $CHECK -ne 0 ] && [ $CHECK2 -eq 0 ] ; then                ###
Added a condition
            eval `echo args$i`=`cygpath --path --ignore --mixed "$arg"`
        else
            eval `echo args$i`="\"$arg\""
        fi
        i=$((i+1))
```

```bash
    done
    case $i in
        (0) set -- ;;
        (1) set -- "$args0" ;;
        (2) set -- "$args0" "$args1" ;;
        (3) set -- "$args0" "$args1" "$args2" ;;
        (4) set -- "$args0" "$args1" "$args2" "$args3" ;;
        (5) set -- "$args0" "$args1" "$args2" "$args3" "$args4" ;;
        (6) set -- "$args0" "$args1" "$args2" "$args3" "$args4" "$args5" ;;
        (7) set -- "$args0" "$args1" "$args2" "$args3" "$args4" "$args5"
"$args6" ;;
        (8) set -- "$args0" "$args1" "$args2" "$args3" "$args4" "$args5"
"$args6" "$args7" ;;
        (9) set -- "$args0" "$args1" "$args2" "$args3" "$args4" "$args5"
"$args6" "$args7" "$args8" ;;
    esac
fi

# Split up the JVM_OPTS And GRADLE_OPTS values into an array, following the
shell quoting and substitution rules
function splitJvmOpts() {
    JVM_OPTS=("$@")
}
eval splitJvmOpts $DEFAULT_JVM_OPTS $JAVA_OPTS $GRADLE_OPTS
JVM_OPTS[${#JVM_OPTS[*]}]="-Dorg.gradle.appname=$APP_BASE_NAME"

exec "$JAVACMD" "${JVM_OPTS[@]}" -classpath "$CLASSPATH"
org.gradle.wrapper.GradleWrapperMain "$@"
```


gradlew.bat

https://raw.githubusercontent.com/textbrowser/smokestack/master/SmokeStack/gradlew.bat

```bat
@if "%DEBUG%" == "" @echo off
@rem
@rem ##########################################################################
@rem
@rem  Gradle startup script for Windows
@rem
@rem
@rem ##########################################################################

@rem Set local scope for the variables with windows NT shell
if "%OS%"=="Windows_NT" setlocal

@rem Add default JVM options here. You can also use JAVA_OPTS and GRADLE_OPTS
to pass JVM options to this script.
set DEFAULT_JVM_OPTS=

set DIRNAME=%~dp0
if "%DIRNAME%" == "" set DIRNAME=.
set APP_BASE_NAME=%~n0
set APP_HOME=%DIRNAME%

@rem Find java.exe
if defined JAVA_HOME goto findJavaFromJavaHome

set JAVA_EXE=java.exe
%JAVA_EXE% -version >NUL 2>&1
if "%ERRORLEVEL%" == "0" goto init
```

```bat
echo.
echo ERROR: JAVA_HOME is not set and no 'java' command could be found in your
PATH.
echo.
echo Please set the JAVA_HOME variable in your environment to match the
echo location of your Java installation.

goto fail

:findJavaFromJavaHome
set JAVA_HOME=%JAVA_HOME:"=%
set JAVA_EXE=%JAVA_HOME%/bin/java.exe

if exist "%JAVA_EXE%" goto init

echo.
echo ERROR: JAVA_HOME is set to an invalid directory: %JAVA_HOME%
echo.
echo Please set the JAVA_HOME variable in your environment to match the
echo location of your Java installation.

goto fail

:init
@rem Get command-line arguments, handling Windowz variants

if not "%OS%" == "Windows_NT" goto win9xME_args
if "%@eval[2+2]" == "4" goto 4NT_args

:win9xME_args
@rem Slurp the command line arguments.
set CMD_LINE_ARGS=
set _SKIP=2

:win9xME_args_slurp
if "x%~1" == "x" goto execute

set CMD_LINE_ARGS=%*
goto execute

:4NT_args
@rem Get arguments from the 4NT Shell from JP Software
set CMD_LINE_ARGS=%$

:execute
@rem Setup the command line

set CLASSPATH=%APP_HOME%\gradle\wrapper\gradle-wrapper.jar

@rem Execute Gradle
"%JAVA_EXE%" %DEFAULT_JVM_OPTS% %JAVA_OPTS% %GRADLE_OPTS% "-
Dorg.gradle.appname=%APP_BASE_NAME%" -classpath "%CLASSPATH%"
org.gradle.wrapper.GradleWrapperMain %CMD_LINE_ARGS%

:end
@rem End local scope for the variables with windows NT shell
if "%ERRORLEVEL%"=="0" goto mainEnd

:fail
rem Set variable GRADLE_EXIT_CONSOLE if you need the _script_ return code
instead of
rem the _cmd.exe /c_ return code!
if  not "" == "%GRADLE_EXIT_CONSOLE%" exit 1
```

```
exit /b 1

:mainEnd
if "%OS%"=="Windows_NT" endlocal

:omega
```

settings.gradle

https://raw.githubusercontent.com/textbrowser/smokestack/master/SmokeStack/settings.gradle
```
include ':app'
```

.gitignore

https://raw.githubusercontent.com/textbrowser/smokestack/master/SmokeStack/app/.gitignore
```
/build
```

build.gradle

https://raw.githubusercontent.com/textbrowser/smokestack/master/SmokeStack/app/build.gradle

```
apply plugin: 'com.android.application'

android {
    compileSdkVersion 25
    defaultConfig {
        buildConfigField "long", "BUILD_TIME", System.currentTimeMillis() + "L"
        applicationId "org.purple.smokestack"
        minSdkVersion 19
        multiDexEnabled true
        targetSdkVersion 26
        testInstrumentationRunner "android.support.test.runner.AndroidJUnitRunner"
        versionCode 20201115
        versionName "2020.11.15"
    }
    dexOptions {
        javaMaxHeapSize "8g"
    }
    buildTypes {
        android.applicationVariants.all { variant ->
            variant.outputs.all {
                outputFileName = "./apk/smokestack.apk"
            }
        }

        release {
            minifyEnabled false
            proguardFiles getDefaultProguardFile('proguard-android.txt'),
'proguard-rules.pro'
        }
    }
}
```

```gradle
dependencies {
    androidTestImplementation('com.android.support.test.espresso:espresso-
core:2.2.2', {
        exclude group: 'com.android.support', module: 'support-annotations'
    })
    implementation 'com.android.support.constraint:constraint-layout:1.1.2'
    implementation 'com.android.support:appcompat-v7:25.4.0'
    implementation 'com.android.support:design:25.4.0'
    implementation 'com.android.support:support-v4:25.4.0'
    implementation fileTree(include: ['*.jar'], dir: 'libs')
    implementation files('libs/bcpkix-jdk15on-167.jar')
    implementation files('libs/bcprov-ext-jdk15on-167.jar')
    testImplementation 'junit:junit:4.12'
}

tasks.withType(JavaCompile) {
    options.compilerArgs << "-Xlint:all"
}
```

proguard-rules.pro

https://raw.githubusercontent.com/textbrowser/smokestack/master/SmokeStack/app/proguard-rules.pro

```
# Add project specific ProGuard rules here.
# By default, the flags in this file are appended to flags specified
# in /home/pluto/Android/Sdk/tools/proguard/proguard-android.txt
# You can edit the include path and order by changing the proguardFiles
# directive in build.gradle.
#
# For more details, see
#   http://developer.android.com/guide/developing/tools/proguard.html

# Add any project specific keep options here:

# If your project uses WebView with JS, uncomment the following
# and specify the fully qualified class name to the JavaScript interface
# class:
#-keepclassmembers class fqcn.of.javascript.interface.for.webview {
#    public *;
#}
```

Libs

https://github.com/textbrowser/smokestack/tree/master/SmokeStack/app/libs

```
12.11.2020   14:09      <DIR>              .
12.11.2020   14:09      <DIR>              ..
12.11.2020   14:09               887.810 bcpkix-jdk15on-167.jar
12.11.2020   14:09             1.616.435 bcpkix-jdk15on-167.tar.gz
12.11.2020   14:09             6.031.520 bcprov-ext-jdk15on-167.jar
12.11.2020   14:09             9.715.254 bcprov-jdk15on-167.tar.gz
                4 File(s),    18.251.019 Bytes
```

AndroidManifest.xml


```xml
<?xml version="1.0" encoding="utf-8"?>
<manifest xmlns:android="http://schemas.android.com/apk/res/android"
    package="org.purple.smokestack">

    <uses-permission android:name="android.permission.ACCESS_NETWORK_STATE" />
    <uses-permission android:name="android.permission.INTERNET" />
    <uses-permission android:name="android.permission.WAKE_LOCK" />

    <application
        android:name=".SmokeStack"
        android:allowBackup="true"
        android:icon="@drawable/smokestack"
        android:label="@string/app_name"
      android:largeHeap="true"
        android:supportsRtl="true"
        android:theme="@style/AppTheme">
        <activity
            android:name=".Authenticate"
            android:label="SmokeStack"
            android:noHistory="true" />
        <activity
            android:name=".Settings"
            android:label="@string/app_name"
            android:noHistory="true">
            <intent-filter>
                <action android:name="android.intent.action.MAIN" />
                <category android:name="android.intent.category.LAUNCHER" />
            </intent-filter>
        </activity>
        <activity
            android:name=".Steam"
            android:label="SmokeStack"
            android:noHistory="true" />
        <service android:enabled="true"
                android:exported="false"
                android:name=".SmokeStackService" />
    </application>

</manifest>
```


/*About.java


```java
** Copyright (c) Alexis Megas.
** All rights reserved.
**
** Redistribution and use in source and binary forms, with or without
** modification, are permitted provided that the following conditions
** are met:
** 1. Redistributions of source code must retain the above copyright
**    notice, this list of conditions and the following disclaimer.
** 2. Redistributions in binary form must reproduce the above copyright
**    notice, this list of conditions and the following disclaimer in the
**    documentation and/or other materials provided with the distribution.
** 3. The name of the author may not be used to endorse or promote products
**    derived from SmokeStack without specific prior written permission.
```

```java
**
** SMOKESTACK IS PROVIDED BY THE AUTHOR ``AS IS'' AND ANY EXPRESS OR
** IMPLIED WARRANTIES, INCLUDING, BUT NOT LIMITED TO, THE IMPLIED WARRANTIES
** OF MERCHANTABILITY AND FITNESS FOR A PARTICULAR PURPOSE ARE DISCLAIMED.
** IN NO EVENT SHALL THE AUTHOR BE LIABLE FOR ANY DIRECT, INDIRECT,
** INCIDENTAL, SPECIAL, EXEMPLARY, OR CONSEQUENTIAL DAMAGES (INCLUDING, BUT
** NOT LIMITED TO, PROCUREMENT OF SUBSTITUTE GOODS OR SERVICES; LOSS OF USE,
** DATA, OR PROFITS; OR BUSINESS INTERRUPTION) HOWEVER CAUSED AND ON ANY
** THEORY OF LIABILITY, WHETHER IN CONTRACT, STRICT LIABILITY, OR TORT
** (INCLUDING NEGLIGENCE OR OTHERWISE) ARISING IN ANY WAY OUT OF THE USE OF
** SMOKESTACK, EVEN IF ADVISED OF THE POSSIBILITY OF SUCH DAMAGE.
*/

package org.purple.smokestack;

import android.os.Build;
import java.text.SimpleDateFormat;
import java.util.Date;
import java.util.Locale;
import java.util.TimeZone;
import org.bouncycastle.jce.provider.BouncyCastleProvider;

public class About
{
    private static String s_about = "";

    private About()
    {
    }

    public static synchronized String about()
    {
      try
      {
          if(s_about.isEmpty())
          {
            SimpleDateFormat simpleDateFormat = new
                SimpleDateFormat("yyyy-MM-dd h:mm:ss", Locale.getDefault());

            simpleDateFormat.setTimeZone(TimeZone.getTimeZone("UTC"));

            // Must agree with SmokeStack/app/build.gradle.

            s_about = "Bouncy Castle Version " +
                new BouncyCastleProvider().getVersion() +
                "\nSmokeStack Version 2020.11.15 Stack Smash " +
                (BuildConfig.DEBUG ? "(Debug) " : "(Release)") +
                "\nBuild Date " +
                simpleDateFormat.format(new Date(BuildConfig.BUILD_TIME)) +
                " UTC\nAndroid " + Build.VERSION.RELEASE +
                (Build.VERSION.SDK_INT < Build.VERSION_CODES.LOLLIPOP ?
                 "\nAndroid version not supported." : "");
          }
      }
      catch(Exception exception)
      {
          if(s_about.isEmpty())
            s_about = "SmokeStack Version 2020.11.15 Stack Smash";
      }

      return s_about;
    }
}
```

```java
/* Authenticate.java

https://raw.githubusercontent.com/textbrowser/smokestack/master/SmokeStack/app
/src/main/java/org/purple/smokestack/Authenticate.java
** Copyright (c) Alexis Megas.
** All rights reserved.
**
** Redistribution and use in source and binary forms, with or without
** modification, are permitted provided that the following conditions
** are met:
** 1. Redistributions of source code must retain the above copyright
**    notice, this list of conditions and the following disclaimer.
** 2. Redistributions in binary form must reproduce the above copyright
**    notice, this list of conditions and the following disclaimer in the
**    documentation and/or other materials provided with the distribution.
** 3. The name of the author may not be used to endorse or promote products
**    derived from SmokeStack without specific prior written permission.
**
** SMOKESTACK IS PROVIDED BY THE AUTHOR ``AS IS'' AND ANY EXPRESS OR
** IMPLIED WARRANTIES, INCLUDING, BUT NOT LIMITED TO, THE IMPLIED WARRANTIES
** OF MERCHANTABILITY AND FITNESS FOR A PARTICULAR PURPOSE ARE DISCLAIMED.
** IN NO EVENT SHALL THE AUTHOR BE LIABLE FOR ANY DIRECT, INDIRECT,
** INCIDENTAL, SPECIAL, EXEMPLARY, OR CONSEQUENTIAL DAMAGES (INCLUDING, BUT
** NOT LIMITED TO, PROCUREMENT OF SUBSTITUTE GOODS OR SERVICES; LOSS OF USE,
** DATA, OR PROFITS; OR BUSINESS INTERRUPTION) HOWEVER CAUSED AND ON ANY
** THEORY OF LIABILITY, WHETHER IN CONTRACT, STRICT LIABILITY, OR TORT
** (INCLUDING NEGLIGENCE OR OTHERWISE) ARISING IN ANY WAY OUT OF THE USE OF
** SMOKESTACK, EVEN IF ADVISED OF THE POSSIBILITY OF SUCH DAMAGE.
*/

package org.purple.smokestack;

import android.app.ProgressDialog;
import android.content.DialogInterface;
import android.content.Intent;
import android.os.Bundle;
import android.support.v7.app.AppCompatActivity;
import android.util.Base64;
import android.view.Menu;
import android.view.MenuItem;
import android.view.View;
import android.widget.Button;
import android.widget.TextView;
import javax.crypto.SecretKey;

public class Authenticate extends AppCompatActivity
{
    private Database m_databaseHelper = null;
    private final static Cryptography s_cryptography =
      Cryptography.getInstance();

    private void prepareListeners()
    {
        final Button button1 = (Button) findViewById(R.id.authenticate);

        button1.setOnClickListener(new View.OnClickListener()
        {
            public void onClick(View view)
            {
                if(Authenticate.this.isFinishing())
                    return;

                byte encryptionSalt[] = Base64.decode
```

```java
        (m_databaseHelper.
         readSetting(null, "encryptionSalt").getBytes(),
         Base64.DEFAULT);
    final TextView textView1 = (TextView) findViewById
        (R.id.password);

    textView1.setSelectAllOnFocus(true);

    if(encryptionSalt == null)
    {
        Miscellaneous.showErrorDialog
          (Authenticate.this,
           "The encryption salt value is zero. System failure.");
        textView1.requestFocus();
        return;
    }

    byte macSalt[] = Base64.decode
        (m_databaseHelper.readSetting(null, "macSalt").getBytes(),
         Base64.DEFAULT);

    if(macSalt == null)
    {
        Miscellaneous.showErrorDialog
          (Authenticate.this,
           "The mac salt value is zero. System failure.");
        textView1.requestFocus();
        return;
    }

    byte saltedPassword[] = Cryptography.sha512
        (textView1.getText().toString().getBytes(),
         encryptionSalt,
         macSalt);

    if(saltedPassword == null)
    {
        Miscellaneous.showErrorDialog
          (Authenticate.this,
           "An error occurred with sha512(). System failure.");
        textView1.requestFocus();
        return;
    }

    int iterationCount = 1000;

    try
    {
        iterationCount = Integer.parseInt
          (m_databaseHelper.readSetting(null, "iterationCount"));
    }
    catch(Exception exception)
    {
        iterationCount = -1;
    }

    if(iterationCount == -1)
    {
        Miscellaneous.showErrorDialog
          (Authenticate.this,
           "Invalid iteration count. System failure.");
        textView1.requestFocus();
        return;
```

```java
        }

        if(!Cryptography.memcmp(m_databaseHelper.
                        readSetting(null,"saltedPassword").
                        getBytes(),
                        Base64.encode(saltedPassword,
                                Base64.DEFAULT)))
        {
            Miscellaneous.showErrorDialog
              (Authenticate.this,
               "Incorrect password. Please try again.");
            textView1.setText("");
            textView1.requestFocus();
            return;
        }

        final ProgressDialog dialog = new ProgressDialog
            (Authenticate.this);

        dialog.setCancelable(false);
        dialog.setIndeterminate(true);
        dialog.setMessage
            ("Generating confidential data. Please be patient " +
             "and do not rotate the device while the process " +
             "executes.");
        dialog.show();

        class SingleShot implements Runnable
        {
            private String m_error = "";
            private String m_password = "";
            private byte m_encryptionSalt[] = null;
            private byte m_macSalt[] = null;
            private int m_iterationCount = 1000;

            SingleShot(String password,
                       byte encryptionSalt[],
                       byte macSalt[],
                       int iterationCount)
            {
              m_encryptionSalt = encryptionSalt;
              m_iterationCount = iterationCount;
              m_macSalt = macSalt;
              m_password = password;
            }

            @Override
            public void run()
            {
              SecretKey encryptionKey = null;
              SecretKey macKey = null;

              try
              {
                  encryptionKey = Cryptography.generateEncryptionKey
                    (m_encryptionSalt,
                     m_password.toCharArray(),
                     m_iterationCount);
                  macKey = Cryptography.generateMacKey
                    (m_macSalt,
                     m_password.toCharArray(),
                     m_iterationCount);
```

```java
            if(encryptionKey != null && macKey != null)
            {
              s_cryptography.setEncryptionKey(encryptionKey);
              s_cryptography.setMacKey(macKey);
            }
            else
            {
              if(encryptionKey == null)
                  m_error = "generateEncryptionKey() " +
                    "failure";
              else
                  m_error = "generateMacKey() failure";

              s_cryptography.reset();
            }
        }
        catch(Exception exception)
        {
            m_error = exception.getMessage().toLowerCase().
              trim();
            s_cryptography.reset();
        }

        Authenticate.this.runOnUiThread(new Runnable()
        {
            @Override
            public void run()
            {
              try
              {
                  dialog.dismiss();

                  if(!m_error.isEmpty())
                    Miscellaneous.showErrorDialog
                        (Authenticate.this,
                         "An error (" + m_error +
                         ") occurred while " +
                         "generating the confidential " +
                         "data.");
                  else
                  {
                    m_databaseHelper.cleanNeighborStatistics
                        (s_cryptography);
                    Kernel.getInstance();
                    State.getInstance().setAuthenticated
                        (true);

                    /*
                    ** Disable some widgets.
                    */

                    button1.setEnabled(false);
                    textView1.setEnabled(false);
                    textView1.setText("");
                    showSettingsActivity();
                  }
              }
              catch(Exception exception)
              {
              }
            }
        });
```

```java
                m_password = "";
            }
        }

        Thread thread = new Thread
            (new SingleShot(textView1.getText().toString(),
                        encryptionSalt,
                        macSalt,
                        iterationCount));

        thread.start();
        }
    });

    final DialogInterface.OnCancelListener listener1 =
        new DialogInterface.OnCancelListener()
    {
        public void onCancel(DialogInterface dialog)
        {
          if(State.getInstance().getString("dialog_accepted").
             equals("true"))
          {
              State.getInstance().reset();
              m_databaseHelper.resetAndDrop();
              s_cryptography.reset();

              Intent intent = new Intent
                (Authenticate.this, Settings.class);

              startActivity(intent);
              finish();
          }
        }
    };

    Button button2 = (Button) findViewById(R.id.reset);

    button2.setOnClickListener(new View.OnClickListener()
    {
        public void onClick(View view)
        {
          Miscellaneous.showPromptDialog
              (Authenticate.this,
               listener1,
               "Are you sure that you " +
               "wish to reset SmokeStack? All " +
               "of the data will be removed.");
        }
    });
    }

    private void showSettingsActivity()
    {
      Intent intent = new Intent(Authenticate.this, Settings.class);

      startActivity(intent);
      finish();
    }

    @Override
    protected void onCreate(Bundle savedInstanceState)
    {
      super.onCreate(savedInstanceState);
```

```java
    SmokeStackService.stopForegroundTask(getApplicationContext());

    try
    {
        getSupportActionBar().setTitle("SmokeStack | Authenticate");
    }
    catch(Exception exception)
    {
    }

      setContentView(R.layout.activity_authenticate);

    boolean isAuthenticated = State.getInstance().isAuthenticated();
    Button button1 = (Button) findViewById(R.id.authenticate);

    button1.setEnabled(!isAuthenticated);

    TextView textView1 = (TextView) findViewById(R.id.password);

    textView1.setEnabled(!isAuthenticated);
  }

  @Override
  protected void onStart()
  {
    super.onStart();
    m_databaseHelper = Database.getInstance(getApplicationContext());
    m_databaseHelper.clearTable("log");
    m_databaseHelper.clearTable("routing_identities");
    prepareListeners();
  }

  @Override
  public boolean onCreateOptionsMenu(Menu menu)
  {
      getMenuInflater().inflate(R.menu.authenticate_menu, menu);
      return true;
  }

  @Override
  public boolean onOptionsItemSelected(MenuItem item)
  {
    if(item != null)
        switch(item.getItemId())
        {
        case R.id.action_exit:
          SmokeStack.exit(Authenticate.this);
          return true;
        case R.id.action_settings:
          showSettingsActivity();
          return true;
        default:
          break;
        }

      return super.onOptionsItemSelected(item);
  }

  @Override
  public boolean onPrepareOptionsMenu(Menu menu)
  {
    boolean isAuthenticated = State.getInstance().isAuthenticated();
```

```
        if(!m_databaseHelper.accountPrepared())
            /*
            ** The database may have been modified or removed.
            */

            isAuthenticated = true;

          menu.findItem(R.id.action_settings).setEnabled(isAuthenticated);
          return true;
        }
    }




```

/* ClientBubble.java

https://raw.githubusercontent.com/textbrowser/smokestack/master/SmokeStack/app/src/main/java/org/purple/smokestack/ClientBubble.java

```
** Copyright (c) Alexis Megas.
** All rights reserved.
**
** Redistribution and use in source and binary forms, with or without
** modification, are permitted provided that the following conditions
** are met:
** 1. Redistributions of source code must retain the above copyright
**    notice, this list of conditions and the following disclaimer.
** 2. Redistributions in binary form must reproduce the above copyright
**    notice, this list of conditions and the following disclaimer in the
**    documentation and/or other materials provided with the distribution.
** 3. The name of the author may not be used to endorse or promote products
**    derived from Smoke without specific prior written permission.
**
** SMOKESTACK IS PROVIDED BY THE AUTHOR ``AS IS'' AND ANY EXPRESS OR
** IMPLIED WARRANTIES, INCLUDING, BUT NOT LIMITED TO, THE IMPLIED WARRANTIES
** OF MERCHANTABILITY AND FITNESS FOR A PARTICULAR PURPOSE ARE DISCLAIMED.
** IN NO EVENT SHALL THE AUTHOR BE LIABLE FOR ANY DIRECT, INDIRECT,
** INCIDENTAL, SPECIAL, EXEMPLARY, OR CONSEQUENTIAL DAMAGES (INCLUDING, BUT
** NOT LIMITED TO, PROCUREMENT OF SUBSTITUTE GOODS OR SERVICES; LOSS OF USE,
** DATA, OR PROFITS; OR BUSINESS INTERRUPTION) HOWEVER CAUSED AND ON ANY
** THEORY OF LIABILITY, WHETHER IN CONTRACT, STRICT LIABILITY, OR TORT
** (INCLUDING NEGLIGENCE OR OTHERWISE) ARISING IN ANY WAY OUT OF THE USE OF
** SMOKESTACK, EVEN IF ADVISED OF THE POSSIBILITY OF SUCH DAMAGE.
*/

package org.purple.smokestack;

import android.content.Context;
import android.view.LayoutInflater;
import android.view.View;
import android.view.ViewGroup;
import android.widget.TextView;

public class ClientBubble extends View
{
    private View m_view = null;

    public ClientBubble(Context context,
                Settings settings,
                ViewGroup viewGroup)
    {
      super(context);

        LayoutInflater inflater = (LayoutInflater) context.getSystemService
```

```java
                (Context.LAYOUT_INFLATER_SERVICE);

      m_view = inflater.inflate(R.layout.client_bubble, viewGroup, false);
    }

    public View view()
    {
      return m_view;
    }

    public void setAddress(String address)
    {
      TextView textView = (TextView) m_view.findViewById(R.id.address);

      textView.setText(address);
    }
}
```

/* ClientElement.java

```java
https://raw.githubusercontent.com/textbrowser/smokestack/master/SmokeStack/app
/src/main/java/org/purple/smokestack/ClientElement.java
** Copyright (c) Alexis Megas.
** All rights reserved.
**
** Redistribution and use in source and binary forms, with or without
** modification, are permitted provided that the following conditions
** are met:
** 1. Redistributions of source code must retain the above copyright
**    notice, this list of conditions and the following disclaimer.
** 2. Redistributions in binary form must reproduce the above copyright
**    notice, this list of conditions and the following disclaimer in the
**    documentation and/or other materials provided with the distribution.
** 3. The name of the author may not be used to endorse or promote products
**    derived from SmokeStack without specific prior written permission.
**
** SMOKESTACK IS PROVIDED BY THE AUTHOR ``AS IS'' AND ANY EXPRESS OR
** IMPLIED WARRANTIES, INCLUDING, BUT NOT LIMITED TO, THE IMPLIED WARRANTIES
** OF MERCHANTABILITY AND FITNESS FOR A PARTICULAR PURPOSE ARE DISCLAIMED.
** IN NO EVENT SHALL THE AUTHOR BE LIABLE FOR ANY DIRECT, INDIRECT,
** INCIDENTAL, SPECIAL, EXEMPLARY, OR CONSEQUENTIAL DAMAGES (INCLUDING, BUT
** NOT LIMITED TO, PROCUREMENT OF SUBSTITUTE GOODS OR SERVICES; LOSS OF USE,
** DATA, OR PROFITS; OR BUSINESS INTERRUPTION) HOWEVER CAUSED AND ON ANY
** THEORY OF LIABILITY, WHETHER IN CONTRACT, STRICT LIABILITY, OR TORT
** (INCLUDING NEGLIGENCE OR OTHERWISE) ARISING IN ANY WAY OUT OF THE USE OF
** SMOKESTACK, EVEN IF ADVISED OF THE POSSIBILITY OF SUCH DAMAGE.
*/

package org.purple.smokestack;

public class ClientElement
{
    public String m_address = "";

    public ClientElement()
    {
    }
}
```

```java
/* Cryptography.java
https://raw.githubusercontent.com/textbrowser/smokestack/master/SmokeStack/app
/src/main/java/org/purple/smokestack/Cryptography.java
** Copyright (c) Alexis Megas.
** All rights reserved.
**
** Redistribution and use in source and binary forms, with or without
** modification, are permitted provided that the following conditions
** are met:
** 1. Redistributions of source code must retain the above copyright
**    notice, this list of conditions and the following disclaimer.
** 2. Redistributions in binary form must reproduce the above copyright
**    notice, this list of conditions and the following disclaimer in the
**    documentation and/or other materials provided with the distribution.
** 3. The name of the author may not be used to endorse or promote products
**    derived from SmokeStack without specific prior written permission.
**
** SMOKESTACK IS PROVIDED BY THE AUTHOR ``AS IS'' AND ANY EXPRESS OR
** IMPLIED WARRANTIES, INCLUDING, BUT NOT LIMITED TO, THE IMPLIED WARRANTIES
** OF MERCHANTABILITY AND FITNESS FOR A PARTICULAR PURPOSE ARE DISCLAIMED.
** IN NO EVENT SHALL THE AUTHOR BE LIABLE FOR ANY DIRECT, INDIRECT,
** INCIDENTAL, SPECIAL, EXEMPLARY, OR CONSEQUENTIAL DAMAGES (INCLUDING, BUT
** NOT LIMITED TO, PROCUREMENT OF SUBSTITUTE GOODS OR SERVICES; LOSS OF USE,
** DATA, OR PROFITS; OR BUSINESS INTERRUPTION) HOWEVER CAUSED AND ON ANY
** THEORY OF LIABILITY, WHETHER IN CONTRACT, STRICT LIABILITY, OR TORT
** (INCLUDING NEGLIGENCE OR OTHERWISE) ARISING IN ANY WAY OUT OF THE USE OF
** SMOKESTACK, EVEN IF ADVISED OF THE POSSIBILITY OF SUCH DAMAGE.
*/

package org.purple.smokestack;

import android.util.Base64;
import java.nio.charset.StandardCharsets;
import java.security.KeyFactory;
import java.security.KeyPair;
import java.security.KeyPairGenerator;
import java.security.MessageDigest;
import java.security.NoSuchAlgorithmException;
import java.security.PrivateKey;
import java.security.PublicKey;
import java.security.SecureRandom;
import java.security.Security;
import java.security.Signature;
import java.security.spec.EncodedKeySpec;
import java.security.spec.InvalidKeySpecException;
import java.security.spec.KeySpec;
import java.security.spec.PKCS8EncodedKeySpec;
import java.security.spec.X509EncodedKeySpec;
import java.util.Arrays;
import java.util.concurrent.locks.ReentrantReadWriteLock;
import javax.crypto.Cipher;
import javax.crypto.Mac;
import javax.crypto.SecretKey;
import javax.crypto.SecretKeyFactory;
import javax.crypto.spec.IvParameterSpec;
import javax.crypto.spec.PBEKeySpec;
import javax.crypto.spec.SecretKeySpec;
import org.bouncycastle.pqc.asn1.PQCObjectIdentifiers;
import org.bouncycastle.pqc.jcajce.provider.BouncyCastlePQCProvider;

public class Cryptography
{
```

```java
static
{
  Security.addProvider(new BouncyCastlePQCProvider());
}

private SecretKey m_encryptionKey = null;
private SecretKey m_macKey = null;
private final ReentrantReadWriteLock m_encryptionKeyMutex =
  new ReentrantReadWriteLock();
private final ReentrantReadWriteLock m_macKeyMutex =
  new ReentrantReadWriteLock();
private final static String HASH_ALGORITHM = "SHA-512";
private final static String HMAC_ALGORITHM = "HmacSHA512";
private final static String PKI_ECDSA_SIGNATURE_ALGORITHM =
  "SHA512withECDSA";
private final static String PKI_RSA_SIGNATURE_ALGORITHM =
  /*
  ** SHA512withRSA/PSS requires API 23+.
  */

  "SHA512withRSA";
private final static String SYMMETRIC_ALGORITHM = "AES";
private final static String SYMMETRIC_CIPHER_TRANSFORMATION =
  "AES/CBC/PKCS7Padding";
private final static int OZONE_STREAM_CREATION_ITERATION_COUNT = 4096;
private final static int SIPHASH_STREAM_CREATION_ITERATION_COUNT = 4096;
private static Cryptography s_instance = null;
private static SecureRandom s_secureRandom = null;
public final static int CIPHER_KEY_LENGTH = 32;
public final static int HASH_KEY_LENGTH = 64;

// 0000-0000-0000-0000-0000-0000-0000-0000

public final static int SIPHASH_IDENTITY_LENGTH = 7 + 4 * 8;
public final static int SIPHASH_OUTPUT_LENGTH = 16; // Bytes (128 bits).

private Cryptography()
{
  prepareSecureRandom();
}

private static synchronized void prepareSecureRandom()
{
  if(s_secureRandom != null)
      return;

  try
  {
      s_secureRandom = new SecureRandom();
  }
  catch(Exception exception)
  {
  }
}

public byte[] etm(byte data[]) // Encrypt-Then-MAC
{
  /*
  ** Encrypt-then-MAC.
  */

  if(data == null)
      return null;
```

```java
        m_encryptionKeyMutex.readLock().lock();

        try
        {
            if(m_encryptionKey == null)
              return null;
        }
        finally
        {
            m_encryptionKeyMutex.readLock().unlock();
        }

        m_macKeyMutex.readLock().lock();

        try
        {
            if(m_macKey == null)
              return null;
        }
        finally
        {
            m_macKeyMutex.readLock().unlock();
        }

        byte bytes[] = null;

        m_encryptionKeyMutex.readLock().lock();

        try
        {
            if(m_encryptionKey == null)
              return null;

            byte iv[] = new byte[16];

            s_secureRandom.nextBytes(iv);

            Cipher cipher = Cipher.getInstance
              (SYMMETRIC_CIPHER_TRANSFORMATION);

            cipher.init
              (Cipher.ENCRYPT_MODE, m_encryptionKey, new IvParameterSpec(iv));
            bytes = cipher.doFinal(data);
            bytes = Miscellaneous.joinByteArrays(iv, bytes);
        }
        catch(Exception exception)
        {
            return null;
        }
        finally
        {
            m_encryptionKeyMutex.readLock().unlock();
        }

        m_macKeyMutex.readLock().lock();

        try
        {
            if(m_macKey == null)
              return null;

            Mac mac = Mac.getInstance(HMAC_ALGORITHM);
```

```java
      mac.init(m_macKey);
      return Miscellaneous.joinByteArrays(bytes, mac.doFinal(bytes));
    }
    catch(Exception exception)
    {
    }
    finally
    {
        m_macKeyMutex.readLock().unlock();
    }

    return null;
  }

  public byte[] hmac(byte data[])
  {
    if(data == null)
        return null;

    m_macKeyMutex.readLock().lock();

    try
    {
        if(m_macKey == null)
          return null;

        Mac mac = Mac.getInstance(HMAC_ALGORITHM);

        mac.init(m_macKey);
        return mac.doFinal(data);
    }
    catch(Exception exception)
    {
    }
    finally
    {
        m_macKeyMutex.readLock().unlock();
    }

    return null;
  }

  public byte[] mtd(byte data[]) // MAC-Then-Decrypt
  {
    /*
    ** MAC-then-decrypt.
    */

    if(data == null)
        return null;

    m_encryptionKeyMutex.readLock().lock();

    try
    {
        if(m_encryptionKey == null)
          return null;
    }
    finally
    {
        m_encryptionKeyMutex.readLock().unlock();
    }
```

```java
        m_macKeyMutex.readLock().lock();

        try
        {
            if(m_macKey == null)
              return null;
        }
        finally
        {
            m_macKeyMutex.readLock().unlock();
        }

        try
        {
            /*
            ** Verify the computed digest with the provided digest.
            */

            byte digest1[] = null; // Provided digest.
            byte digest2[] = null; // Computed digest.

            digest1 = Arrays.copyOfRange
              (data, data.length - 512 / 8, data.length);
            m_macKeyMutex.readLock().lock();

            try
            {
              if(m_macKey == null)
                  return null;

              Mac mac = Mac.getInstance(HMAC_ALGORITHM);

              mac.init(m_macKey);
              digest2 = mac.doFinal
                  (Arrays.copyOf(data, data.length - 512 / 8));
            }
            catch(Exception exception)
            {
              return null;
            }
            finally
            {
              m_macKeyMutex.readLock().unlock();
            }

            if(!memcmp(digest1, digest2))
              return null;
        }
        catch(Exception exception)
        {
            return null;
        }

        m_encryptionKeyMutex.readLock().lock();

        try
        {
            if(m_encryptionKey == null)
              return null;

            Cipher cipher = Cipher.getInstance(SYMMETRIC_CIPHER_TRANSFORMATION);
            byte iv[] = Arrays.copyOf(data, 16);
```

```java
      cipher.init
        (Cipher.DECRYPT_MODE, m_encryptionKey, new IvParameterSpec(iv));
      return cipher.doFinal
        (Arrays.copyOfRange(data, 16, data.length - 512 / 8));
  }
  catch(Exception exception)
  {
  }
  finally
  {
      m_encryptionKeyMutex.readLock().unlock();
  }

  return null;
}

public static KeyPair generatePrivatePublicKeyPair
  (String algorithm, int keySize)
{
  prepareSecureRandom();

  try
  {
      KeyPairGenerator keyPairGenerator = KeyPairGenerator.
        getInstance(algorithm);

      keyPairGenerator.initialize(keySize, s_secureRandom);
      return keyPairGenerator.generateKeyPair();
  }
  catch(Exception exception)
  {
  }

  return null;
}

public static KeyPair generatePrivatePublicKeyPair(String algorithm,
                                  byte privateBytes[],
                                  byte publicBytes[])
{
  try
  {
      EncodedKeySpec privateKeySpec = new PKCS8EncodedKeySpec
        (privateBytes);
      EncodedKeySpec publicKeySpec = new X509EncodedKeySpec(publicBytes);
      KeyFactory keyFactory = KeyFactory.getInstance(algorithm);
      PrivateKey privateKey = null;
      PublicKey publicKey = null;

      privateKey = keyFactory.generatePrivate(privateKeySpec);
      publicKey = keyFactory.generatePublic(publicKeySpec);
      return new KeyPair(publicKey, privateKey);
  }
  catch(Exception exception)
  {
      Database.getInstance().writeLog
        ("Cryptography::generatePrivatePublicKeyPair(): " +
        "exception raised.");
  }

  return null;
}
```

```java
    public static PublicKey publicKeyFromBytes(byte publicBytes[])
    {
      if(publicBytes == null)
          return null;

      try
      {
          EncodedKeySpec publicKeySpec = new X509EncodedKeySpec(publicBytes);

          for(int i = 0; i < 3; i++)
            try
              {
                  KeyFactory keyFactory = null;

                  switch(i)
                  {
                  case 0:
                    keyFactory = KeyFactory.getInstance("EC");
                    break;
                  case 1:
                    keyFactory = KeyFactory.getInstance
                        (PQCObjectIdentifiers.mcElieceCca2.getId());
                    break;
                  default:
                    keyFactory = KeyFactory.getInstance("RSA");
                    break;
                  }

                  return keyFactory.generatePublic(publicKeySpec);
            }
            catch(Exception exception)
              {
              }
      }
      catch(Exception exception)
      {
      }

      return null;
    }

    public static SecretKey generateEncryptionKey(byte salt[],
                                    char password[],
                                    int iterations)
      throws InvalidKeySpecException, NoSuchAlgorithmException
    {
      if(salt == null)
          return null;

      KeySpec keySpec = new PBEKeySpec(password, salt, iterations, 256);
      SecretKeyFactory secretKeyFactory = SecretKeyFactory.getInstance
          ("PBKDF2WithHmacSHA1");

      return secretKeyFactory.generateSecret(keySpec);
    }

    public static SecretKey generateMacKey(byte salt[],
                                char password[],
                                int iterations)
      throws InvalidKeySpecException, NoSuchAlgorithmException
    {
      if(salt == null)
```

```java
          return null;

  KeySpec keySpec = new PBEKeySpec(password, salt, iterations, 512);
  SecretKeyFactory secretKeyFactory = SecretKeyFactory.getInstance
      ("PBKDF2WithHmacSHA1");

  return secretKeyFactory.generateSecret(keySpec);
}

public static String fingerPrint(byte bytes[])
{
  String fingerprint =
      "cf83e1357eefb8bdf1542850d66d8007d620e4050b5715dc" +
      "83f4a921d36ce9ce47d0d13c5d85f2b0ff8318d2877eec2f63b931bd4" +
      "7417a81a538327af927da3e";
  StringBuilder stringBuilder = new StringBuilder();

  if(bytes != null)
  {
      bytes = sha512(bytes);

      if(bytes != null)
        fingerprint = Miscellaneous.byteArrayAsHexString(bytes);
  }

  try
  {
      int length = fingerprint.length();

      for(int i = 0; i < length; i += 2)
        if(i < length - 2)
            stringBuilder.append(fingerprint, i, i + 2).append(":");
        else
            stringBuilder.append(fingerprint.substring(i));
  }
  catch(Exception exception)
  {
  }

  return stringBuilder.toString();
}

public static boolean memcmp(byte a[], byte b[])
{
  if(a == null || b == null)
      return false;

  int rc = 0;
  int size = java.lang.Math.max(a.length, b.length);

  for(int i = 0; i < size; i++)
      rc |= (i < a.length ? a[i] : 0) ^ (i < b.length ? b[i] : 0);

  return rc == 0;
}

public static boolean verifySignature(PublicKey publicKey,
                          byte bytes[],
                          byte data[])
{
  if(bytes == null || data == null || publicKey == null)
      return false;
```

```java
    try
    {
        Signature signature = null;

        if(publicKey.getAlgorithm().equals("EC"))
          signature = Signature.getInstance
              (PKI_ECDSA_SIGNATURE_ALGORITHM);
        else
          signature = Signature.getInstance(PKI_RSA_SIGNATURE_ALGORITHM);

        signature.initVerify(publicKey);
        signature.update(data);
        return signature.verify(bytes);
    }
    catch(Exception exception)
    {
    }

    return false;
}

public static byte[] decrypt(byte data[], byte keyBytes[])
{
  if(data == null || keyBytes == null)
      return null;

  try
  {
      Cipher cipher = Cipher.getInstance(SYMMETRIC_CIPHER_TRANSFORMATION);
      SecretKey secretKey = new SecretKeySpec
        (keyBytes, SYMMETRIC_ALGORITHM);
      byte iv[] = Arrays.copyOf(data, 16);

      cipher.init
        (Cipher.DECRYPT_MODE, secretKey, new IvParameterSpec(iv));
      return cipher.doFinal
        (Arrays.copyOfRange(data, 16, data.length));
  }
  catch(Exception exception)
  {
  }

  return null;
}

public static byte[] encrypt(byte data[], byte keyBytes[])
{
  if(data == null || keyBytes == null)
      return null;

  prepareSecureRandom();

  try
  {
      SecretKey secretKey = new SecretKeySpec
        (keyBytes, SYMMETRIC_ALGORITHM);
      byte bytes[] = null;
      byte iv[] = new byte[16];

      s_secureRandom.nextBytes(iv);

      Cipher cipher = Cipher.getInstance(SYMMETRIC_CIPHER_TRANSFORMATION);
```

```java
        cipher.init
          (Cipher.ENCRYPT_MODE, secretKey, new IvParameterSpec(iv));
        bytes = cipher.doFinal(data);
        return Miscellaneous.joinByteArrays(iv, bytes);
    }
  catch(Exception exception)
    {
    }

  return null;
}

public static byte[] generateOzone(String string)
{
  if(string == null || string.trim().isEmpty())
      return null;

  try
    {
      byte bytes[] = null;
      byte salt[] = sha512
        (string.trim().getBytes(StandardCharsets.UTF_8));

      if(salt != null)
        bytes = pbkdf2
            (salt,
             string.trim().toCharArray(),
             OZONE_STREAM_CREATION_ITERATION_COUNT,
             160); // SHA-1

      if(bytes != null)
        bytes = pbkdf2(salt,
                    Base64.encodeToString(bytes, Base64.NO_WRAP).
                    toCharArray(),
                    1,
                    768); // 8 * (32 + 64) bits.

      return bytes;
    }
  catch(Exception exception)
    {
    }

  return null;
}

public static byte[] keyForSipHash(byte data[])
{
  if(data == null)
      return null;

  return pbkdf2(sha512(data),
              Miscellaneous.byteArrayAsHexString(data).toCharArray(),
              SIPHASH_STREAM_CREATION_ITERATION_COUNT,
              8 * SipHash.KEY_LENGTH);
}

public static byte[] hmac(byte data[], byte keyBytes[])
{
  if(data == null || keyBytes == null)
      return null;

  try
```

```java
        {
            Mac mac = Mac.getInstance(HMAC_ALGORITHM);
            SecretKey key = new SecretKeySpec(keyBytes, HASH_ALGORITHM);

            mac.init(key);
            return mac.doFinal(data);
        }
        catch(Exception exception)
        {
        }

        return null;
    }

    public static byte[] pbkdf2(byte salt[],
                     char password[],
                     int iterations,
                     int length)
    {
      if(password == null || salt == null)
          return null;

      try
      {
          KeySpec keySpec = new PBEKeySpec
            (password, salt, iterations, length);
          SecretKeyFactory secretKeyFactory = SecretKeyFactory.getInstance
            ("PBKDF2WithHmacSHA1");

          return secretKeyFactory.generateSecret(keySpec).getEncoded();
      }
      catch(Exception exception)
      {
      }

      return null;
    }

    public static byte[] randomBytes(int length)
    {
      if(length <= 0)
          return null;

      prepareSecureRandom();

      try
      {
          byte bytes[] = new byte[length];

          s_secureRandom.nextBytes(bytes);
          return bytes;
      }
      catch(Exception exception)
      {
      }

      return null;
    }

    public static byte[] sha512(byte[] ... data)
    {
      try
      {
```

```java
        MessageDigest messageDigest = MessageDigest.getInstance("SHA-512");

        for(byte b[] : data)
          if(b != null)
              messageDigest.update(b);

        return messageDigest.digest();
    }
    catch(Exception exception)
    {
    }

    return null;
  }

  public static byte[] sipHashIdStream(String sipHashId)
  {
    try
    {
        byte bytes[] = null;
        byte salt[] = sha512(sipHashId.getBytes(StandardCharsets.UTF_8));
        byte temporary[] = pbkdf2(salt,
                          sipHashId.toCharArray(),
                          SIPHASH_STREAM_CREATION_ITERATION_COUNT,
                          160); // SHA-1

        if(temporary != null)
          bytes = pbkdf2
              (salt,
               Base64.encodeToString(temporary, Base64.NO_WRAP).
               toCharArray(),
               1,
               768); // 8 * (32 + 64) bits.

        return bytes;
    }
    catch(Exception exception)
    {
    }

    return null;
  }

  public static synchronized Cryptography getInstance()
  {
    if(s_instance == null)
        s_instance = new Cryptography();

    return s_instance;
  }

  public void reset()
  {
    m_encryptionKeyMutex.writeLock().lock();

    try
    {
        m_encryptionKey = null;
    }
    finally
    {
        m_encryptionKeyMutex.writeLock().unlock();
    }
```

```java
      m_macKeyMutex.writeLock().lock();

      try
      {
          m_macKey = null;
      }
      finally
      {
          m_macKeyMutex.writeLock().unlock();
      }
    }

    public void setEncryptionKey(SecretKey key)
    {
      m_encryptionKeyMutex.writeLock().lock();

      try
      {
          m_encryptionKey = key;
      }
      finally
      {
          m_encryptionKeyMutex.writeLock().unlock();
      }
    }

    public void setMacKey(SecretKey key)
    {
      m_macKeyMutex.writeLock().lock();

      try
      {
          m_macKey = key;
      }
      finally
      {
          m_macKeyMutex.writeLock().unlock();
      }
    }
}
```

/* Database.java

```java
** IMPLIED WARRANTIES, INCLUDING, BUT NOT LIMITED TO, THE IMPLIED WARRANTIES
** OF MERCHANTABILITY AND FITNESS FOR A PARTICULAR PURPOSE ARE DISCLAIMED.
** IN NO EVENT SHALL THE AUTHOR BE LIABLE FOR ANY DIRECT, INDIRECT,
** INCIDENTAL, SPECIAL, EXEMPLARY, OR CONSEQUENTIAL DAMAGES (INCLUDING, BUT
** NOT LIMITED TO, PROCUREMENT OF SUBSTITUTE GOODS OR SERVICES; LOSS OF USE,
** DATA, OR PROFITS; OR BUSINESS INTERRUPTION) HOWEVER CAUSED AND ON ANY
** THEORY OF LIABILITY, WHETHER IN CONTRACT, STRICT LIABILITY, OR TORT
** (INCLUDING NEGLIGENCE OR OTHERWISE) ARISING IN ANY WAY OUT OF THE USE OF
** SMOKESTACK, EVEN IF ADVISED OF THE POSSIBILITY OF SUCH DAMAGE.
*/

package org.purple.smokestack;

import android.content.ContentValues;
import android.content.Context;
import android.database.Cursor;
import android.database.sqlite.SQLiteConstraintException;
import android.database.sqlite.SQLiteDatabase;
import android.database.sqlite.SQLiteOpenHelper;
import android.util.Base64;
import android.util.Patterns;
import android.util.SparseArray;
import android.util.SparseIntArray;
import java.net.InetAddress;
import java.nio.charset.StandardCharsets;
import java.security.KeyFactory;
import java.security.PublicKey;
import java.security.spec.X509EncodedKeySpec;
import java.text.SimpleDateFormat;
import java.util.ArrayList;
import java.util.Arrays;
import java.util.Collections;
import java.util.Comparator;
import java.util.Date;
import java.util.Locale;
import java.util.TimeZone;
import java.util.UUID;
import java.util.concurrent.atomic.AtomicLong;
import java.util.concurrent.locks.ReentrantReadWriteLock;
import java.util.regex.Matcher;

public class Database extends SQLiteOpenHelper
{
    private SQLiteDatabase m_db = null;
    private final AtomicLong m_cursorsClosed = new AtomicLong(0L);
    private final AtomicLong m_cursorsOpened = new AtomicLong(0L);
    private final static Comparator<ListenerElement>
      s_readListenersComparator = new Comparator<ListenerElement> ()
      {
          @Override
          public int compare(ListenerElement e1, ListenerElement e2)
          {
            /*
            ** Sort by IP address, port, and scope ID.
            */

              try
              {
                  byte bytes1[] = InetAddress.getByName(e1.m_localIpAddress).
                  getAddress();
                  byte bytes2[] = InetAddress.getByName(e2.m_localIpAddress).
                  getAddress();
                  int length = Math.max(bytes1.length, bytes2.length);
```

```java
                    for(int i = 0; i < length; i++)
                    {
                      byte b1 = (i >= length - bytes1.length) ?
                          bytes1[i - (length - bytes1.length)] : 0;
                       byte b2 = (i >= length - bytes2.length) ?
                          bytes2[i - (length - bytes2.length)] : 0;

                       if(b1 != b2)
                           return (0xff & b1) - (0xff & b2);
                    }
                }
            catch(Exception exception)
            {
            }

            int i = e1.m_localPort.compareTo(e2.m_localPort);

            if(i != 0)
                return i;

            return e1.m_localScopeId.compareTo(e2.m_localScopeId);
        }
    };
    private final static Comparator<NeighborElement>
      s_readNeighborsComparator = new Comparator<NeighborElement> ()
      {
        @Override
        public int compare(NeighborElement e1, NeighborElement e2)
        {
          /*
          ** Sort by IP address, port, and transport.
          */

            try
            {
                byte bytes1[] = InetAddress.getByName(e1.m_remoteIpAddress).
                getAddress();
                byte bytes2[] = InetAddress.getByName(e2.m_remoteIpAddress).
                getAddress();
                int length = Math.max(bytes1.length, bytes2.length);

                for(int i = 0; i < length; i++)
                {
                  byte b1 = (i >= length - bytes1.length) ?
                      bytes1[i - (length - bytes1.length)] : 0;
                   byte b2 = (i >= length - bytes2.length) ?
                      bytes2[i - (length - bytes2.length)] : 0;

                   if(b1 != b2)
                       return (0xff & b1) - (0xff & b2);
                }
            }
            catch(Exception exception)
            {
            }

            int i = e1.m_remotePort.compareTo(e2.m_remotePort);

            if(i != 0)
                return i;

            return e1.m_transport.compareTo(e2.m_transport);
```

```java
        }
    };
  private final static Comparator<OzoneElement>
    s_readOzonesComparator = new Comparator<OzoneElement> ()
    {
        @Override
        public int compare(OzoneElement e1, OzoneElement e2)
        {
          if(e1 == null || e2 == null)
              return -1;

          /*
          ** Sort by address.
          */

          return e1.m_address.compareTo(e2.m_address);
        }
    };
  private final static Comparator<SipHashIdElement>
    s_readSipHashIdsComparator = new Comparator<SipHashIdElement> ()
    {
        @Override
        public int compare(SipHashIdElement e1, SipHashIdElement e2)
        {
          if(e1 == null || e2 == null)
              return -1;

          /*
          ** Sort by name and Smoke identity.
          */

          int i = e1.m_name.compareTo(e2.m_name);

          if(i != 0)
              return i;

          return e1.m_sipHashId.compareTo(e2.m_sipHashId);
        }
    };
  private final static ReentrantReadWriteLock s_congestionControlMutex =
    new ReentrantReadWriteLock();
  private final static String DATABASE_NAME = "smokestack.db";
  private final static int DATABASE_VERSION = 1;
  private final static int SIPHASH_STREAM_CREATION_ITERATION_COUNT = 4096;
  private final static long ONE_WEEK = 604800000L;
  private final static long WRITE_PARTICIPANT_TIME_DELTA =
    60000L; // 60 Seconds
  private static Database s_instance = null;

  private Database(Context context)
  {
      super(context, DATABASE_NAME, null, DATABASE_VERSION);

    try
    {
        m_db = getWritableDatabase();
    }
    catch(Exception exception)
    {
        m_db = null;
    }
  }
```

```java
public boolean authenticate(Cryptography cryptography,
                            String data,
                            StringBuffer stringBuffer)
{
  if(cryptography == null ||
     data == null ||
     data.length() == 0 ||
     m_db == null ||
     stringBuffer == null ||
     stringBuffer.length() == 0)
      return false;

  Cursor cursor = null;

  try
  {
      byte buffer[] = Base64.decode(data.getBytes(), Base64.NO_WRAP);

      if(buffer.length < 129)
        // Random (64) + Signature Key Digest (64) + Signature (?)
        return false;

      byte random[] = Arrays.copyOfRange(buffer, 0, 64);

      if(Cryptography.memcmp(random, stringBuffer.toString().getBytes()))
        return false;

      byte signature[] = Arrays.copyOfRange(buffer, 128, buffer.length);
      byte signatureKeyDigest[] = Arrays.copyOfRange(buffer, 64, 128);

      cursor = m_db.rawQuery
        ("SELECT signature_public_key FROM participants " +
         "WHERE signature_public_key_digest = ?",
         new String[] {Base64.encodeToString(signatureKeyDigest,
                               Base64.DEFAULT)});

      if(cursor != null)
        m_cursorsOpened.getAndIncrement();

      while(cursor != null && cursor.moveToNext())
      {
        PublicKey publicKey = null;
        byte bytes[] = cryptography.mtd
            (Base64.decode(cursor.getString(0).getBytes(),
                     Base64.DEFAULT));

        if(bytes != null)
            for(int i = 0; i < 2; i++)
              try
              {
                  if(i == 0)
                    publicKey = KeyFactory.getInstance("EC").
                        generatePublic
                        (new X509EncodedKeySpec(bytes));
                  else
                    publicKey = KeyFactory.getInstance("RSA").
                        generatePublic
                        (new X509EncodedKeySpec(bytes));

                  break;
              }
              catch(Exception exception)
              {
```

```java
                    }

            if(publicKey != null)
            {
                buffer = Miscellaneous.joinByteArrays
                  (random,
                   signatureKeyDigest,
                   stringBuffer.toString().getBytes());

                if(Cryptography.
                   verifySignature(publicKey, signature, buffer))
                  return true;
            }
        }
    }
    catch(Exception exception)
    {
    }
    finally
    {
        if(cursor != null)
        {
          cursor.close();

          if(cursor.isClosed())
             m_cursorsClosed.getAndIncrement();
        }
    }

    return false;
}

public boolean toggleListenerPrivacy(Cryptography cryptography, int oid)
{
  if(cryptography == null || m_db == null)
      return false;

  try
  {
      ArrayList<ListenerElement> arrayList = readListeners
        (cryptography, oid);

      if(arrayList == null || arrayList.isEmpty())
        throw new Exception();

      byte bytes[] = cryptography.etm
        (arrayList.get(0).m_isPrivate ?
         "false".getBytes() : "true".getBytes());

      if(bytes == null)
        throw new Exception();

      ContentValues values = new ContentValues();

      values.put
        ("is_private", Base64.encodeToString(bytes, Base64.DEFAULT));
      m_db.update
        ("listeners",
         values,
         "OID = ?",
         new String[] {String.valueOf(oid)});
  }
  catch(Exception exception)
```

```
            {
                return false;
            }

          return true;
        }

      public boolean writePublicKeyPairs
        (Cryptography cryptography, String sipHashId, String strings[])
      {
        if(cryptography == null ||
           m_db == null ||
           sipHashId == null ||
           sipHashId.length() != Cryptography.SIPHASH_IDENTITY_LENGTH ||
           strings == null ||
           strings.length != Messages.EPKS_GROUP_ONE_ELEMENT_COUNT)
            return false;

        /*
        ** Do not prepare a database transaction.
        */

        try
        {
            ContentValues values = new ContentValues();
            SparseArray<String> sparseArray = new SparseArray<> ();
            byte bytes[] = null;

            /*
            ** strings[0] - A Timestamp
            ** strings[1] - Key Type
            ** strings[2] - Sender's Smoke Identity
            ** strings[3] - Public Key
            ** strings[4] - Public Key Signature
            ** strings[5] - Signature Public Key
            ** strings[6] - Signature Public Key Signature
            */

            bytes = cryptography.etm(strings[1].getBytes());
            values.put
              ("key_type", Base64.encodeToString(bytes, Base64.DEFAULT));
            sparseArray.append(0, "public_key_string");
            sparseArray.append(1, "public_key_signature_string");
            sparseArray.append(2, "signature_public_key_string");
            sparseArray.append(3, "signature_public_key_signature_string");

            int size = sparseArray.size();

            for(int i = 0; i < size; i++)
            {
              bytes = cryptography.etm(strings[i + 3].getBytes());
              values.put
                  (sparseArray.get(i),
                   Base64.encodeToString(bytes, Base64.DEFAULT));
            }

            bytes = cryptography.etm
              (sipHashId.toUpperCase().trim().
               getBytes(StandardCharsets.UTF_8));
            values.put
              ("siphash_id", Base64.encodeToString(bytes, Base64.DEFAULT));
            values.put
              ("siphash_id_digest",
```

```
            Base64.encodeToString
              (cryptography.hmac(sipHashId.toUpperCase().trim().
                          getBytes(StandardCharsets.UTF_8)),
               Base64.DEFAULT)));
          m_db.replace("public_key_pairs", null, values);
          sparseArray.clear();
      }
    catch(Exception exception)
      {
          return false;
      }

      return true;
    }

    private void updateRoutingIdentityTimestamp(String clientIdentity,
                                 String identity)
    {
      if(m_db == null)
          return;

      Cursor cursor = null;

      m_db.beginTransactionNonExclusive();

      try
      {
          cursor = m_db.rawQuery
            ("UPDATE routing_identities SET " +
             "timestamp = CURRENT_TIMESTAMP " +
             "WHERE client_identity = ? AND identity = ?",
             new String[] {clientIdentity, identity});

          if(cursor != null)
            m_cursorsOpened.getAndIncrement();

          m_db.setTransactionSuccessful();
      }
    catch(Exception exception)
      {
      }
    finally
      {
          if(cursor != null)
          {
            cursor.close();

            if(cursor.isClosed())
                m_cursorsClosed.getAndIncrement();
          }

          m_db.endTransaction();
      }
    }

    public ArrayList<byte[]> readIdentities(int limit)
    {
      if(m_db == null)
          return null;

      Cursor cursor = null;
      ArrayList<byte[]> arrayList = null;
```

```java
    try
    {
        if(limit > 0)
          cursor = m_db.rawQuery
              ("SELECT DISTINCT(identity) FROM routing_identities " +
               "ORDER BY timestamp DESC LIMIT ?",
               new String[] {String.valueOf(limit)});
        else
          cursor = m_db.rawQuery
              ("SELECT DISTINCT(identity) FROM routing_identities " +
               "ORDER BY timestamp DESC", null);

        if(cursor != null)
          m_cursorsOpened.getAndIncrement();

        arrayList = new ArrayList<> ();

        while(cursor != null && cursor.moveToNext())
        {
          byte bytes[] = Base64.decode
              (cursor.getString(0).getBytes(), Base64.DEFAULT);

          if(bytes != null)
              arrayList.add(bytes);
        }

        if(arrayList.isEmpty())
          arrayList = null;
    }
    catch(Exception exception)
    {
        if(arrayList != null)
          arrayList.clear();

        arrayList = null;
    }
    finally
    {
        if(cursor != null)
        {
          cursor.close();

          if(cursor.isClosed())
              m_cursorsClosed.getAndIncrement();
        }
    }

    return arrayList;
  }

  public ArrayList<ListenerElement> readListeners
    (Cryptography cryptography, int listenerOid)
  {
    if(cryptography == null || m_db == null)
        return null;

    Cursor cursor = null;
    ArrayList<ListenerElement> arrayList = null;

    try
    {
        if(listenerOid == -1)
          cursor = m_db.rawQuery
```

```java
                ("SELECT " +
                 "certificate, " +
                 "ip_version, " +
                 "is_private, " +
                 "last_error, " +
                 "local_ip_address, " +
                 "local_port, " +
                 "local_scope_id, " +
                 "peers_count, " +
                 "private_key, " +
                 "public_key, " +
                 "status, " +
                 "status_control, " +
                 "uptime, " +
                 "OID " +
                 "FROM listeners", null);
            else
              cursor = m_db.rawQuery
                ("SELECT " +
                 "certificate, " +
                 "ip_version, " +
                 "is_private, " +
                 "last_error, " +
                 "local_ip_address, " +
                 "local_port, " +
                 "local_scope_id, " +
                 "peers_count, " +
                 "private_key, " +
                 "public_key, " +
                 "status, " +
                 "status_control, " +
                 "uptime, " +
                 "OID " +
                 "FROM listeners WHERE OID = ?",
                 new String[] {String.valueOf(listenerOid)});

        if(cursor != null)
          m_cursorsOpened.getAndIncrement();

        arrayList = new ArrayList<> ();

        while(cursor != null && cursor.moveToNext())
        {
          ListenerElement listenerElement = new ListenerElement();
          int count = cursor.getColumnCount();
          int oid = cursor.getInt(count - 1);

          for(int i = 0; i < count; i++)
          {
              if(i == count - 1)
              {
                listenerElement.m_oid = cursor.getInt(i);
                continue;
              }

              byte bytes[] = cryptography.mtd
                (Base64.decode(cursor.getString(i).getBytes(),
                            Base64.DEFAULT));

              if(bytes == null)
              {
                StringBuilder stringBuilder = new StringBuilder();
```

```java
                    stringBuilder.append("Database::readListeners(): ");
                    stringBuilder.append("error on column ");
                    stringBuilder.append(cursor.getColumnName(i));
                    stringBuilder.append(".");
                    writeLog(stringBuilder.toString());
                }

                switch(i)
                {
                case 0:
                  if(bytes != null)
                      listenerElement.m_certificate = bytes;

                  break;
                case 1:
                  if(bytes != null)
                      listenerElement.m_ipVersion = new String(bytes);
                  else
                      listenerElement.m_ipVersion =
                        "error (" + oid + ")";

                  break;
                case 2:
                  if(bytes != null)
                      listenerElement.m_isPrivate =
                        new String(bytes).equals("true");
                  else
                      listenerElement.m_isPrivate = false;

                  break;
                case 3:
                  if(bytes != null)
                      listenerElement.m_error = new String(bytes);
                  else
                      listenerElement.m_error = "error (" + oid + ")";

                  break;
                case 4:
                  if(bytes != null)
                      listenerElement.m_localIpAddress = new String
                        (bytes);
                  else
                      listenerElement.m_localIpAddress =
                        "error (" + oid + ")";

                  break;
                case 5:
                  if(bytes != null)
                      listenerElement.m_localPort = new String(bytes);
                  else
                      listenerElement.m_localPort =
                        "error (" + oid + ")";

                  break;
                case 6:
                  if(bytes != null)
                      listenerElement.m_localScopeId = new String
                        (bytes);
                  else
                      listenerElement.m_localScopeId =
                        "error (" + oid + ")";

                  break;
```

```java
            case 7:
              try
              {
                  if(bytes != null)
                    listenerElement.m_peersCount =
                        Long.parseLong(new String(bytes));
                  else
                    listenerElement.m_peersCount = 0;
              }
              catch(Exception exception)
              {
                  listenerElement.m_peersCount = 0;
              }

              break;
            case 8:
              if(bytes != null)
                  listenerElement.m_privateKey = bytes;

              break;
            case 9:
              if(bytes != null)
                  listenerElement.m_publicKey = bytes;

              break;
            case 10:
              if(bytes != null)
                  listenerElement.m_status = new String(bytes);
              else
                  listenerElement.m_status =
                    "error (" + oid + ")";

              break;
            case 11:
              if(bytes != null)
                  listenerElement.m_statusControl = new String
                    (bytes);
              else
                  listenerElement.m_statusControl =
                    "error (" + oid + ")";

              break;
            case 12:
              if(bytes != null)
                  listenerElement.m_uptime = new String(bytes);
              else
                  listenerElement.m_uptime =
                    "error (" + oid + ")";

              break;
            }
          }

        arrayList.add(listenerElement);
        }

    if(arrayList.isEmpty())
      arrayList = null;
    else if(arrayList.size() > 1)
      Collections.sort(arrayList, s_readListenersComparator);
  }
catch(Exception exception)
  {
```

```java
        if(arrayList != null)
          arrayList.clear();

      arrayList = null;
    }
    finally
    {
        if(cursor != null)
        {
          cursor.close();

          if(cursor.isClosed())
              m_cursorsClosed.getAndIncrement();
        }
    }

    return arrayList;
  }

  public ArrayList<NeighborElement> readNeighborOids
    (Cryptography cryptography)
  {
    if(cryptography == null || m_db == null)
        return null;

    Cursor cursor = null;
    ArrayList<NeighborElement> arrayList = null;

    try
    {
        cursor = m_db.rawQuery
          ("SELECT status_control, OID FROM neighbors", null);

        if(cursor != null)
          m_cursorsOpened.getAndIncrement();

        arrayList = new ArrayList<> ();

        while(cursor != null && cursor.moveToNext())
        {
          NeighborElement neighborElement = new NeighborElement();
          boolean error = false;
          int count = cursor.getColumnCount();

          for(int i = 0; i < count; i++)
          {
              if(i == count - 1)
              {
                neighborElement.m_oid = cursor.getInt(i);
                continue;
              }

              byte bytes[] = cryptography.mtd
                (Base64.decode(cursor.getString(i).getBytes(),
                          Base64.DEFAULT));

              if(bytes == null)
              {
                error = true;

                StringBuilder stringBuilder = new StringBuilder();

                stringBuilder.append
```

```java
                    ("Database::readNeighborOids(): ");
                  stringBuilder.append("error on column ");
                  stringBuilder.append(cursor.getColumnName(i));
                  stringBuilder.append(".");
                  writeLog(stringBuilder.toString());
                  break;
                }

                switch(i)
                {
                case 0:
                  neighborElement.m_statusControl = new String(bytes);
                  break;
                }
            }

            if(!error)
                arrayList.add(neighborElement);
        }

        if(arrayList.isEmpty())
          arrayList = null;
    }
    catch(Exception exception)
    {
        if(arrayList != null)
          arrayList.clear();

        arrayList = null;
    }
    finally
    {
        if(cursor != null)
        {
          cursor.close();

          if(cursor.isClosed())
              m_cursorsClosed.getAndIncrement();
        }
    }

    return arrayList;
  }

  public ArrayList<NeighborElement> readNeighbors(Cryptography cryptography)
  {
    if(!State.getInstance().isAuthenticated())
        return null;

    if(cryptography == null || m_db == null)
        return null;

    Cursor cursor = null;
    ArrayList<NeighborElement> arrayList = null;

    try
    {
        cursor = m_db.rawQuery
          ("SELECT " +
            "(SELECT COUNT(*) FROM outbound_queue o WHERE " +
            "o.echo_queue = 0 AND o.neighbor_oid = n.OID), " +
            "(SELECT COUNT(*) FROM outbound_queue o WHERE " +
            "o.echo_queue = 1 AND o.neighbor_oid = n.OID), " +
```

```java
                "n.bytes_buffered, " +
                "n.bytes_read, " +
                "n.bytes_written, " +
                "n.ip_version, " +
                "n.last_error, " +
                "n.local_ip_address, " +
                "n.local_port, " +
                "n.proxy_ip_address, " +
                "n.proxy_port, " +
                "n.proxy_type, " +
                "n.queue_size, " +
                "n.remote_certificate, " +
                "n.remote_ip_address, " +
                "n.remote_port, " +
                "n.remote_scope_id, " +
                "n.session_cipher, " +
                "n.status, " +
                "n.status_control, " +
                "n.transport, " +
                "n.uptime, " +
                "n.OID " +
                "FROM neighbors n ORDER BY n.OID", null);

        if(cursor != null)
          m_cursorsOpened.getAndIncrement();

        arrayList = new ArrayList<> ();

        while(cursor != null && cursor.moveToNext())
        {
          NeighborElement neighborElement = new NeighborElement();
          int count = cursor.getColumnCount();
          int oid = cursor.getInt(count - 1);

          for(int i = 0; i < count; i++)
          {
              if(i == count - 1)
              {
                neighborElement.m_oid = cursor.getInt(i);
                continue;
              }

              byte bytes[] - null;

              if(i != 0 && i != 1)
                bytes = cryptography.mtd
                    (Base64.decode(cursor.getString(i).getBytes(),
                             Base64.DEFAULT));

              if(bytes == null && i != 0 && i != 1)
              {
                StringBuilder stringBuilder = new StringBuilder();

                stringBuilder.append("Database::readNeighbors(): ");
                stringBuilder.append("error on column ");
                stringBuilder.append(cursor.getColumnName(i));
                stringBuilder.append(".");
                writeLog(stringBuilder.toString());
              }

              switch(i)
              {
              case 0:
```

```java
              neighborElement.m_outboundQueued = cursor.
                  getLong(i);
            break;
          case 1:
            neighborElement.m_outboundEchoQueued =
                cursor.getLong(i);
            break;
          case 2:
            if(bytes != null)
                neighborElement.m_bytesBuffered =
                  new String(bytes);
            else
                neighborElement.m_bytesBuffered =
                  "error (" + oid + ")";

            break;
          case 3:
            if(bytes != null)
                neighborElement.m_bytesRead = new String(bytes);
            else
                neighborElement.m_bytesRead =
                  "error (" + oid + ")";

            break;
          case 4:
            if(bytes != null)
                neighborElement.m_bytesWritten =
                  new String(bytes);
            else
                neighborElement.m_bytesWritten =
                  "error (" + oid + ")";

            break;
          case 5:
            if(bytes != null)
                neighborElement.m_ipVersion = new String(bytes);
            else
                neighborElement.m_ipVersion =
                  "error (" + oid + ")";

            break;
          case 6:
            if(bytes != null)
                neighborElement.m_error = new String(bytes);
            else
                neighborElement.m_error =
                  "error (" + oid + ")";

            break;
          case 7:
            if(bytes != null)
                neighborElement.m_localIpAddress =
                  new String(bytes);
            else
                neighborElement.m_localIpAddress =
                  "error (" + oid + ")";

            break;
          case 8:
            if(bytes != null)
                neighborElement.m_localPort = new String(bytes);
            else
                neighborElement.m_localPort =
```

```java
              "error (" + oid + ")";

          break;
        case 9:
         if(bytes != null)
            neighborElement.m_proxyIpAddress =
              new String(bytes);
          else
            neighborElement.m_proxyIpAddress =
              "error (" + oid + ")";

          break;
        case 10:
         if(bytes != null)
            neighborElement.m_proxyPort = new String(bytes);
          else
            neighborElement.m_proxyPort =
              "error (" + oid + ")";

          break;
        case 11:
         if(bytes != null)
            neighborElement.m_proxyType = new String(bytes);
          else
            neighborElement.m_proxyType =
              "error (" + oid + ")";

          break;
        case 12:
         if(bytes != null)
            neighborElement.m_queueSize = new String(bytes);
          else
            neighborElement.m_queueSize =
              "error (" + oid + ")";

          break;
        case 13:
         if(bytes != null)
            neighborElement.m_remoteCertificate = bytes;

          break;
        case 14:
         if(bytes != null)
            neighborElement.m_remoteIpAddress =
              new String(bytes);
          else
            neighborElement.m_remoteIpAddress =
              "error (" + oid + ")";

          break;
        case 15:
         if(bytes != null)
            neighborElement.m_remotePort =
              new String(bytes);
          else
            neighborElement.m_remotePort =
              "error (" + oid + ")";

          break;
        case 16:
         if(bytes != null)
            neighborElement.m_remoteScopeId =
              new String(bytes);
```

```java
                    else
                        neighborElement.m_remoteScopeId =
                          "error (" + oid + ")";

                    break;
                  case 17:
                    if(bytes != null)
                        neighborElement.m_sessionCipher =
                          new String(bytes);
                    else
                        neighborElement.m_sessionCipher =
                          "error (" + oid + ")";

                    break;
                  case 18:
                    if(bytes != null)
                        neighborElement.m_status = new String(bytes);
                    else
                        neighborElement.m_status =
                          "error (" + oid + ")";

                    break;
                  case 19:
                    if(bytes != null)
                        neighborElement.m_statusControl =
                          new String(bytes);
                    else
                        neighborElement.m_statusControl =
                          "error (" + oid + ")";

                    break;
                  case 20:
                    if(bytes != null)
                        neighborElement.m_transport = new String(bytes);
                    else
                        neighborElement.m_transport =
                          "error (" + oid + ")";

                    break;
                  case 21:
                    if(bytes != null)
                        neighborElement.m_uptime = new String(bytes);
                    else
                        neighborElement.m_uptime =
                          "error (" + oid + ")";

                    break;
                }
            }

          arrayList.add(neighborElement);
        }

        if(arrayList.isEmpty())
          arrayList = null;
        else if(arrayList.size() > 1)
          Collections.sort(arrayList, s_readNeighborsComparator);
    }
    catch(Exception exception)
    {
        if(arrayList != null)
          arrayList.clear();
```

```java
            arrayList = null;
    }
    finally
    {
        if(cursor != null)
        {
          cursor.close();

          if(cursor.isClosed())
              m_cursorsClosed.getAndIncrement();
        }
    }

    return arrayList;
  }

  public ArrayList<OzoneElement> readOzones(Cryptography cryptography)
  {
    if(cryptography == null || m_db == null)
        return null;

    ArrayList<OzoneElement> arrayList = null;
    Cursor cursor = null;

    try
    {
        cursor = m_db.rawQuery
          ("SELECT " +
           "ozone_address, " +
           "ozone_address_stream, " +
           "OID " +
           "FROM ozones", null);

        if(cursor != null)
          m_cursorsOpened.getAndIncrement();

        arrayList = new ArrayList<> ();

        while(cursor != null && cursor.moveToNext())
        {
          OzoneElement ozoneElement = new OzoneElement();
          int count = cursor.getColumnCount();
          int oid = cursor.getInt(count - 1);

          for(int i = 0; i < count; i++)
          {
              if(i == count - 1)
              {
                ozoneElement.m_oid = cursor.getInt(i);
                continue;
              }

              byte bytes[] = cryptography.mtd
                (Base64.decode(cursor.getString(i).getBytes(),
                         Base64.DEFAULT));

              if(bytes == null)
              {
                StringBuilder stringBuilder = new StringBuilder();

                stringBuilder.append
                    ("Database::readOzones(): ");
                stringBuilder.append("error on column ");
```

```java
                    stringBuilder.append(cursor.getColumnName(i));
                    stringBuilder.append(".");
                    writeLog(stringBuilder.toString());
                }

                switch(i)
                {
                case 0:
                  if(bytes != null)
                      ozoneElement.m_address = new String(bytes);
                  else
                      ozoneElement.m_address =
                        "error (" + oid + ")";

                  break;
                case 1:
                  if(bytes != null)
                      ozoneElement.m_addressStream = bytes;

                  break;
                }
            }

            arrayList.add(ozoneElement);
          }

        if(arrayList.isEmpty())
          arrayList = null;
        else if(arrayList.size() > 1)
          Collections.sort(arrayList, s_readOzonesComparator);
      }
    catch(Exception exception)
    {
        if(arrayList != null)
          arrayList.clear();

        arrayList = null;
    }
    finally
    {
        if(cursor != null)
        {
          cursor.close();

          if(cursor.isClosed())
              m_cursorsClosed.getAndIncrement();
        }
    }

    return arrayList;
    }

    public ArrayList<SipHashIdElement> readSipHashIds(Cryptography
cryptography)
    {
      if(cryptography == null || m_db == null)
          return null;

      ArrayList<SipHashIdElement> arrayList = null;
      Cursor cursor = null;

      try
      {
```

```java
cursor = m_db.rawQuery
  ("SELECT " +
   "(SELECT EXISTS(SELECT 1 FROM participants p " +
   "WHERE p.siphash_id_digest = si.siphash_id_digest)) AS a, " +
   "(SELECT p.encryption_public_key_digest FROM participants p " +
   "WHERE p.siphash_id_digest = si.siphash_id_digest) AS b, " +
   "(SELECT COUNT(p.OID) FROM public_key_pairs p " +
   "WHERE p.siphash_id_digest = si.siphash_id_digest) AS c, " +
   "(SELECT COUNT(s.OID) FROM stack s WHERE " +
   "s.siphash_id_digest = si.siphash_id_digest AND " +
   "s.timestamp IS NULL) AS d, " +
   "(SELECT COUNT(s.OID) FROM stack s WHERE " +
   "s.siphash_id_digest = si.siphash_id_digest AND " +
   "s.timestamp IS NOT NULL) AS e, " +
   "si.accept_without_signatures, " +
   "si.name, " +
   "si.siphash_id, " +
   "si.stream, " +
   "si.timestamp, " +
   "si.OID " +
   "FROM siphash_ids si ORDER BY si.OID", null);

if(cursor != null)
  m_cursorsOpened.getAndIncrement();

arrayList = new ArrayList<> ();

while(cursor != null && cursor.moveToNext())
{
  SipHashIdElement sipHashIdElement = new SipHashIdElement();
  int count = cursor.getColumnCount();
  int oid = cursor.getInt(count - 1);

  for(int i = 0; i < count; i++)
  {
      switch(i)
      {
      case 0:
        sipHashIdElement.m_epksCompleted =
            cursor.getInt(i) > 0;
        continue;
      case 1:
        if(cursor.isNull(i) || cursor.getString(i).isEmpty())
        {
            sipHashIdElement.m_chatEncryptionKeyDigest = null;
            continue;
        }

        sipHashIdElement.m_chatEncryptionKeyDigest =
            Base64.decode(cursor.getString(i), Base64.DEFAULT);
        continue;
      case 2:
        sipHashIdElement.m_keysSigned = cursor.getLong(i) > 0L;
        continue;
      case 3:
        sipHashIdElement.m_inMessages = cursor.getLong(i);
        continue;
      case 4:
        sipHashIdElement.m_outMessages = cursor.getLong(i);
        sipHashIdElement.m_totalMessages =
            sipHashIdElement.m_inMessages +
            sipHashIdElement.m_outMessages;
        continue;
```

```java
          case 9:
            sipHashIdElement.m_timestamp = cursor.getString(i);
            continue;
          default:
            break;
          }

          if(i == count - 1)
          {
            sipHashIdElement.m_oid = cursor.getInt(i);
            continue;
          }

          byte bytes[] = cryptography.mtd
            (Base64.decode(cursor.getString(i).getBytes(),
                       Base64.DEFAULT));

          if(bytes == null)
          {
            StringBuilder stringBuilder = new StringBuilder();

            stringBuilder.append
                ("Database::readSipHashIds(): ");
            stringBuilder.append("error on column ");
            stringBuilder.append(cursor.getColumnName(i));
            stringBuilder.append(".");
            writeLog(stringBuilder.toString());
          }

          switch(i)
          {
          case 0:
          case 1:
          case 2:
          case 3:
          case 4:
            break;
          case 5:
            if(bytes != null)
                sipHashIdElement.m_acceptWithoutSignatures =
                  new String(bytes).equals("true");

            break;
          case 6:
            if(bytes != null)
                sipHashIdElement.m_name = new String(bytes);
            else
                sipHashIdElement.m_name =
                  "error (" + oid + ")";

            break;
          case 7:
            if(bytes != null)
                sipHashIdElement.m_sipHashId = new String
                  (bytes, StandardCharsets.UTF_8);
            else
                sipHashIdElement.m_sipHashId =
                  "error (" + oid + ")";

            break;
          case 8:
            if(bytes != null)
                sipHashIdElement.m_stream = bytes;
```

```java
                break;
              default:
                break;
            }
          }

          arrayList.add(sipHashIdElement);
        }

      if(arrayList.isEmpty())
        arrayList = null;
      else if(arrayList.size() > 1)
        Collections.sort(arrayList, s_readSipHashIdsComparator);
    }
  catch(Exception exception)
    {
        if(arrayList != null)
          arrayList.clear();

        arrayList = null;
    }
  finally
    {
        if(cursor != null)
        {
          cursor.close();

          if(cursor.isClosed())
              m_cursorsClosed.getAndIncrement();
        }
    }

  return arrayList;
  }

  public ArrayList<byte[]> readTaggedMessage(String sipHashIdDigest,
                                 Cryptography cryptography,
                                 int oid)
  {
    if(cryptography == null || m_db == null)
        return null;

    ArrayList<byte[]> arrayList = null;
    Cursor cursor = null;

    try
    {
        cursor = m_db.rawQuery
          ("SELECT message, message_digest, OID " +
           "FROM stack WHERE siphash_id_digest = ? AND " +
           "timestamp IS NULL AND verified_digest = ? AND " +
           "OID > CAST(? AS INTEGER) ORDER BY OID",
           new String[] {sipHashIdDigest,
                       Base64.
                       encodeToString(cryptography.
                                hmac("true".getBytes()),
                                Base64.DEFAULT),
                     String.valueOf(oid)});

        if(cursor != null)
          m_cursorsOpened.getAndIncrement();
```

```java
        arrayList = new ArrayList<> ();

        while(cursor != null && cursor.moveToNext())
        {
          boolean error = false;
          int count = cursor.getColumnCount();

          for(int i = 0; i < count; i++)
          {
              byte bytes[] = null;

              switch(i)
              {
              case 0:
                bytes = cryptography.mtd
                    (Base64.decode(cursor.getString(i).getBytes(),
                            Base64.DEFAULT));

                if(bytes != null)
                    arrayList.add(bytes);
                else
                    error = true;

                break;
              case 1:
                arrayList.add(cursor.getString(i).getBytes());
                break;
              case 2:
                arrayList.add
                    (Miscellaneous.intToByteArray(cursor.getInt(i)));
                break;
              }

              if(error)
                break;
          }

          if(error)
              arrayList.clear();
          else
              break;
        }

        if(arrayList.isEmpty())
          arrayList = null;
    }
    catch(Exception exception)
    {
        if(arrayList != null)
          arrayList.clear();

        arrayList = null;
    }
    finally
    {
        if(cursor != null)
        {
          cursor.close();

          if(cursor.isClosed())
              m_cursorsClosed.getAndIncrement();
        }
    }
```

```java
    return arrayList;
  }

  public MessageTotals readMessageTotals(String oid)
  {
    if(m_db == null)
        return null;

    Cursor cursor = null;
    MessageTotals messageTotals = null;

    try
    {
        cursor = m_db.rawQuery
          ("SELECT (SELECT COUNT(s.OID) FROM stack s WHERE " +
            "s.siphash_id_digest = si.siphash_id_digest AND " +
            "s.timestamp IS NULL) AS a, " +
            "(SELECT COUNT(s.OID) FROM stack s WHERE " +
            "s.siphash_id_digest = si.siphash_id_digest AND " +
            "s.timestamp IS NOT NULL) AS b, " +
            "si.OID " +
            "FROM siphash_ids si WHERE si.OID = ? ORDER BY si.OID",
            new String[] {oid});

        if(cursor != null)
          m_cursorsOpened.getAndIncrement();

        if(cursor != null && cursor.moveToFirst())
        {
          messageTotals = new MessageTotals();
          messageTotals.m_inMessages = cursor.getLong(0);
          messageTotals.m_outMessages = cursor.getLong(1);
          messageTotals.m_totalMessages = messageTotals.m_inMessages +
              messageTotals.m_outMessages;
        }
    }
    catch(Exception exception)
    {
        messageTotals = null;
    }
    finally
    {
        if(cursor != null)
        {
          cursor.close();

          if(cursor.isClosed())
              m_cursorsClosed.getAndIncrement();
        }
    }

    return messageTotals;
  }

  public PublicKey signatureKeyForDigest(Cryptography cryptography,
                          byte digest[])
  {
    if(cryptography == null ||
        digest == null ||
        digest.length == 0 ||
        m_db == null)
        return null;
```

```java
        Cursor cursor = null;
        PublicKey publicKey = null;

        try
        {
            cursor = m_db.rawQuery
              ("SELECT " +
               "signature_public_key " +
               "FROM participants WHERE encryption_public_key_digest = ?",
               new String[] {Base64.encodeToString(digest, Base64.DEFAULT)});

            if(cursor != null)
              m_cursorsOpened.getAndIncrement();

            if(cursor != null && cursor.moveToFirst())
            {
              byte bytes[] = cryptography.mtd
                    (Base64.decode(cursor.getString(0).getBytes(),
                            Base64.DEFAULT));

              if(bytes != null)
                  for(int i = 0; i < 2; i++)
                    try
                    {
                        if(i == 0)
                          publicKey = KeyFactory.getInstance("EC").
                              generatePublic
                              (new X509EncodedKeySpec(bytes));
                        else
                          publicKey = KeyFactory.getInstance("RSA").
                              generatePublic
                              (new X509EncodedKeySpec(bytes));

                        break;
                    }
                    catch(Exception exception)
                    {
                    }
            }
        }
        catch(Exception exception)
        {
            publicKey = null;
        }
        finally
        {
            if(cursor != null)
            {
              cursor.close();

              if(cursor.isClosed())
                  m_cursorsClosed.getAndIncrement();
            }
        }

        return publicKey;
    }

    public SparseIntArray readNeighborOids()
    {
      if(m_db == null)
          return null;
```

```java
        Cursor cursor = null;
        SparseIntArray sparseArray = null;

        try
        {
            cursor = m_db.rawQuery("SELECT OID FROM neighbors", null);

            if(cursor != null)
              m_cursorsOpened.getAndIncrement();

            int index = -1;

            sparseArray = new SparseIntArray();

            while(cursor != null && cursor.moveToNext())
            {
              index += 1;
              sparseArray.append(index, cursor.getInt(0));
            }

            if(index == -1)
              sparseArray = null;
        }
        catch(Exception exception)
        {
            if(sparseArray != null)
              sparseArray.clear();

            sparseArray = null;
        }
        finally
        {
            if(cursor != null)
            {
              cursor.close();

              if(cursor.isClosed())
                  m_cursorsClosed.getAndIncrement();
            }
        }

        return sparseArray;
    }

    public String nameFromSipHashId(Cryptography cryptography, String
sipHashId)
    {
      if(cryptography == null || m_db == null)
          return "";

      Cursor cursor = null;
      String name = "";

      try
      {
          cursor = m_db.rawQuery
            ("SELECT name FROM siphash_ids WHERE siphash_id_digest = ?",
             new String[] {Base64.
                        encodeToString
                          (cryptography.
                        hmac(sipHashId.toUpperCase().trim().
                            getBytes(StandardCharsets.UTF_8)),
```

```java
                    Base64.DEFAULT)});

        if(cursor != null)
          m_cursorsOpened.getAndIncrement();

        if(cursor != null && cursor.moveToFirst())
        {
          byte bytes[] = cryptography.mtd
              (Base64.decode(cursor.getString(0).getBytes(),
                       Base64.DEFAULT));

          if(bytes != null)
              name = new String(bytes);
        }
    }
    catch(Exception exception)
    {
    }
    finally
    {
        if(cursor != null)
        {
          cursor.close();

          if(cursor.isClosed())
              m_cursorsClosed.getAndIncrement();
        }
    }

    return name;
}

public String readListenerNeighborStatusControl
  (Cryptography cryptography, String table, int oid)
{
  if(cryptography == null || m_db == null)
      return null;

  Cursor cursor = null;
  String status = "";

  try
  {
      cursor = m_db.rawQuery
        ("SELECT status_control FROM " + table + " WHERE OID = ?",
         new String[] {String.valueOf(oid)});

      if(cursor != null)
        m_cursorsOpened.getAndIncrement();

      if(cursor != null && cursor.moveToFirst())
      {
        byte bytes[] = cryptography.mtd
            (Base64.decode(cursor.getString(0).getBytes(),
                     Base64.DEFAULT));

        if(bytes != null)
            status = new String(bytes);
      }
  }
  catch(Exception exception)
  {
  }
```

```java
    finally
    {
        if(cursor != null)
        {
          cursor.close();

          if(cursor.isClosed())
              m_cursorsClosed.getAndIncrement();
        }
    }

    return status;
    }

    public String readSetting(Cryptography cryptography, String name)
    {
      if(m_db == null)
          return "";

      Cursor cursor = null;
      String str = "";

      try
      {
          if(cryptography == null)
            cursor = m_db.rawQuery
                ("SELECT value FROM settings WHERE name = ?",
                 new String[] {name});
          else
          {
            byte bytes[] = cryptography.hmac(name.getBytes());

            if(bytes != null)
                cursor = m_db.rawQuery
                  ("SELECT value FROM settings WHERE name_digest = ?",
                   new String[] {Base64.encodeToString(bytes,
                                          Base64.DEFAULT)});
          }

          if(cursor != null)
            m_cursorsOpened.getAndIncrement();

          if(cursor != null && cursor.moveToFirst())
            if(cryptography == null)
                str = cursor.getString(0);
            else
            {
                byte bytes[] = cryptography.mtd
                  (Base64.decode(cursor.getString(0).getBytes(),
                            Base64.DEFAULT));

                if(bytes != null)
                  str = new String(bytes);
            }
      }
      catch(Exception exception)
      {
          str = "";
      }
      finally
      {
          if(cursor != null)
          {
```

```java
        cursor.close();

        if(cursor.isClosed())
            m_cursorsClosed.getAndIncrement();
      }
    }

    /*
    ** Default values.
    */

    if(name.equals("show_chat_icons") && str.isEmpty())
        return "true";

    return str;
  }

  public String sipHashIdDigestFromDigest(Cryptography cryptography,
                                          byte digest[])
  {
    if(cryptography == null ||
       digest == null ||
       digest.length == 0 ||
       m_db == null)
        return "";

    Cursor cursor = null;
    String sipHashIdDigest = "";

    try
    {
        cursor = m_db.rawQuery
          ("SELECT siphash_id_digest " +
           "FROM participants WHERE encryption_public_key_digest = ?",
           new String[] {Base64.encodeToString(digest, Base64.DEFAULT)});

        if(cursor != null)
          m_cursorsOpened.getAndIncrement();

        if(cursor != null && cursor.moveToFirst())
          sipHashIdDigest = cursor.getString(0);
    }
    catch(Exception exception)
    {
        sipHashIdDigest = "";
    }
    finally
    {
        if(cursor != null)
        {
          cursor.close();

          if(cursor.isClosed())
              m_cursorsClosed.getAndIncrement();
        }
    }

    return sipHashIdDigest;
  }

  public String[] readOutboundMessage(boolean echo, int oid)
  {
    if(m_db == null)
```

```java
      return null;

    Cursor cursor = null;
    String array[] = null;

    try
    {
        cursor = m_db.rawQuery
          ("SELECT message, OID FROM outbound_queue WHERE " +
           "echo_queue = ? AND neighbor_oid = ? ORDER BY OID LIMIT 1",
           new String[] {String.valueOf(echo ? 1 : 0),
                         String.valueOf(oid)});

        if(cursor != null)
          m_cursorsOpened.getAndIncrement();

        if(cursor != null && cursor.moveToFirst())
        {
          array = new String[2];
          array[0] = cursor.getString(0);
          array[1] = String.valueOf(cursor.getInt(1));
        }
    }
    catch(Exception exception)
    {
        array = null;
    }
    finally
    {
        if(cursor != null)
        {
          cursor.close();

          if(cursor.isClosed())
              m_cursorsClosed.getAndIncrement();
        }
    }

    return array;
  }

  public String[] readPublicKeyPair(Cryptography cryptography,
                         String sipHashId)
  {
    if(cryptography == null || m_db == null)
        return null;

    Cursor cursor = null;
    String array[] = null;

    try
    {
        cursor = m_db.rawQuery
          ("SELECT " +
           "key_type, " +
           "public_key_string, " +
           "public_key_signature_string, " +
           "signature_public_key_string, " +
           "signature_public_key_signature_string " +
           "FROM public_key_pairs WHERE siphash_id_digest = ?",
           new String[] {Base64.
                         encodeToString
                         (cryptography.
```

```java
                        hmac(sipHashId.toUpperCase().trim().
                            getBytes(StandardCharsets.UTF_8)),
                    Base64.DEFAULT)});

        if(cursor != null)
          m_cursorsOpened.getAndIncrement();

        if(cursor != null && cursor.moveToFirst())
        {
          boolean error = false;
          int count = cursor.getColumnCount();

          array = new String[count + 1];

          for(int i = 0; i < count; i++)
          {
              byte bytes[] = cryptography.mtd
                (Base64.decode(cursor.getString(i).getBytes(),
                        Base64.DEFAULT));

              if(bytes == null)
              {
                error = true;

                StringBuilder stringBuilder = new StringBuilder();

                stringBuilder.append("Database::readPublicKeyPair(): ");
                stringBuilder.append("error on column ");
                stringBuilder.append(cursor.getColumnName(i));
                stringBuilder.append(".");
                writeLog(stringBuilder.toString());
                break;
              }
              else
                array[i] = new String(bytes);
          }

          if(!error)
              array[count] = Base64.encodeToString
                (sipHashId.getBytes(StandardCharsets.UTF_8),
                 Base64.NO_WRAP);

          if(error)
              array = null;
        }
    }
    catch(Exception exception)
    {
        array = null;
    }
    finally
    {
        if(cursor != null)
        {
          cursor.close();

          if(cursor.isClosed())
              m_cursorsClosed.getAndIncrement();
        }
    }

    return array;
}
```

```java
public boolean accountPrepared()
{
  return !readSetting(null, "encryptionSalt").isEmpty() &&
      !readSetting(null, "macSalt").isEmpty() &&
      !readSetting(null, "saltedPassword").isEmpty();
}

public boolean containsCongestionDigest(long value)
{
  if(m_db == null)
      return false;

  boolean contains = false;

  s_congestionControlMutex.readLock().lock();

  try
  {
      Cursor cursor = null;

      try
      {
        cursor = m_db.rawQuery
            ("SELECT EXISTS(SELECT 1 FROM " +
             "congestion_control WHERE digest = ?)",
             new String[] {Base64.
                       encodeToString(Miscellaneous.
                                 longToByteArray(value),
                                 Base64.DEFAULT)});

        if(cursor != null)
            m_cursorsOpened.getAndIncrement();

        if(cursor != null && cursor.moveToFirst())
            contains = cursor.getInt(0) == 1;
      }
      catch(Exception exception)
      {
      }
      finally
      {
        if(cursor != null)
        {
            cursor.close();

            if(cursor.isClosed())
              m_cursorsClosed.getAndIncrement();
        }
      }
  }
  finally
  {
      s_congestionControlMutex.readLock().unlock();
  }

  return contains;
}

public boolean containsRoutingIdentity(String clientIdentity,
                           String message)
{
  if(clientIdentity == null ||
```

```java
      clientIdentity.length() == 0 ||
     m_db == null ||
     message == null ||
     message.trim().isEmpty())
      return false;

  Cursor cursor = null;

  try
  {
      String strings[] = Messages.stripMessage(message).split("\\n");
      byte array1[] = null;
      byte array2[] = null;

      if(strings != null && strings.length == 3) // Buzz, Fire
      {
        array1 = Miscellaneous.joinByteArrays
            (Base64.decode(strings[0], Base64.NO_WRAP),
             Base64.decode(strings[1], Base64.NO_WRAP));
        array2 = Base64.decode(strings[2], Base64.NO_WRAP);
      }
      else
      {
        byte data[] = Base64.decode
            (Messages.stripMessage(message), Base64.DEFAULT);

        array1 = Arrays.copyOfRange(data, 0, data.length - 64);
        array2 = Arrays.copyOfRange
            (data, data.length - 64, data.length);
      }

      cursor = m_db.rawQuery
        ("SELECT identity FROM routing_identities WHERE " +
         "client_identity = ?", new String[] {clientIdentity});

      if(cursor != null)
        m_cursorsOpened.getAndIncrement();

      while(cursor != null && cursor.moveToNext())
      {
        byte bytes[] = Base64.decode
            (cursor.getString(0), Base64.DEFAULT);

        if(Cryptography.
           memcmp(Cryptography.hmac(array1, bytes), array2))
        {
            updateRoutingIdentityTimestamp
              (clientIdentity, cursor.getString(0));
            return true;
        }
      }
  }
  catch(Exception exception)
  {
  }
  finally
  {
      if(cursor != null)
      {
        cursor.close();

        if(cursor.isClosed())
            m_cursorsClosed.getAndIncrement();
```

```java
        }
    }

    return false;
  }

  public boolean deleteEntry(String oid, String table)
  {
    if(m_db == null)
        return false;

    boolean ok = false;

    m_db.beginTransactionNonExclusive();

    try
    {
        ok = m_db.delete(table, "OID = ?", new String[] {oid}) > 0;
        m_db.setTransactionSuccessful();
    }
    catch(Exception exception)
    {
        ok = false;
    }
    finally
    {
        m_db.endTransaction();
    }

    return ok;
  }

  public boolean deleteOzone(Cryptography cryptography,
                    ListenerElement listenerElement)
  {
    if(cryptography == null || listenerElement == null || m_db == null)
        return false;

    String ozone = listenerElement.m_localIpAddress +
        ":" +
        listenerElement.m_localPort +
        ":TCP";
    String ozoneAddressDigest = Base64.encodeToString
        (cryptography.
         hmac(ozone.getBytes(StandardCharsets.UTF_8)), Base64.DEFAULT);
    boolean ok = true;

    m_db.beginTransactionNonExclusive();

    try
    {
        ok = m_db.delete
          ("ozones",
           "ozone_address_digest = ?",
           new String[] {ozoneAddressDigest}) > 0;
        m_db.setTransactionSuccessful();
    }
    catch(Exception exception)
    {
        ok = false;
    }
    finally
    {
```

```java
        m_db.endTransaction();
    }

    return ok;
  }

  public boolean deleteOzoneAndSipHashId(String oid)
  {
    if(m_db == null)
        return false;

    boolean ok = false;

    m_db.beginTransactionNonExclusive();

    try
    {
        m_db.execSQL
          ("DELETE FROM ozones WHERE ozone_address_digest IN " +
            "(SELECT siphash_id_digest FROM siphash_ids WHERE OID = ?)",
            new String[] {oid});
        ok = m_db.delete("siphash_ids", "OID = ?", new String[] {oid}) > 0;
        m_db.setTransactionSuccessful();
    }
    catch(Exception exception)
    {
        ok = false;
    }
    finally
    {
        m_db.endTransaction();
    }

    return ok;
  }

  public boolean removeMessages()
  {
    if(m_db == null)
        return false;

    boolean ok = false;

    m_db.beginTransactionNonExclusive();

    try
    {
        ok = m_db.delete("stack", null, null) > 0;
        m_db.setTransactionSuccessful();
    }
    catch(Exception exception)
    {
        ok = false;
    }
    finally
    {
        m_db.endTransaction();
    }

    return ok;
  }

  public boolean removeMessages(String oid)
```

```java
{
  if(m_db == null)
      return false;

  boolean ok = false;

  m_db.beginTransactionNonExclusive();

  try
  {
      ok = m_db.delete
        ("stack",
         "siphash_id_digest = (SELECT siphash_id_digest " +
         "FROM siphash_ids WHERE OID = ?)",
         new String[] {oid}) > 0;
      m_db.setTransactionSuccessful();
  }
  catch(Exception exception)
  {
      ok = false;
  }
  finally
  {
      m_db.endTransaction();
  }

  return ok;
}

public boolean resetRetrievalState(Cryptography cryptography,
                          String oid)
{
  if(cryptography == null || m_db == null)
      return false;

  boolean ok = false;

  m_db.beginTransactionNonExclusive();

  try
  {
      ContentValues values = new ContentValues();

      values.put
        ("verified_digest",
         Base64.encodeToString(cryptography.
                      hmac("false".getBytes()),
                      Base64.DEFAULT));
      values.putNull("timestamp");
      ok = m_db.update
        ("stack",
         values,
         "siphash_id_digest = (SELECT siphash_id_digest " +
         "FROM siphash_ids WHERE OID = ?)",
         new String[] {oid}) > 0;
      m_db.setTransactionSuccessful();
  }
  catch(Exception exception)
  {
      ok = false;
  }
  finally
  {
```

```java
            m_db.endTransaction();
    }

    return ok;
}

public boolean writeListener(Cryptography cryptography,
                             String ipAddress,
                             String ipPort,
                             String ipScopeId,
                             String version,
                             boolean isPrivate)
{
    if(cryptography == null || m_db == null)
        return false;

    ContentValues values = null;
    boolean ok = true;

    try
    {
        values = new ContentValues();
    }
    catch(Exception exception)
    {
        ok = false;
    }

    if(!ok)
        return ok;

    /*
    ** Content values should prevent SQL injections.
    */

    try
    {
        SparseArray<String> sparseArray = new SparseArray<> ();
        byte bytes[] = null;

        sparseArray.append(0, "certificate");
        sparseArray.append(1, "ip_version");
        sparseArray.append(2, "is_private");
        sparseArray.append(3, "last_error");
        sparseArray.append(4, "local_ip_address");
        sparseArray.append(5, "local_ip_address_digest");
        sparseArray.append(6, "local_port");
        sparseArray.append(7, "local_port_digest");
        sparseArray.append(8, "local_scope_id");
        sparseArray.append(9, "peers_count");
        sparseArray.append(10, "private_key");
        sparseArray.append(11, "public_key");
            sparseArray.append(12, "status");
            sparseArray.append(13, "status_control");
        sparseArray.append(14, "uptime");

        if(!ipAddress.toLowerCase().trim().matches(".*[a-z].*"))
        {
          Matcher matcher = Patterns.IP_ADDRESS.matcher(ipAddress.trim());

            if(!matcher.matches())
            {
                if(version.toLowerCase().equals("ipv4"))
```

```java
                    ipAddress = "0.0.0.0";
                else
                    ipAddress = "0:0:0:0:0:ffff:0:0";
            }
        }

        int size = sparseArray.size();

        for(int i = 0; i < size; i++)
        {
          switch(sparseArray.get(i))
          {
          case "ip_version":
              bytes = cryptography.etm(version.trim().getBytes());
              break;
          case "is_private":
              bytes = cryptography.etm
                (isPrivate ? "true".getBytes() : "false".getBytes());
              break;
          case "local_ip_address":
              bytes = cryptography.etm(ipAddress.trim().getBytes());
              break;
          case "local_ip_address_digest":
              bytes = cryptography.hmac(ipAddress.trim().getBytes());
              break;
          case "local_port":
              bytes = cryptography.etm(ipPort.trim().getBytes());
              break;
          case "local_port_digest":
              bytes = cryptography.hmac(ipPort.trim().getBytes());
              break;
          case "local_scope_id":
              bytes = cryptography.etm(ipScopeId.trim().getBytes());
              break;
          case "peers_count":
              bytes = cryptography.etm("0".getBytes());
              break;
          case "status":
              bytes = cryptography.etm("disconnected".getBytes());
              break;
          case "status_control":
              bytes = cryptography.etm("listen".getBytes());
              break;
          default:
              bytes = cryptography.etm("".getBytes());
              break;
          }

          if(bytes == null)
          {
              sparseArray.clear();

              StringBuilder stringBuilder = new StringBuilder();

              stringBuilder.append
                ("Database::writeListener(): error with ");
              stringBuilder.append(sparseArray.get(i));
              stringBuilder.append(" field.");
              writeLog(stringBuilder.toString());
              throw new Exception();
          }

          String str = Base64.encodeToString(bytes, Base64.DEFAULT);
```

```java
            values.put(sparseArray.get(i), str);
        }

        sparseArray.clear();
    }
    catch(Exception exception)
    {
        ok = false;
    }

    m_db.beginTransactionNonExclusive();

    try
    {
        if(ok)
        {
          m_db.insertOrThrow("listeners", null, values);
          m_db.setTransactionSuccessful();
        }
    }
    catch(SQLiteConstraintException exception)
    {
        ok = exception.getMessage().toLowerCase().contains("unique");
    }
    catch(Exception exception)
      {
        ok = false;
    }
    finally
    {
        m_db.endTransaction();
    }

    return ok;
}

public boolean writeNeighbor(Cryptography cryptography,
                    String proxyIpAddress,
                    String proxyPort,
                    String proxyType,
                    String remoteIpAddress,
                    String remoteIpPort,
                    String remoteIpScopeId,
                    String transport,
                    String version)
{
  if(cryptography == null || m_db == null)
      return false;

  ContentValues values = null;
  boolean ok = true;

  try
  {
      values = new ContentValues();
  }
  catch(Exception exception)
  {
      ok = false;
  }

  if(!ok)
```

```java
        return ok;

    /*
    ** Content values should prevent SQL injections.
    */

    try
    {
        SparseArray<String> sparseArray = new SparseArray<> ();
        byte bytes[] = null;

        sparseArray.append(0, "bytes_buffered");
        sparseArray.append(1, "bytes_read");
        sparseArray.append(2, "bytes_written");
        sparseArray.append(3, "ip_version");
        sparseArray.append(4, "last_error");
        sparseArray.append(5, "local_ip_address");
        sparseArray.append(6, "local_ip_address_digest");
        sparseArray.append(7, "local_port");
        sparseArray.append(8, "local_port_digest");
        sparseArray.append(9, "proxy_ip_address");
        sparseArray.append(10, "proxy_port");
        sparseArray.append(11, "proxy_type");
        sparseArray.append(12, "queue_size");
        sparseArray.append(13, "remote_certificate");
        sparseArray.append(14, "remote_ip_address");
        sparseArray.append(15, "remote_ip_address_digest");
        sparseArray.append(16, "remote_port");
          sparseArray.append(17, "remote_port_digest");
          sparseArray.append(18, "remote_scope_id");
          sparseArray.append(19, "session_cipher");
          sparseArray.append(20, "status");
          sparseArray.append(21, "status_control");
          sparseArray.append(22, "transport");
          sparseArray.append(23, "transport_digest");
          sparseArray.append(24, "uptime");
          sparseArray.append(25, "user_defined_digest");

        /*
        ** Proxy information.
        */

        proxyIpAddress = proxyIpAddress.trim();

        if(proxyIpAddress.isEmpty())
          proxyPort = "";

        if(!remoteIpAddress.toLowerCase().trim().matches(".*[a-z].*"))
        {
          Matcher matcher = Patterns.IP_ADDRESS.matcher
              (remoteIpAddress.trim());

          if(!matcher.matches())
          {
              if(version.toLowerCase().equals("ipv4"))
                remoteIpAddress = "0.0.0.0";
              else
                remoteIpAddress = "0:0:0:0:0:ffff:0:0";
          }
        }

        int size = sparseArray.size();
```

```java
for(int i = 0; i < size; i++)
{
  switch(sparseArray.get(i))
  {
  case "ip_version":
      bytes = cryptography.etm(version.trim().getBytes());
      break;
  case "last_error":
      bytes = cryptography.etm("".getBytes());
      break;
  case "local_ip_address_digest":
      bytes = cryptography.hmac("".getBytes());
      break;
  case "local_port_digest":
      bytes = cryptography.hmac("".getBytes());
      break;
  case "proxy_ip_address":
      bytes = cryptography.etm(proxyIpAddress.getBytes());
      break;
  case "proxy_port":
      bytes = cryptography.etm(proxyPort.getBytes());
      break;
  case "proxy_type":
      bytes = cryptography.etm(proxyType.getBytes());
      break;
  case "remote_ip_address":
      bytes = cryptography.etm
        (remoteIpAddress.trim().getBytes());
      break;
  case "remote_ip_address_digest":
      bytes = cryptography.hmac
        (remoteIpAddress.trim().getBytes());
      break;
  case "remote_port":
      bytes = cryptography.etm(remoteIpPort.trim().getBytes());
      break;
  case "remote_port_digest":
      bytes = cryptography.hmac(remoteIpPort.trim().getBytes());
      break;
  case "remote_scope_id":
      bytes = cryptography.etm
        (remoteIpScopeId.trim().getBytes());
      break;
  case "status":
      bytes = cryptography.etm("disconnected".getBytes());
      break;
  case "status_control":
      bytes = cryptography.etm("connect".getBytes());
      break;
  case "transport":
      bytes = cryptography.etm(transport.trim().getBytes());
      break;
  case "transport_digest":
      bytes = cryptography.hmac(transport.trim().getBytes());
      break;
  case "user_defined_digest":
      bytes = cryptography.hmac("true".getBytes());
      break;
  default:
      bytes = cryptography.etm("".getBytes());
      break;
  }
```

```java
            if(bytes == null)
            {
                sparseArray.clear();

                StringBuilder stringBuilder = new StringBuilder();

                stringBuilder.append
                    ("Database::writeNeighbor(): error with ");
                stringBuilder.append(sparseArray.get(i));
                stringBuilder.append(" field.");
                writeLog(stringBuilder.toString());
                throw new Exception();
            }

            String str = Base64.encodeToString(bytes, Base64.DEFAULT);

            values.put(sparseArray.get(i), str);
        }

        sparseArray.clear();
    }
    catch(Exception exception)
    {
        ok = false;
    }

    m_db.beginTransactionNonExclusive();

    try
    {
        if(ok)
        {
          m_db.insertOrThrow("neighbors", null, values);
          m_db.setTransactionSuccessful();
        }
    }
    catch(SQLiteConstraintException exception)
    {
        ok = exception.getMessage().toLowerCase().contains("unique");
    }
    catch(Exception exception)
      {
        ok = false;
    }
    finally
    {
        m_db.endTransaction();
    }

    return ok;
}

public boolean writeOzone(Cryptography cryptography,
                 String address,
                 byte addressStream[])
{
  if(address == null ||
     address.trim().isEmpty() ||
     addressStream == null ||
     addressStream.length == 0 ||
     cryptography == null ||
     m_db == null)
      return false;
```

```java
ContentValues values = null;
boolean ok = true;

try
{
    values = new ContentValues();
}
catch(Exception exception)
{
    ok = false;
}

if(!ok)
    return ok;

/*
** Content values should prevent SQL injections.
*/

try
{
    SparseArray<String> sparseArray = new SparseArray<> ();
    byte bytes[] = null;

    sparseArray.append(0, "ozone_address");
    sparseArray.append(1, "ozone_address_digest");
    sparseArray.append(2, "ozone_address_stream");

    int size = sparseArray.size();

    for(int i = 0; i < size; i++)
    {
      switch(sparseArray.get(i))
       {
      case "ozone_address":
          bytes = cryptography.etm
            (address.trim().getBytes(StandardCharsets.UTF_8));
          break;
      case "ozone_address_digest":
          bytes = cryptography.hmac
            (address.trim().getBytes(StandardCharsets.UTF_8));
          break;
      default:
          bytes = cryptography.etm(addressStream);
          break;
       }

      if(bytes == null)
      {
          sparseArray.clear();

          StringBuilder stringBuilder = new StringBuilder();

          stringBuilder.append
            ("Database::writeOzone(): error with ");
          stringBuilder.append(sparseArray.get(i));
          stringBuilder.append(" field.");
          writeLog(stringBuilder.toString());
          throw new Exception();
      }

      String str = Base64.encodeToString(bytes, Base64.DEFAULT);
```

```java
            values.put(sparseArray.get(i), str);
        }

        sparseArray.clear();
    }
    catch(Exception exception)
    {
        ok = false;
    }

    m_db.beginTransactionNonExclusive();

    try
    {
        if(ok)
        {
            if(m_db.replace("ozones", null, values) == -1)
                ok = false;

            m_db.setTransactionSuccessful();
        }
    }
    catch(Exception exception)
      {
        ok = false;
    }
    finally
    {
        m_db.endTransaction();
    }

    return ok;
}

public boolean writeParticipant(Cryptography cryptography,
                    boolean ignoreSignatures,
                    byte data[])
{
  if(cryptography == null ||
     data == null ||
     data.length == 0 ||
     m_db == null)
      return false;

  ContentValues values = null;
  Cursor cursor = null;

  try
  {
      String strings[] = new String(data).split("\\n");

      if(strings.length != Messages.EPKS_GROUP_ONE_ELEMENT_COUNT)
        return false;

      PublicKey encryptionKey = null;
      PublicKey signatureKey = null;
      String sipHashId = "";
      boolean exists = false;
      byte keyType[] = null;
      byte encryptionKeySignature[] = null;
      byte signatureKeySignature[] = null;
      byte sipHashIdBytes[] = null;
```

```java
        int ii = 0;

    for(String string : strings)
      switch(ii)
      {
      case 0:
          long current = System.currentTimeMillis();
          long timestamp = Miscellaneous.byteArrayToLong
            (Base64.decode(string.getBytes(), Base64.NO_WRAP));

          if(current - timestamp < 0L)
          {
            if(timestamp - current > WRITE_PARTICIPANT_TIME_DELTA)
                return false;
          }
          else if(current - timestamp > WRITE_PARTICIPANT_TIME_DELTA)
            return false;

          ii += 1;
          break;
      case 1:
          keyType = Base64.decode
            (string.getBytes(), Base64.NO_WRAP);

          if(keyType == null ||
             keyType.length != 1 ||
             keyType[0] != Messages.CHAT_KEY_TYPE[0])
           return false;

          ii += 1;
          break;
      case 2:
          /*
          ** Sender's Smoke Identity!
          */

          sipHashId = new String
            (Base64.decode(string.getBytes(StandardCharsets.UTF_8),
                      Base64.NO_WRAP),
             StandardCharsets.UTF_8);
          sipHashIdBytes = sipHashId.getBytes(StandardCharsets.UTF_8);
          ii += 1;
          break;
      case 3:
          cursor = m_db.rawQuery
            ("SELECT EXISTS(SELECT 1 " +
             "FROM participants WHERE " +
             "encryption_public_key_digest = ?)",
             new String[] {Base64.
                        encodeToString(Cryptography.
                                sha512(Base64.
                                    decode(string.
                                        getBytes(),
                                        Base64.
                                        NO_WRAP)),
                                Base64.DEFAULT)});

          if(cursor != null)
            m_cursorsOpened.getAndIncrement();

          if(cursor != null && cursor.moveToFirst())
            if(cursor.getInt(0) == 1)
                exists = true;
```

```java
        if(cursor != null)
        {
          cursor.close();

          if(cursor.isClosed())
              m_cursorsClosed.getAndIncrement();

          cursor = null;
        }

        encryptionKey = Cryptography.publicKeyFromBytes
          (Base64.decode(string.getBytes(), Base64.NO_WRAP));

        if(encryptionKey == null)
          return false;

        ii += 1;
        break;
    case 4:
        encryptionKeySignature = Base64.decode
          (string.getBytes(), Base64.NO_WRAP);
        ii += 1;
        break;
    case 5:
        cursor = m_db.rawQuery
          ("SELECT EXISTS(SELECT 1 " +
          "FROM participants WHERE " +
          "signature_public_key_digest = ?)",
          new String[] {Base64.
                        encodeToString(Cryptography.
                                sha512(Base64.
                                       decode(string.
                                              getBytes(),
                                              Base64.
                                              NO_WRAP)),
                                Base64.DEFAULT)});

        if(cursor != null)
          m_cursorsOpened.getAndIncrement();

        if(cursor != null && cursor.moveToFirst())
          if(cursor.getInt(0) == 1)
              if(exists)
                return false;

        if(cursor != null)
        {
          cursor.close();

          if(cursor.isClosed())
              m_cursorsClosed.getAndIncrement();

          cursor = null;
        }

        signatureKey = Cryptography.publicKeyFromBytes
          (Base64.decode(string.getBytes(), Base64.NO_WRAP));

        if(signatureKey == null)
          return false;

        ii += 1;
```

```java
            break;
          case 6:
              signatureKeySignature = Base64.decode
                (string.getBytes(), Base64.NO_WRAP);

              if(!encryptionKey.getAlgorithm().equals("McEliece-CCA2"))
                if(!Cryptography.
                    verifySignature(encryptionKey,
                              encryptionKeySignature,
                              Miscellaneous.
                              joinByteArrays(sipHashIdBytes,
                                    encryptionKey.
                                    getEncoded(),
                                    signatureKey.
                                    getEncoded()))))
                {
                    if(!ignoreSignatures)
                      return false;
                }

              if(!Cryptography.
                  verifySignature(signatureKey,
                            signatureKeySignature,
                            Miscellaneous.
                            joinByteArrays(sipHashIdBytes,
                                  encryptionKey.
                                  getEncoded(),
                                  signatureKey.
                                  getEncoded()))))
                {
                  if(!ignoreSignatures)
                      return false;
                }

              break;
          }

      String name = nameFromSipHashId(cryptography, sipHashId).trim();

      if(name.isEmpty())
        return false;

      if(!writePublicKeyPairs(cryptography, sipHashId, strings))
        return false;

      values = new ContentValues();

      SparseArray<String> sparseArray = new SparseArray<> ();

      sparseArray.append(0, "encryption_public_key");
      sparseArray.append(1, "encryption_public_key_digest");
      sparseArray.append(2, "function_digest");
      sparseArray.append(3, "signature_public_key");
      sparseArray.append(4, "signature_public_key_digest");
      sparseArray.append(5, "siphash_id");
      sparseArray.append(6, "siphash_id_digest");

      int size = sparseArray.size();

      for(int i = 0; i < size; i++)
      {
        byte bytes[] = null;
```

```java
        switch(sparseArray.get(i))
        {
        case "encryption_public_key":
            bytes = cryptography.etm(encryptionKey.getEncoded());
            break;
        case "encryption_public_key_digest":
            bytes = Cryptography.sha512(encryptionKey.getEncoded());
            break;
        case "function_digest":
            bytes = cryptography.hmac("chat".getBytes());
            break;
        case "signature_public_key":
            bytes = cryptography.etm(signatureKey.getEncoded());
            break;
        case "signature_public_key_digest":
            bytes = Cryptography.sha512(signatureKey.getEncoded());
            break;
        case "siphash_id":
            bytes = cryptography.etm
              (sipHashId.getBytes(StandardCharsets.UTF_8));
            break;
        case "siphash_id_digest":
            bytes = cryptography.hmac
              (sipHashId.getBytes(StandardCharsets.UTF_8));
            break;
        }

        if(bytes == null)
        {
            sparseArray.clear();
            return false;
        }

        values.put(sparseArray.get(i),
                Base64.encodeToString(bytes, Base64.DEFAULT));
        }

        sparseArray.clear();
    }
    catch(Exception exception)
    {
        return false;
    }
    finally
    {
        if(cursor != null)
        {
          cursor.close();

          if(cursor.isClosed())
              m_cursorsClosed.getAndIncrement();
        }
    }

    if(values == null)
        return false;

    m_db.beginTransactionNonExclusive();

    try
    {
        m_db.insertOrThrow("participants", null, values);
        m_db.setTransactionSuccessful();
```

```java
      }
    catch(SQLiteConstraintException exception)
    {
        return exception.getMessage().toLowerCase().contains("unique");
    }
    catch(Exception exception)
    {
        return false;
    }
    finally
    {
        m_db.endTransaction();
    }

    return true;
  }

  public boolean writeParticipantName(Cryptography cryptography,
                                      String name,
                                      int oid)
  {
    if(cryptography == null ||
       m_db == null ||
       name == null ||
       name.trim().isEmpty())
        return false;

    m_db.beginTransactionNonExclusive();

    try
    {
        ContentValues values = new ContentValues();

        values.put
          ("name",
           Base64.encodeToString(cryptography.etm(name.trim().getBytes()),
                      Base64.DEFAULT));
        m_db.update("siphash_ids", values, "OID = ?",
                new String[] {String.valueOf(oid)});
        m_db.setTransactionSuccessful();
    }
    catch(Exception exception)
    {
        return false;
    }
    finally
    {
        m_db.endTransaction();
    }

    return true;
  }

  public boolean writeSipHashParticipant(Cryptography cryptography,
                                         String name,
                                         String sipHashId,
                                         boolean acceptWithoutSignatures)
  {
    if(cryptography == null || m_db == null)
        return false;

    ContentValues values = null;
    boolean ok = true;
```

```java
        try
        {
            values = new ContentValues();
        }
        catch(Exception exception)
        {
            ok = false;
        }

        if(!ok)
            return ok;

        /*
        ** Content values should prevent SQL injections.
        */

        try
        {
            SparseArray<String> sparseArray = new SparseArray<> ();
            byte bytes[] = null;

            name = name.trim();

            if(name.isEmpty())
              name = "unknown";

            sipHashId = sipHashId.toUpperCase().trim();
            sparseArray.append(0, "accept_without_signatures");
            sparseArray.append(1, "name");
            sparseArray.append(2, "siphash_id");
            sparseArray.append(3, "siphash_id_digest");
            sparseArray.append(4, "stream");
            sparseArray.append(5, "timestamp");

            int size = sparseArray.size();

            for(int i = 0; i < size; i++)
            {
              switch(sparseArray.get(i))
              {
              case "accept_without_signatures":
                  bytes = cryptography.etm
                    (acceptWithoutSignatures ?
                     "true".getBytes() : "false".getBytes());
                  break;
              case "name":
                  bytes = cryptography.etm(name.getBytes());
                  break;
              case "siphash_id":
                  bytes = cryptography.etm
                    (sipHashId.getBytes(StandardCharsets.UTF_8));
                  break;
              case "siphash_id_digest":
                  bytes = cryptography.hmac
                    (sipHashId.getBytes(StandardCharsets.UTF_8));
                  break;
              case "timestamp":
                  SimpleDateFormat simpleDateFormat = new SimpleDateFormat
                    ("yyyy-MM-dd HH:mm:ss", Locale.getDefault());

                  simpleDateFormat.setTimeZone(TimeZone.getTimeZone("GMT"));
                  values.put
```

```java
                        (sparseArray.get(i),
                         simpleDateFormat.format(new Date())));
                    continue;
                default:
                    byte salt[] = Cryptography.sha512
                        (sipHashId.trim().getBytes(StandardCharsets.UTF_8));
                    byte temporary[] = Cryptography.
                        pbkdf2(salt,
                                sipHashId.toCharArray(),
                                SIPHASH_STREAM_CREATION_ITERATION_COUNT,
                                160); // SHA-1

                    if (temporary != null)
                        bytes = cryptography.etm
                            (Cryptography.
                              pbkdf2(salt,
                                    Base64.encodeToString(temporary,
                                                Base64.NO_WRAP).
                                    toCharArray(),
                                    1,
                                    768)); // 8 * (32 + 64) bits.

                    break;
                }

                if(bytes == null)
                {
                    sparseArray.clear();

                    StringBuilder stringBuilder = new StringBuilder();

                    stringBuilder.append
                        ("Database::writeSipHashParticipant(): error with ");
                    stringBuilder.append(sparseArray.get(i));
                    stringBuilder.append(" field.");
                    writeLog(stringBuilder.toString());
                    throw new Exception();
                }

                String str = Base64.encodeToString(bytes, Base64.DEFAULT);

                values.put(sparseArray.get(i), str);
            }

        sparseArray.clear();
    }
    catch(Exception exception)
    {
        ok = false;
    }

    m_db.beginTransactionNonExclusive();

    try
    {
        if(ok)
        {
            if(m_db.
                update("siphash_ids",
                        values,
                        "siphash_id_digest = ?",
                        new String[] {Base64.
                                encodeToString
```

```java
                                (cryptography.
                                 hmac(sipHashId.toUpperCase().trim().
                                     getBytes(StandardCharsets.UTF_8)),
                                 Base64.DEFAULT)}) <= 0)
               if(m_db.replace("siphash_ids", null, values) == -1)
                 ok = false;

            m_db.setTransactionSuccessful();
          }
      }
    catch(Exception exception)
       {
          ok = false;
       }
    finally
       {
          m_db.endTransaction();
       }

    return ok;
  }

  public byte[] neighborRemoteCertificate(Cryptography cryptography,
                                int oid)
  {
    if(cryptography == null || m_db == null)
        return null;

    Cursor cursor = null;
    byte bytes[] = null;

    try
    {
        cursor = m_db.rawQuery
          ("SELECT remote_certificate FROM neighbors WHERE OID = ?",
           new String[] {String.valueOf(oid)});

        if(cursor != null)
          m_cursorsOpened.getAndIncrement();

        if(cursor != null && cursor.moveToFirst())
          bytes = cryptography.mtd
               (Base64.decode(cursor.getString(0).getBytes(),
                       Base64.DEFAULT));
    }
    catch(Exception exception)
    {
        bytes = null;
    }
    finally
    {
        if(cursor != null)
        {
          cursor.close();

          if(cursor.isClosed())
             m_cursorsClosed.getAndIncrement();
        }
    }

    return bytes;
  }
```

```java
public long count(String table)
{
  if(m_db == null)
      return -1L;

  Cursor cursor = null;
  long c = 0L;

  try
  {
      StringBuilder stringBuilder = new StringBuilder();

      stringBuilder.append("SELECT COUNT(*) FROM ");
      stringBuilder.append(table);
      cursor = m_db.rawQuery(stringBuilder.toString(), null);

      if(cursor != null)
        m_cursorsOpened.getAndIncrement();

      if(cursor != null && cursor.moveToFirst())
        c = cursor.getLong(0);
  }
  catch(Exception exception)
  {
      c = -1L;
  }
  finally
  {
      if(cursor != null)
      {
        cursor.close();

        if(cursor.isClosed())
            m_cursorsClosed.getAndIncrement();
      }
  }

  return c;
}

public long cursorsClosed()
{
  return m_cursorsClosed.get();
}

public long cursorsOpened()
{
  return m_cursorsOpened.get();
}

public static synchronized Database getInstance()
{
  return s_instance; // Should never be null.
}

public static synchronized Database getInstance(Context context)
{
  if(s_instance == null)
      s_instance = new Database(context.getApplicationContext());

  return s_instance;
}
```

```java
public static void releaseMemory()
{
  SQLiteDatabase.releaseMemory();
}

public void cleanDanglingMessages()
{
  if(m_db == null)
      return;

  Cursor cursor = null;

  m_db.beginTransactionNonExclusive();

  try
  {
      cursor = m_db.rawQuery
        ("DELETE FROM stack WHERE siphash_id_digest " +
         "NOT IN (SELECT siphash_id_digest FROM siphash_ids)",
         null);

      if(cursor != null)
        m_cursorsOpened.getAndIncrement();

      m_db.setTransactionSuccessful();
  }
  catch(Exception exception)
  {
  }
  finally
  {
      if(cursor != null)
      {
        cursor.close();

        if(cursor.isClosed())
            m_cursorsClosed.getAndIncrement();
      }

      m_db.endTransaction();
  }
}

public void cleanDanglingOutboundQueued()
{
  if(m_db == null)
      return;

  Cursor cursor = null;

  m_db.beginTransactionNonExclusive();

  try
  {
      cursor = m_db.rawQuery
        ("DELETE FROM outbound_queue WHERE neighbor_oid " +
         "NOT IN (SELECT OID FROM neighbors)",
         null);

      if(cursor != null)
        m_cursorsOpened.getAndIncrement();

      m_db.setTransactionSuccessful();
```

```java
            }
    catch(Exception exception)
        {
    }
    finally
    {
        if(cursor != null)
        {
          cursor.close();

          if(cursor.isClosed())
              m_cursorsClosed.getAndIncrement();
        }

        m_db.endTransaction();
    }
}

public void cleanDanglingParticipants()
{
  if(m_db == null)
      return;

  Cursor cursor = null;

  m_db.beginTransactionNonExclusive();

  try
  {
      cursor = m_db.rawQuery
        ("DELETE FROM participants WHERE siphash_id_digest " +
         "NOT IN (SELECT siphash_id_digest FROM siphash_ids)",
         null);

      if(cursor != null)
        m_cursorsOpened.getAndIncrement();

      m_db.setTransactionSuccessful();
  }
  catch(Exception exception)
      {
  }
  finally
  {
      if(cursor != null)
      {
        cursor.close();

        if(cursor.isClosed())
            m_cursorsClosed.getAndIncrement();
      }

      m_db.endTransaction();
  }

  cursor = null;
  m_db.beginTransactionNonExclusive();

  try
  {
      cursor = m_db.rawQuery
        ("DELETE FROM public_key_pairs WHERE siphash_id_digest " +
         "NOT IN (SELECT siphash_id_digest FROM siphash_ids)",
```

```java
                    null);

          if(cursor != null)
            m_cursorsOpened.getAndIncrement();

          m_db.setTransactionSuccessful();
      }
    catch(Exception exception)
        {
      }
    finally
        {
          if(cursor != null)
            {
              cursor.close();

              if(cursor.isClosed())
                  m_cursorsClosed.getAndIncrement();
            }

          m_db.endTransaction();
      }
    }

    public void cleanNeighborStatistics(Cryptography cryptography)
    {
      ArrayList<NeighborElement> arrayList = readNeighborOids(cryptography);

      if(arrayList == null || arrayList.isEmpty())
          return;

      for(NeighborElement neighborElement : arrayList)
          if(neighborElement != null)
            saveNeighborInformation(cryptography,
                            "0",              // Bytes Buffered
                            "0",              // Bytes Read
                            "0",              // Bytes Written
                            "",               // Error
                            "",               // IP Address
                            "0",              // Port
                            "0",              // Queue Size
                            "",               // Session Cipher
                            "disconnected",   // Status
                            "0",              // Uptime
                            String.valueOf(neighborElement.m_oid));

      arrayList.clear();
    }

    public void clearTable(String table)
    {
      if(m_db == null)
          return;

      m_db.beginTransactionNonExclusive();

      try
        {
          m_db.delete(table, null, null);
          m_db.setTransactionSuccessful();
      }
    catch(Exception exception)
        {
```

```java
        }
    finally
    {
        m_db.endTransaction();
    }
}

public void deleteEchoQueue()
{
  if(m_db == null)
      return;

  m_db.beginTransactionNonExclusive();

  try
  {
      m_db.delete("outbound_queue", "echo_queue = 1", null);
      m_db.setTransactionSuccessful();
  }
  catch(Exception exception)
  {
  }
  finally
  {
      m_db.endTransaction();
  }
}

public void deleteEchoQueue(int oid)
{
  if(m_db == null)
      return;

  m_db.beginTransactionNonExclusive();

  try
  {
      m_db.delete("outbound_queue",
              "echo_queue = 1 AND neighbor_oid = ?",
              new String[] {String.valueOf(oid)});
      m_db.setTransactionSuccessful();
  }
  catch(Exception exception)
  {
  }
  finally
  {
      m_db.endTransaction();
  }
}

public void deleteRoutingEntry(String clientIdentity)
{
  if(m_db == null)
      return;

  m_db.beginTransactionNonExclusive();

  try
  {
      m_db.delete("routing_identities", "client_identity = ?",
              new String[] {clientIdentity});
      m_db.setTransactionSuccessful();
```

```java
        }
      catch(Exception exception)
      {
      }
      finally
      {
          m_db.endTransaction();
      }
    }

    public void deleteSetting(String name)
    {
      if(m_db == null)
          return;

      m_db.beginTransactionNonExclusive();

      try
      {
          m_db.delete("settings", "name = ?", new String[] {name});
          m_db.setTransactionSuccessful();
      }
      catch(Exception exception)
      {
      }
      finally
      {
          m_db.endTransaction();
      }
    }

    public void enqueueOutboundMessage(Cryptography cryptography,
                                       String message,
                                       boolean echo,
                                       int oid)
    {
      if(cryptography == null ||
         message == null ||
         message.trim().isEmpty() ||
         m_db == null)
          return;

      m_db.beginTransactionNonExclusive();

      try
      {
          ContentValues values = new ContentValues();

          values.put("echo_queue", echo ? 1 : 0);
          values.put("message", message);
          values.put
            ("message_digest",
             Base64.encodeToString(cryptography.hmac(message.getBytes()),
                       Base64.DEFAULT));
          values.put("neighbor_oid", oid);
          m_db.insertOrThrow("outbound_queue", null, values);
          m_db.setTransactionSuccessful();
      }
      catch(Exception exception)
        {
      }
      finally
        {
```

```java
      m_db.endTransaction();
   }
}


public void listenerNeighborControlStatus(Cryptography cryptography,
                                          String controlStatus,
                                          String oid,
                                          String table)
{
  if(cryptography == null || m_db == null)
     return;

  m_db.beginTransactionNonExclusive();

  try
  {
     ContentValues values = new ContentValues();

     values.put
       ("status_control",
        Base64.encodeToString(cryptography.
                              etm(controlStatus.trim().getBytes()),
                              Base64.DEFAULT));
     m_db.update(table, values, "OID = ?", new String[] {oid});
     m_db.setTransactionSuccessful();
  }
  catch(Exception exception)
  {
  }
  finally
  {
     m_db.endTransaction();
  }
}

public void neighborRecordCertificate(Cryptography cryptography,
                             String oid,
                             byte certificate[])
{
  if(cryptography == null || m_db == null)
     return;

  m_db.beginTransactionNonExclusive();

  try
  {
     ContentValues values = new ContentValues();

     if(certificate == null)
       values.put
           ("remote_certificate",
            Base64.encodeToString(cryptography.etm("".getBytes()),
                       Base64.DEFAULT));
     else
       values.put
           ("remote_certificate",
            Base64.encodeToString(cryptography.etm(certificate),
                       Base64.DEFAULT));

     m_db.update("neighbors", values, "OID = ?", new String[] {oid});
     m_db.setTransactionSuccessful();
  }
  catch(Exception exception)
```

```java
    {
    }
    finally
    {
        m_db.endTransaction();
    }
}

@Override
public void onConfigure(SQLiteDatabase db)
{
  try
  {
      db.enableWriteAheadLogging();
  }
  catch(Exception exception)
  {
  }

  try
  {
      db.execSQL("VACUUM");
      db.execSQL("PRAGMA auto_vacuum = Full", null);
  }
  catch(Exception exception)
  {
  }

  try
  {
      db.execSQL("PRAGMA secure_delete = True", null);
  }
  catch(Exception exception)
  {
  }

  try
  {
      db.setForeignKeyConstraintsEnabled(true);
    }
  catch(Exception exception)
  {
  }
}

@Override
public void onCreate(SQLiteDatabase db)
{
  String str = "";

  /*
  ** Order is critical.
  */

  /*
  ** Create the siphash_ids table.
  */

  str = "CREATE TABLE IF NOT EXISTS siphash_ids (" +
      "accept_without_signatures TEXT NOT NULL, " +
      "name TEXT NOT NULL, " +
      "siphash_id TEXT NOT NULL, " +
      "siphash_id_digest TEXT NOT NULL PRIMARY KEY, " +
```

```java
            "stream TEXT NOT NULL, " +
            "timestamp DATETIME DEFAULT CURRENT_TIMESTAMP)";

        try
        {
            db.execSQL(str);
        }
        catch(Exception exception)
        {
        }

        /*
        ** Create the congestion_control table.
        */

        str = "CREATE TABLE IF NOT EXISTS congestion_control (" +
            "digest TEXT NOT NULL PRIMARY KEY, " +
            "timestamp DATETIME DEFAULT CURRENT_TIMESTAMP)";

        try
        {
            db.execSQL(str);
        }
        catch(Exception exception)
        {
        }

        /*
        ** Create the listeners table.
        */

        str = "CREATE TABLE IF NOT EXISTS listeners (" +
            "certificate TEXT NOT NULL, " +
            "ip_version TEXT NOT NULL, " +
            "is_private TEXT NOT NULL, " +
            "last_error TEXT NOT NULL, " +
            "local_ip_address TEXT NOT NULL, " +
            "local_ip_address_digest TEXT NOT NULL, " +
            "local_port TEXT NOT NULL, " +
            "local_port_digest TEXT NOT NULL, " +
            "local_scope_id TEXT NOT NULL, " +
            "peers_count TEXT NOT NULL, " +
            "private_key TEXT NOT NULL, " +
            "public_key TEXT NOT NULL, " +
            "status TEXT NOT NULL, " +
            "status_control TEXT NOT NULL, " +
            "uptime TEXT NOT NULL, " +
            "PRIMARY KEY (local_ip_address_digest, " +
            "local_port_digest))";

        try
        {
            db.execSQL(str);
        }
        catch(Exception exception)
        {
        }

        /*
        ** Create the log table.
        */

        str = "CREATE TABLE IF NOT EXISTS log (" +
```

```
        "event TEXT NOT NULL, " +
        "timestamp DATETIME DEFAULT CURRENT_TIMESTAMP)";

    try
    {
        db.execSQL(str);
    }
    catch(Exception exception)
    {
    }

    /*
    ** Create the neighbors table.
    */

    str = "CREATE TABLE IF NOT EXISTS neighbors (" +
        "bytes_buffered TEXT NOT NULL, " +
        "bytes_read TEXT NOT NULL, " +
        "bytes_written TEXT NOT NULL, " +
        "ip_version TEXT NOT NULL, " +
        "last_error TEXT NOT NULL, " +
        "local_ip_address TEXT NOT NULL, " +
        "local_ip_address_digest TEXT NOT NULL, " +
        "local_port TEXT NOT NULL, " +
        "local_port_digest TEXT NOT NULL, " +
        "proxy_ip_address TEXT NOT NULL, " +
        "proxy_port TEXT NOT NULL, " +
        "proxy_type TEXT NOT NULL, " +
        "queue_size TEXT NOT NULL, " +
        "remote_certificate TEXT NOT NULL, " +
        "remote_ip_address TEXT NOT NULL, " +
        "remote_ip_address_digest TEXT NOT NULL, " +
        "remote_port TEXT NOT NULL, " +
        "remote_port_digest TEXT NOT NULL, " +
        "remote_scope_id TEXT NOT NULL, " +
        "session_cipher TEXT NOT NULL, " +
        "status TEXT NOT NULL, " +
        "status_control TEXT NOT NULL, " +
        "transport TEXT NOT NULL, " +
        "transport_digest TEXT NOT NULL, " +
        "uptime TEXT NOT NULL, " +
        "user_defined_digest TEXT NOT NULL, " +
        "PRIMARY KEY (remote_ip_address_digest, " +
        "remote_port_digest, " +
        "transport_digest))";

    try
    {
        db.execSQL(str);
    }
    catch(Exception exception)
    {
    }

    /*
    ** Create the outbound_queue table.
    */

    str = "CREATE TABLE IF NOT EXISTS outbound_queue (" +
        "echo_queue INTEGER NOT NULL DEFAULT 0, " +
        "message TEXT NOT NULL, " +
        "message_digest TEXT NOT NULL, " +
        "neighbor_oid INTEGER NOT NULL, " +
```

```java
		"PRIMARY KEY (message_digest, neighbor_oid))";

	try
	{
	    db.execSQL(str);
	}
	catch(Exception exception)
	{
	}

	/*
	** Create the ozones table.
	*/

	str = "CREATE TABLE IF NOT EXISTS ozones (" +
	    "ozone_address TEXT NOT NULL, " +
	    "ozone_address_digest TEXT NOT NULL PRIMARY KEY, " +
	    "ozone_address_stream TEXT NOT NULL)";

	try
	{
	    db.execSQL(str);
	}
	catch(Exception exception)
	{
	}

	/*
	** Create the participants table.
	*/

	str = "CREATE TABLE IF NOT EXISTS participants (" +
	    "encryption_public_key TEXT NOT NULL, " +
	    "encryption_public_key_digest TEXT NOT NULL, " +
	    "function_digest NOT NULL, " + // chat, e-mail, etc.
	    "signature_public_key TEXT NOT NULL, " +
	    "signature_public_key_digest TEXT NOT NULL, " +
	    "siphash_id TEXT NOT NULL, " +
	    "siphash_id_digest TEXT NOT NULL, " +
	    "FOREIGN KEY (siphash_id_digest) REFERENCES " +
	    "siphash_ids (siphash_id_digest) ON DELETE CASCADE, " +
	    "PRIMARY KEY (encryption_public_key_digest, " +
	    "signature_public_key_digest))";

	try
	{
	    db.execSQL(str);
	}
	catch(Exception exception)
	{
	}

	/*
	** Create the public_key_pairs table.
	*/

	str = "CREATE TABLE IF NOT EXISTS public_key_pairs (" +
	    "key_type TEXT NOT NULL, " +
	    "public_key_signature_string TEXT NOT NULL, " +
	    "public_key_string TEXT NOT NULL, " +
	    "signature_public_key_signature_string TEXT NOT NULL, " +
	    "signature_public_key_string TEXT NOT NULL, " +
	    "siphash_id TEXT NOT NULL, " +
```

```java
        "siphash_id_digest TEXT NOT NULL PRIMARY KEY, " +
        "FOREIGN KEY (siphash_id_digest) REFERENCES " +
        "siphash_ids (siphash_id_digest) ON DELETE CASCADE)";

    try
    {
        db.execSQL(str);
    }
    catch(Exception exception)
    {
    }

    /*
    ** Create the routing_identities table.
    */

    str = "CREATE TABLE IF NOT EXISTS routing_identities (" +
        "algorithm TEXT NOT NULL, " +
        "client_identity TEXT NOT NULL, " +
        "identity TEXT NOT NULL, " +
        "timestamp DATETIME DEFAULT CURRENT_TIMESTAMP, " +
        "PRIMARY KEY (client_identity, identity))";

    try
    {
        db.execSQL(str);
    }
    catch(Exception exception)
    {
    }

    /*
    ** Create the settings table.
    */

    str = "CREATE TABLE IF NOT EXISTS settings (" +
        "name TEXT NOT NULL, " +
        "name_digest TEXT NOT NULL PRIMARY KEY, " +
        "value TEXT NOT NULL)";

    try
    {
        db.execSQL(str);
    }
    catch(Exception exception)
    {
    }

    /*
    ** Create the stack table.
    */

    str = "CREATE TABLE IF NOT EXISTS stack (" +
        "message TEXT NOT NULL, " +
        "message_digest TEXT NOT NULL, " +
        "siphash_id TEXT NOT NULL, " +
        "siphash_id_digest TEXT NOT NULL, " +
        "timestamp TEXT DEFAULT NULL, " +
        "verified_digest TEXT NOT NULL, " +
        "PRIMARY KEY (message_digest, siphash_id_digest), " +
        "FOREIGN KEY (siphash_id_digest) REFERENCES " +
        "siphash_ids (siphash_id_digest) ON DELETE CASCADE)";
```

```java
    try
    {
        db.execSQL(str);
    }
    catch(Exception exception)
    {
    }
}

@Override
public void onDowngrade(SQLiteDatabase db, int oldVersion, int newVersion)
{
    onUpgrade(db, oldVersion, newVersion);
}

@Override
public void onUpgrade(SQLiteDatabase db, int oldVersion, int newVersion)
{
    onCreate(db);
}

public void purgeCongestion(int lifetime)
{
  if(m_db == null)
      return;

  m_db.beginTransactionNonExclusive();

  try
  {
      /*
      ** The bound string value must be cast to an integer.
      */

      m_db.delete
        ("congestion_control",
         "ABS(STRFTIME('%s', 'now') - STRFTIME('%s', timestamp)) > " +
         "CAST(? AS INTEGER)",
         new String[] {String.valueOf(lifetime)});
      m_db.setTransactionSuccessful();
  }
  catch(Exception exception)
  {
  }
  finally
  {
      m_db.endTransaction();
  }
}

public void purgeExpiredRoutingEntries(int lifetime)
{
  if(m_db == null)
      return;

  m_db.beginTransactionNonExclusive();

  try
  {
      /*
      ** The bound string value must be cast to an integer.
      */
```

```java
        m_db.delete
          ("routing_identities",
           "ABS(STRFTIME('%s', 'now') - STRFTIME('%s', timestamp)) > " +
           "CAST(? AS INTEGER)",
           new String[] {String.valueOf(lifetime)});
        m_db.setTransactionSuccessful();
    }
    catch(Exception exception)
    {
    }
    finally
    {
        m_db.endTransaction();
    }
}

public void purgeReleasedMessages(Cryptography cryptography)
{
    if(cryptography == null || m_db == null)
        return;

    m_db.beginTransactionNonExclusive();

    Cursor cursor = null;

    try
    {
        cursor = m_db.rawQuery
          ("SELECT timestamp, OID " +
           "FROM stack WHERE timestamp IS NOT NULL AND " +
           "verified_digest = ?",
           new String[] {Base64.
                      encodeToString(cryptography.
                                  hmac("true".getBytes()),
                                  Base64.DEFAULT)});

        if(cursor != null)
          m_cursorsOpened.getAndIncrement();

        while(cursor != null && cursor.moveToNext())
        {
          String oid = String.valueOf(cursor.getInt(1));
          byte bytes[] = cryptography.mtd
              (Base64.decode(cursor.getString(0).getBytes(),
                      Base64.DEFAULT));

          if(bytes == null)
              m_db.delete("stack", "OID = ?", new String[] {oid});
          else
          {
              long timestamp = Miscellaneous.byteArrayToLong(bytes);

              if(Math.abs(System.currentTimeMillis() - timestamp) >
                 ONE_WEEK)
                m_db.delete("stack", "OID = ?", new String[] {oid});
          }
        }

        m_db.setTransactionSuccessful();
    }
    catch(Exception exception)
    {
    }
```

```java
    finally
    {
        if(cursor != null)
        {
          cursor.close();

          if(cursor.isClosed())
              m_cursorsClosed.getAndIncrement();
        }

        m_db.endTransaction();
    }
}

public void reset()
{
  if(m_db == null)
      return;

  m_db.beginTransactionNonExclusive();

  try
  {
      String tables[] = new String[]
        {"congestion_control",
         "listeners",
         "log",
         "neighbors",
         "outbound_queue",
         "ozones",
         "participants",
         "public_key_pairs",
         "routing_identities",
         "settings",
         "siphash_ids",
         "stack"};

      for(String string : tables)
        try
        {
            m_db.delete(string, null, null);
        }
        catch(Exception exception)
        {
        }

      m_db.setTransactionSuccessful();
  }
  catch(Exception exception)
  {
  }
  finally
  {
      m_db.endTransaction();
  }
}

public void resetAndDrop()
{
  reset();

  if(m_db == null)
      return;
```

```java
        String strings[] = new String[]
            {"DROP TABLE IF EXISTS congestion_control",
             "DROP TABLE IF EXISTS listeners",
             "DROP TABLE IF EXISTS log",
             "DROP TABLE IF EXISTS neighbors",
             "DROP TABLE IF EXISTS outbound_queue",
             "DROP TABLE IF EXISTS ozones",
             "DROP TABLE IF EXISTS participants",
             "DROP TABLE IF EXISTS public_key_pairs",
             "DROP TABLE IF EXISTS routing_identities",
             "DROP TABLE IF EXISTS settings",
             "DROP TABLE IF EXISTS siphash_ids",
             "DROP TABLE IF EXISTS stack"};

        for(String string : strings)
            try
            {
                m_db.execSQL(string);
            }
            catch(Exception exception)
            {
            }

        onCreate(m_db);
    }

    public void saveListenerInformation(Cryptography cryptography,
                                        String error,
                                        String peersCount,
                                        String status,
                                        String uptime,
                                        String oid)
    {
        if(cryptography == null || m_db == null)
            return;

        m_db.beginTransactionNonExclusive();

        try
        {
            ContentValues values = new ContentValues();

            if(!status.equals("listening"))
            {
                error = error.trim(); // Do not clear the error.
                peersCount = "";
                uptime = "";
            }

            values.put
                ("last_error",
                 Base64.encodeToString(cryptography.etm(error.getBytes()),
                            Base64.DEFAULT));
            values.put
                ("peers_count",
                 Base64.encodeToString(cryptography.etm(peersCount.getBytes()),
                            Base64.DEFAULT));
            values.put
                ("status",
                 Base64.encodeToString(cryptography.
                            etm(status.trim().getBytes()),
                            Base64.DEFAULT));
```

```java
        values.put
          ("uptime",
           Base64.encodeToString(cryptography.
                                 etm(uptime.trim().getBytes()),
                                 Base64.DEFAULT));
        m_db.update("listeners", values, "OID = ?", new String[] {oid});
        m_db.setTransactionSuccessful();
    }
    catch(Exception exception)
    {
    }
    finally
    {
        m_db.endTransaction();
    }
}

public void saveNeighborInformation(Cryptography cryptography,
                                    String bytesBuffered,
                                    String bytesRead,
                                    String bytesWritten,
                                    String error,
                                    String ipAddress,
                                    String ipPort,
                                    String queueSize,
                                    String sessionCipher,
                                    String status,
                                    String uptime,
                                    String oid)
{
  if(cryptography == null || m_db == null)
      return;

  m_db.beginTransactionNonExclusive();

  try
  {
      ContentValues values = new ContentValues();

      if(!status.equals("connected"))
      {
        bytesRead = "";
        bytesWritten = "";
        error = error.trim(); // Do not clear the error.
        ipAddress = "";
        ipPort = "";
        sessionCipher = "";
        uptime = "";
      }

      values.put
        ("bytes_buffered",
         Base64.encodeToString(cryptography.
                               etm(bytesBuffered.getBytes()),
                               Base64.DEFAULT));
      values.put
        ("bytes_read",
         Base64.encodeToString(cryptography.etm(bytesRead.getBytes()),
                               Base64.DEFAULT));
      values.put
        ("bytes_written",
         Base64.encodeToString(cryptography.etm(bytesWritten.
                                   getBytes()),
```

```java
                                        Base64.DEFAULT));
        values.put
          ("last_error",
           Base64.encodeToString(cryptography.etm(error.getBytes()),
                              Base64.DEFAULT));
        values.put
          ("local_ip_address",
           Base64.encodeToString(cryptography.
                              etm(ipAddress.trim().getBytes()),
                              Base64.DEFAULT));
        values.put
          ("local_ip_address_digest",
           Base64.encodeToString(cryptography.
                              hmac(ipAddress.trim().getBytes()),
                              Base64.DEFAULT));
        values.put
          ("local_port",
           Base64.encodeToString(cryptography.
                              etm(ipPort.trim().getBytes()),
                              Base64.DEFAULT));
        values.put
          ("local_port_digest",
           Base64.encodeToString(cryptography.
                              hmac(ipPort.trim().getBytes()),
                              Base64.DEFAULT));
        values.put
          ("queue_size",
           Base64.encodeToString(cryptography.etm(queueSize.getBytes()),
                              Base64.DEFAULT));
        values.put
          ("session_cipher",
           Base64.encodeToString(cryptography.etm(sessionCipher.
                                   getBytes()),
                              Base64.DEFAULT));
        values.put
          ("status",
           Base64.encodeToString(cryptography.
                              etm(status.trim().getBytes()),
                              Base64.DEFAULT));
        values.put
          ("uptime",
           Base64.encodeToString(cryptography.
                              etm(uptime.trim().getBytes()),
                              Base64.DEFAULT));
        m_db.update("neighbors", values, "OID = ?", new String[] {oid});
        m_db.setTransactionSuccessful();
      }
    catch(Exception exception)
    {
    }
    finally
    {
        m_db.endTransaction();
    }
  }

  public void tagMessagesForRelease(Cryptography cryptography,
                          String sipHashIdDigest)
  {
    if(cryptography == null || m_db == null)
        return;

    m_db.beginTransactionNonExclusive();
```

```java
    try
    {
        ContentValues values = new ContentValues();

        values.put
          ("verified_digest",
           Base64.encodeToString(cryptography.hmac("true".getBytes()),
                        Base64.DEFAULT));
        m_db.update
          ("stack", values, "siphash_id_digest = ? AND " +
           "timestamp IS NULL AND verified_digest = ?",
           new String[] {sipHashIdDigest,
                    Base64.encodeToString(cryptography.
                              hmac("false".getBytes()),
                              Base64.DEFAULT)});
        m_db.setTransactionSuccessful();
    }
    catch(Exception exception)
    {
    }
    finally
    {
        m_db.endTransaction();
    }
}

public void timestampReleasedMessage(Cryptography cryptography,
                        byte digest[])
{
  if(cryptography == null ||
     digest == null ||
     digest.length == 0 ||
     m_db == null)
      return;

  m_db.beginTransactionNonExclusive();

  try
  {
      ContentValues values = new ContentValues();

      values.put
        ("timestamp",
         Base64.
         encodeToString(cryptography.
                   etm(Miscellaneous.
                     longToByteArray(System.
                                currentTimeMillis())),
                 Base64.DEFAULT));
      m_db.update
        ("stack", values, "message_digest = ? AND " +
         "timestamp IS NULL AND verified_digest = ?",
         new String[] {Base64.encodeToString(digest, Base64.DEFAULT),
                  Base64.encodeToString(cryptography.
                               hmac("true".getBytes()),
                               Base64.DEFAULT)});
      m_db.setTransactionSuccessful();
  }
  catch(Exception exception)
  {
  }
  finally
```

```java
        {
            m_db.endTransaction();
        }
    }

    public void updateSipHashIdTimestamp(byte digest[])
    {
      if(digest == null || digest.length == 0 || m_db == null)
          return;

      m_db.beginTransactionNonExclusive();

      try
      {
          ContentValues values = new ContentValues();
          SimpleDateFormat simpleDateFormat = new SimpleDateFormat
            ("yyyy-MM-dd HH:mm:ss", Locale.getDefault());

          simpleDateFormat.setTimeZone(TimeZone.getTimeZone("GMT"));
          values.put
            ("timestamp", simpleDateFormat.format(new Date()));
          m_db.update
            ("siphash_ids", values, "siphash_id_digest = ?",
             new String[] {new String(digest)});
          m_db.setTransactionSuccessful();
      }
      catch(Exception exception)
      {
      }
      finally
      {
          m_db.endTransaction();
      }
    }

    public void writeCongestionDigest(long value)
    {
      if(m_db == null)
          return;

      s_congestionControlMutex.writeLock().lock();

      try
      {
          m_db.beginTransactionNonExclusive();

          try
          {
            ContentValues values = new ContentValues();

            values.put
                ("digest",
                 Base64.encodeToString(Miscellaneous.
                            longToByteArray(value),
                            Base64.DEFAULT));
            m_db.replace("congestion_control", null, values);
            m_db.setTransactionSuccessful();
          }
          catch(Exception exception)
          {
          }
          finally
          {
```

```java
        m_db.endTransaction();
      }
  }
  finally
  {
      s_congestionControlMutex.writeLock().unlock();
  }
}

public void writeIdentities(UUID clientIdentity, byte bytes[])
{
  if(bytes == null ||
     bytes.length == 0 ||
     clientIdentity == null ||
     m_db == null)
      return;

  m_db.beginTransactionNonExclusive();

  try
  {
      ContentValues values = new ContentValues();
      SimpleDateFormat simpleDateFormat = new SimpleDateFormat
        ("yyyy-MM-dd HH:mm:ss", Locale.getDefault());

      simpleDateFormat.setTimeZone(TimeZone.getTimeZone("GMT"));

      int length = bytes.length;

      for(int i = 0; i < length; i += 64)
      {
        values.clear();
        values.put("algorithm", "sha-512");
        values.put("client_identity", clientIdentity.toString());
        values.put
            ("identity",
             Base64.encodeToString(Arrays.copyOfRange(bytes, i, i + 64),
                       Base64.DEFAULT));
        values.put("timestamp", simpleDateFormat.format(new Date()));
        m_db.replace("routing_identities", null, values);
      }

      m_db.setTransactionSuccessful();
  }
  catch(Exception exception)
    {
  }
  finally
  {
      m_db.endTransaction();
  }
}

public void writeIdentity(UUID clientIdentity, String identity)
{
  if(clientIdentity == null ||
     identity == null ||
     identity.length() == 0 ||
     m_db == null)
      return;

  m_db.beginTransactionNonExclusive();
```

```java
        try
        {
            ContentValues values = new ContentValues();
            SimpleDateFormat simpleDateFormat = new SimpleDateFormat
              ("yyyy-MM-dd HH:mm:ss", Locale.getDefault());
            int index = identity.indexOf(";");

            /*
            ** The identity variable may contain preferred algorithms.
            */

            simpleDateFormat.setTimeZone(TimeZone.getTimeZone("GMT"));
            values.put("algorithm", "sha-512");
            values.put("client_identity", clientIdentity.toString());

            if(index > 0)
              values.put("identity", identity.substring(0, index));
            else
              values.put("identity", identity);

            values.put("timestamp", simpleDateFormat.format(new Date()));
            m_db.replace("routing_identities", null, values);
            m_db.setTransactionSuccessful();
        }
      catch(Exception exception)
        {
        }
      finally
        {
            m_db.endTransaction();
        }
    }

    public void writeListenerCertificateDetails(Cryptography cryptography,
                                    byte certificate[],
                                    byte privateKey[],
                                    byte publicKey[],
                                    int oid)
    {
      if(cryptography == null ||
         certificate == null ||
         certificate.length == 0 ||
         m_db == null ||
         privateKey == null ||
         privateKey.length == 0 ||
         publicKey == null ||
         publicKey.length == 0)
          return;

      m_db.beginTransactionNonExclusive();

      try
      {
          ContentValues values = new ContentValues();

          values.put
            ("certificate",
             Base64.encodeToString(cryptography.etm(certificate),
                        Base64.DEFAULT));
          values.put
            ("private_key",
             Base64.encodeToString(cryptography.etm(privateKey),
                        Base64.DEFAULT));
```

```java
      values.put
        ("public_key",
         Base64.encodeToString(cryptography.etm(publicKey),
                        Base64.DEFAULT));
        m_db.update("listeners",
                values,
                "OID = ?",
                new String[] {String.valueOf(oid)});
        m_db.setTransactionSuccessful();
    }
    catch(Exception exception)
    {
    }
    finally
    {
        m_db.endTransaction();
    }
  }

  public void writeLog(String event)
  {
    if(m_db == null)
        return;

    m_db.beginTransactionNonExclusive();

    try
    {
        ContentValues values = new ContentValues();

        values.put("event", event.trim());
        m_db.insert("log", null, values);
        m_db.setTransactionSuccessful();
    }
    catch(Exception exception)
      {
    }
    finally
    {
        m_db.endTransaction();
    }
  }

  public void writeMessage(Cryptography cryptography,
                  String sipHashId,
                  byte message[])
  {
    if(cryptography == null ||
       m_db == null ||
       message == null ||
       message.length == 0)
        return;

    m_db.beginTransactionNonExclusive();

    try
    {
        ContentValues values = new ContentValues();

        values.put
          ("message",
           Base64.encodeToString(cryptography.etm(message),
                        Base64.DEFAULT));
```

```java
            values.put
              ("message_digest",
               Base64.encodeToString(Cryptography.sha512(message),
                          Base64.DEFAULT));
            values.put
              ("siphash_id",
               Base64.encodeToString
               (cryptography.etm(sipHashId.getBytes(StandardCharsets.UTF_8)),
                Base64.DEFAULT));
            values.put
              ("siphash_id_digest",
               Base64.encodeToString
               (cryptography.hmac(sipHashId.getBytes(StandardCharsets.UTF_8)),
                Base64.DEFAULT));
            values.put
              ("verified_digest",
               Base64.encodeToString(cryptography.hmac("false".getBytes()),
                          Base64.DEFAULT));
        m_db.replace("stack", null, values);
        m_db.setTransactionSuccessful();
    }
    catch(Exception exception)
    {
    }
    finally
    {
        m_db.endTransaction();
    }
    }

    public void writeSetting(Cryptography cryptography,
                    String name,
                    String value)
    {
      if(m_db == null)
        return;

      m_db.beginTransactionNonExclusive();

      try
      {
          String a = name.trim();
          String b = name.trim();
          String c = value; // Do not trim.

          if(cryptography != null)
          {
            byte bytes[] = null;

            bytes = cryptography.etm(a.getBytes());

            if(bytes != null)
                a = Base64.encodeToString(bytes, Base64.DEFAULT);
            else
                a = "";

            bytes = cryptography.hmac(b.getBytes());

            if(bytes != null)
                b = Base64.encodeToString(bytes, Base64.DEFAULT);
            else
                b = "";
```

```java
            bytes = cryptography.etm(c.getBytes());

            if(bytes != null)
                c = Base64.encodeToString(bytes, Base64.DEFAULT);
            else
                c = "";

            if(a.isEmpty() || b.isEmpty() || c.isEmpty())
                throw new Exception();
        }

        ContentValues values = new ContentValues();

        values.put("name", a);
        values.put("name_digest", b);
        values.put("value", c);
        m_db.replace("settings", null, values);
        m_db.setTransactionSuccessful();
    }
    catch(Exception exception)
        {
    }
    finally
    {
        m_db.endTransaction();
    }
    }
}
```

/* Kernel.java

```
https://raw.githubusercontent.com/textbrowser/smokestack/master/SmokeStack/app
/src/main/java/org/purple/smokestack/Kernel.java
** Copyright (c) Alexis Megas.
** All rights reserved.
**
** Redistribution and use in source and binary forms, with or without
** modification, are permitted provided that the following conditions
** are met:
** 1. Redistributions of source code must retain the above copyright
**    notice, this list of conditions and the following disclaimer.
** 2. Redistributions in binary form must reproduce the above copyright
**    notice, this list of conditions and the following disclaimer in the
**    documentation and/or other materials provided with the distribution.
** 3. The name of the author may not be used to endorse or promote products
**    derived from SmokeStack without specific prior written permission.
**
** SMOKESTACK IS PROVIDED BY THE AUTHOR ``AS IS'' AND ANY EXPRESS OR
** IMPLIED WARRANTIES, INCLUDING, BUT NOT LIMITED TO, THE IMPLIED WARRANTIES
** OF MERCHANTABILITY AND FITNESS FOR A PARTICULAR PURPOSE ARE DISCLAIMED.
** IN NO EVENT SHALL THE AUTHOR BE LIABLE FOR ANY DIRECT, INDIRECT,
** INCIDENTAL, SPECIAL, EXEMPLARY, OR CONSEQUENTIAL DAMAGES (INCLUDING, BUT
** NOT LIMITED TO, PROCUREMENT OF SUBSTITUTE GOODS OR SERVICES; LOSS OF USE,
** DATA, OR PROFITS; OR BUSINESS INTERRUPTION) HOWEVER CAUSED AND ON ANY
** THEORY OF LIABILITY, WHETHER IN CONTRACT, STRICT LIABILITY, OR TORT
** (INCLUDING NEGLIGENCE OR OTHERWISE) ARISING IN ANY WAY OUT OF THE USE OF
** SMOKESTACK, EVEN IF ADVISED OF THE POSSIBILITY OF SUCH DAMAGE.
*/

package org.purple.smokestack;
```

```java
import android.content.Context;
import android.content.Intent;
import android.net.ConnectivityManager;
import android.net.NetworkInfo;
import android.net.wifi.WifiManager.WifiLock;
import android.net.wifi.WifiManager;
import android.os.PowerManager.WakeLock;
import android.os.PowerManager;
import android.support.v4.content.LocalBroadcastManager;
import android.util.Base64;
import android.util.SparseArray;
import java.net.InetAddress;
import java.nio.charset.StandardCharsets;
import java.security.PublicKey;
import java.util.ArrayList;
import java.util.Arrays;
import java.util.Collections;
import java.util.Hashtable;
import java.util.Iterator;
import java.util.UUID;
import java.util.concurrent.Executors;
import java.util.concurrent.ScheduledExecutorService;
import java.util.concurrent.ScheduledFuture;
import java.util.concurrent.TimeUnit;
import java.util.concurrent.atomic.AtomicInteger;
import java.util.concurrent.locks.ReentrantReadWriteLock;

public class Kernel
{
    private ArrayList<OzoneElement> m_ozones = null;
    private ArrayList<SipHashIdElement> m_sipHashIds = null;
    private Hashtable<String, ScheduledFuture<?> >
      m_releaseMessagesSchedulers = null;
    private ScheduledExecutorService m_congestionScheduler = null;
    private ScheduledExecutorService m_listenersScheduler = null;
    private ScheduledExecutorService m_neighborsScheduler = null;
    private ScheduledExecutorService m_purgeExpiredRoutingEntriesScheduler =
      null;
    private ScheduledExecutorService m_purgeReleasedMessagesScheduler = null;
    private WakeLock m_wakeLock = null;
    private WifiLock m_wifiLock = null;
    private final ReentrantReadWriteLock m_listenersMutex = new
      ReentrantReadWriteLock();
    private final ReentrantReadWriteLock m_ozonesMutex = new
      ReentrantReadWriteLock();
    private final ReentrantReadWriteLock m_releaseMessagesSchedulersMutex =
new
      ReentrantReadWriteLock();
    private final ReentrantReadWriteLock m_sipHashIdsMutex = new
      ReentrantReadWriteLock();
    private final SparseArray<Neighbor> m_neighbors = new SparseArray<> ();
    private final SparseArray<TcpListener> m_listeners = new SparseArray<> ();
    private final static Database s_databaseHelper = Database.getInstance();
    private final static Cryptography s_cryptography =
      Cryptography.getInstance();
    private final static SipHash s_congestionSipHash = new SipHash
      (Cryptography.randomBytes(SipHash.KEY_LENGTH));
    private final static int CONGESTION_LIFETIME = 60;
    private final static int ROUTING_ENTRY_LIFETIME = CONGESTION_LIFETIME;
    private final static long CHAT_MESSAGE_RETRIEVAL_WINDOW = 30000L; /*
                                                     ** 30
                                                     ** Seconds
                                                     */
```

```java
private final static long CONGESTION_INTERVAL = 15000L; // 15 Seconds
private final static long LISTENERS_INTERVAL = 5000L; // 5 Seconds
private final static long NEIGHBORS_INTERVAL = 5000L; // 5 Seconds
private final static long PKP_MESSAGE_RETRIEVAL_WINDOW =
  30000L; // 30 Seconds
private final static long PURGE_RELEASED_MESSAGES_INTERVAL =
  5000L; // 5 Seconds
private final static long ROUTING_INTERVAL = 15000L; // 15 Seconds
private final static long SHARE_SIPHASH_IDENTITY_WINDOW =
  30000L; // 30 Seconds
private static Kernel s_instance = null;

private Kernel()
{
  m_releaseMessagesSchedulers = new Hashtable<> ();

  /*
  ** Never, ever sleep.
  */

  try
  {
      PowerManager powerManager = (PowerManager)
        SmokeStack.getApplication().getApplicationContext().
        getSystemService(Context.POWER_SERVICE);

      if(powerManager != null)
        m_wakeLock = powerManager.newWakeLock
            (PowerManager.PARTIAL_WAKE_LOCK,
             "SmokeStack:SmokeStackWakeLockTag");

      if(m_wakeLock != null)
      {
        m_wakeLock.setReferenceCounted(false);
        m_wakeLock.acquire();
      }
  }
  catch(Exception exception)
  {
  }

  try
  {
      WifiManager wifiManager = (WifiManager)
        SmokeStack.getApplication().getApplicationContext().
        getSystemService(Context.WIFI_SERVICE);

      if(wifiManager != null)
        m_wifiLock = wifiManager.createWifiLock
            (WifiManager.WIFI_MODE_FULL_HIGH_PERF,
             "SmokeStack:SmokeStackWiFiLockTag");

      if(m_wifiLock != null)
      {
        m_wifiLock.setReferenceCounted(false);
        m_wifiLock.acquire();
      }
  }
  catch(Exception exception)
  {
  }

  /*
```

```java
     ** Other tasks.
     */

    populateOzones();
    populateSipHashIds();
    prepareSchedulers();
  }

  public boolean isNetworkAvailable()
  {
    try
    {
        ConnectivityManager connectivityManager = (ConnectivityManager)
          SmokeStack.getApplication().getApplicationContext().
          getSystemService(Context.CONNECTIVITY_SERVICE);
        NetworkInfo networkInfo = connectivityManager.
          getActiveNetworkInfo();

        if(networkInfo.getState() !=
            android.net.NetworkInfo.State.CONNECTED)
          return false;
    }
    catch(Exception exception)
    {
        return false;
    }

    return true;
  }

  private void prepareListeners()
  {
    if(!isNetworkAvailable())
    {
        purgeListeners();
        return;
    }

    ArrayList<ListenerElement> listeners =
        s_databaseHelper.readListeners(s_cryptography, -1);

    if(listeners == null || listeners.size() == 0)
    {
        purgeListeners();
        return;
    }

    m_listenersMutex.writeLock().lock();

    try
    {
        for(int i = m_listeners.size() - 1; i >= 0; i--)
        {
          /*
          ** Remove listener objects which do not exist in the database.
          ** Also removed will be listeners having disconnected statuses.
          */

          boolean found = false;
          int oid = m_listeners.keyAt(i);

          for(ListenerElement listenerElement : listeners)
              if(listenerElement != null && listenerElement.m_oid == oid)
```

```java
        {
          if(!listenerElement.m_statusControl.toLowerCase().
            equals("disconnect"))
            found = true;

          break;
        }

      if(!found)
      {
          if(m_listeners.get(oid) != null)
            m_listeners.get(oid).abort();

          m_listeners.remove(oid);
      }
    }
}
finally
{
    m_listenersMutex.writeLock().unlock();
}

for(ListenerElement listenerElement : listeners)
{
    if(listenerElement == null)
      continue;
    else
    {
      m_listenersMutex.readLock().lock();

      try
      {
          if(m_listeners.get(listenerElement.m_oid) != null)
            continue;
      }
      finally
      {
          m_listenersMutex.readLock().unlock();
      }

      if(listenerElement.m_statusControl.toLowerCase().
          equals("delete") ||
          listenerElement.m_statusControl.toLowerCase().
          equals("disconnect"))
      {
          if(listenerElement.m_statusControl.toLowerCase().
            equals("disconnect"))
            s_databaseHelper.saveListenerInformation
              (s_cryptography,
               "",                  // Error
               "0",                 // Peers Count
               "disconnected",  // Status
               "0",                 // Uptime
               String.valueOf(listenerElement.m_oid));

          continue;
      }
    }

    TcpListener listener = new TcpListener
      (listenerElement.m_localIpAddress,
       listenerElement.m_localPort,
       listenerElement.m_localScopeId,
```

```java
            listenerElement.m_ipVersion,
            listenerElement.m_isPrivate,
            listenerElement.m_certificate,
            listenerElement.m_privateKey,
            listenerElement.m_publicKey,
            listenerElement.m_oid);

        m_listenersMutex.writeLock().lock();

        try
        {
          m_listeners.append(listenerElement.m_oid, listener);
        }
        finally
        {
          m_listenersMutex.writeLock().unlock();
        }
      }

    listeners.clear();
    }

  private void prepareNeighbors()
  {
    if(!isNetworkAvailable())
    {
        purgeNeighbors();
        return;
    }

    ArrayList<NeighborElement> neighbors = purgeDeletedNeighbors();

    if(neighbors == null)
        return;

    for(NeighborElement neighborElement : neighbors)
    {
        if(neighborElement == null)
          continue;
        else
        {
          synchronized(m_neighbors)
          {
              if(m_neighbors.get(neighborElement.m_oid) != null)
                continue;
          }

          if(neighborElement.m_statusControl.toLowerCase().
            equals("delete") ||
            neighborElement.m_statusControl.toLowerCase().
            equals("disconnect"))
          {
              if(neighborElement.m_statusControl.toLowerCase().
                equals("disconnect"))
              {
                s_databaseHelper.deleteEchoQueue
                    (neighborElement.m_oid);
                s_databaseHelper.saveNeighborInformation
                    (s_cryptography,
                      "0",               // Bytes Buffered
                      "0",               // Bytes Read
                      "0",               // Bytes Written
                      "",                // Error
```

```java
                    "",                  // IP Address
                    "0",                 // Port
                    "0",                 // Queue Size
                    "",                  // Session Cipher
                    "disconnected",  // Status
                    "0",                 // Uptime
                    String.valueOf(neighborElement.m_oid));
            }

            continue;
          }
        }

        Neighbor neighbor = null;

        if(neighborElement.m_transport.equals("TCP"))
          neighbor = new TcpNeighbor
              (neighborElement.m_proxyIpAddress,
               neighborElement.m_proxyPort,
               neighborElement.m_proxyType,
               neighborElement.m_remoteIpAddress,
               neighborElement.m_remotePort,
               neighborElement.m_remoteScopeId,
               neighborElement.m_ipVersion,
               neighborElement.m_oid);
        else if(neighborElement.m_transport.equals("UDP"))
        {
          try
          {
              InetAddress inetAddress = InetAddress.getByName
                (neighborElement.m_remoteIpAddress);

              if(inetAddress.isMulticastAddress())
                neighbor = new UdpMulticastNeighbor
                    (neighborElement.m_remoteIpAddress,
                     neighborElement.m_remotePort,
                     neighborElement.m_remoteScopeId,
                     neighborElement.m_ipVersion,
                     neighborElement.m_oid);
              else
                neighbor = new UdpNeighbor
                    (neighborElement.m_remoteIpAddress,
                     neighborElement.m_remotePort,
                     neighborElement.m_remoteScopeId,
                     neighborElement.m_ipVersion,
                     neighborElement.m_oid);
          }
          catch(Exception exception)
          {
          }
        }

        if(neighbor == null)
          continue;

        synchronized(m_neighbors)
        {
          m_neighbors.append(neighborElement.m_oid, neighbor);
        }
    }

    neighbors.clear();
  }
```

```java
    private void prepareReleaseMessagesScheduler(final String sipHashIdDigest,
                                final byte identity[])
    {
      if(!isNetworkAvailable() ||
          identity == null ||
          identity.length == 0 ||
          sipHashIdDigest == null ||
          sipHashIdDigest.isEmpty())
          return;

      m_releaseMessagesSchedulersMutex.writeLock().lock();

      try
      {
          if(m_releaseMessagesSchedulers.containsKey(sipHashIdDigest))
            return;

          m_releaseMessagesSchedulers.put
            (sipHashIdDigest,
             Executors.newSingleThreadScheduledExecutor().
             schedule(new Runnable()
             {
                private AtomicInteger m_oid = new AtomicInteger(-1);

                @Override
                public void run()
                {
                  try
                  {
                      m_oid.set(-1);

                      while(true)
                      {
                        if(!isNetworkAvailable())
                            return;

                        ArrayList<byte[]> arrayList = s_databaseHelper.
                            readTaggedMessage
                            (sipHashIdDigest,
                             s_cryptography,
                             m_oid.get());

                        if(arrayList == null)
                            break;

                        if(arrayList.size() != 3)
                        {
                            arrayList.clear();
                            break;
                        }

                        byte destination[] = Cryptography.hmac
                            (arrayList.get(0), identity);

                        if(destination == null)
                            break;

                        String message = Messages.bytesToMessageString
                            (Miscellaneous.
                             joinByteArrays(arrayList.get(0),
                                    destination));
```

```java
                    enqueueMessage(message);
                    Thread.sleep(250);
                    m_oid.set
                        (Miscellaneous.
                         byteArrayToInt(arrayList.get(2)));
                    arrayList.clear();
                }
            }
            catch(Exception exception)
            {
            }
        }
    }, 5000L, TimeUnit.MILLISECONDS));
}
catch(Exception exception)
{
}
finally
{
    m_releaseMessagesSchedulersMutex.writeLock().unlock();
}

synchronized(m_releaseMessagesSchedulersMutex)
{
    try
    {
      m_releaseMessagesSchedulersMutex.notify();
    }
    catch(Exception exception)
    {
    }
}
}

private void prepareSchedulers()
{
  if(m_congestionScheduler == null)
  {
      m_congestionScheduler = Executors.
        newSingleThreadScheduledExecutor();
      m_congestionScheduler.scheduleAtFixedRate(new Runnable()
      {
        @Override
        public void run()
        {
            try
            {
              s_databaseHelper.purgeCongestion(CONGESTION_LIFETIME);
            }
            catch(Exception exception)
            {
            }
        }
      }, 1500L, CONGESTION_INTERVAL, TimeUnit.MILLISECONDS);
  }

  if(m_listenersScheduler == null)
  {
      m_listenersScheduler = Executors.newSingleThreadScheduledExecutor();
      m_listenersScheduler.scheduleAtFixedRate(new Runnable()
      {
        @Override
        public void run()
```

```java
            {
                try
                {
                  prepareListeners();
                }
                catch(Exception exception)
                {
                }
            }
        }, 1500L, LISTENERS_INTERVAL, TimeUnit.MILLISECONDS);
    }

    if(m_neighborsScheduler == null)
    {
        m_neighborsScheduler = Executors.newSingleThreadScheduledExecutor();
        m_neighborsScheduler.scheduleAtFixedRate(new Runnable()
        {
          @Override
          public void run()
          {
                try
                {
                  prepareNeighbors();
                }
                catch(Exception exception)
                {
                }
            }
        }, 1500L, NEIGHBORS_INTERVAL, TimeUnit.MILLISECONDS);
    }

    if(m_purgeReleasedMessagesScheduler == null)
    {
        m_purgeReleasedMessagesScheduler = Executors.
          newSingleThreadScheduledExecutor();
        m_purgeReleasedMessagesScheduler.scheduleAtFixedRate(new Runnable()
        {
          @Override
          public void run()
          {
                try
                {
                  boolean empty = true;

                  m_releaseMessagesSchedulersMutex.readLock().lock();

                  try
                  {
                      empty = m_releaseMessagesSchedulers.isEmpty();
                  }
                  finally
                  {
                      m_releaseMessagesSchedulersMutex.
                        readLock().unlock();
                  }

                  if(empty)
                      synchronized(m_releaseMessagesSchedulersMutex)
                      {
                        try
                        {
                            m_releaseMessagesSchedulersMutex.wait();
                        }
```

```java
                    catch(Exception exception)
                    {
                    }
                }

            m_releaseMessagesSchedulersMutex.writeLock().lock();

            try
            {
                if(!m_releaseMessagesSchedulers.isEmpty())
                {
                    /*
                    ** Remove completed schedules.
                    */

                    Iterator<Hashtable.
                            Entry<String, ScheduledFuture<?> > >
                        it = m_releaseMessagesSchedulers.entrySet().
                        iterator();

                    while(it.hasNext())
                    {
                        Hashtable.Entry
                          <String, ScheduledFuture<?> >
                          entry = it.next();

                        if(entry.getValue() == null)
                          it.remove();
                        else if(entry.getValue().isDone())
                          it.remove();
                    }
                }
            }
            finally
            {
                m_releaseMessagesSchedulersMutex.
                  writeLock().unlock();
            }
        }
        catch(Exception exception)
        {
        }
      }
    }, 1500L, PURGE_RELEASED_MESSAGES_INTERVAL, TimeUnit.MILLISECONDS);
}

if(m_purgeExpiredRoutingEntriesScheduler == null)
{
    m_purgeExpiredRoutingEntriesScheduler = Executors.
      newSingleThreadScheduledExecutor();
    m_purgeExpiredRoutingEntriesScheduler.scheduleAtFixedRate
      (new Runnable()
    {
      @Override
      public void run()
      {
          try
          {
            s_databaseHelper.purgeExpiredRoutingEntries
                (ROUTING_ENTRY_LIFETIME);
          }
          catch(Exception exception)
          {
```

```java
                }
            }
        }, 1500L, ROUTING_INTERVAL, TimeUnit.MILLISECONDS);
    }
}

    private void purgeListeners()
    {
        /*
        ** Disconnect all existing sockets.
        */

        m_listenersMutex.writeLock().lock();

        try
        {
            int size = m_listeners.size();

            for(int i = 0; i < size; i++)
            {
                int j = m_listeners.keyAt(i);

                if(m_listeners.get(j) != null)
                    m_listeners.get(j).abort();
            }

            m_listeners.clear();
        }
        finally
        {
            m_listenersMutex.writeLock().unlock();
        }
    }

    private void purgeNeighbors()
    {
        /*
        ** Disconnect all non-server sockets.
        */

        synchronized(m_neighbors)
        {
            int size = m_neighbors.size();

            for(int i = 0; i < size; i++)
            {
                int j = m_neighbors.keyAt(i);

                if(m_neighbors.get(j) != null)
                    m_neighbors.get(j).abort();
            }

            m_neighbors.clear();
        }
    }

    public ArrayList<NeighborElement> purgeDeletedNeighbors()
    {
        ArrayList<NeighborElement> neighbors =
            s_databaseHelper.readNeighbors(s_cryptography);

        if(neighbors == null || neighbors.size() == 0)
        {
```

```java
      purgeNeighbors();
      return neighbors;
    }

  synchronized(m_neighbors)
  {
      /*
      ** Remove neighbor objects which do not exist in the database.
      ** Also removed will be neighbors having disconnected statuses.
      */

      for(int i = m_neighbors.size() - 1; i >= 0; i--)
      {
        boolean found = false;
        int oid = m_neighbors.keyAt(i);

        for(NeighborElement neighborElement : neighbors)
            if(neighborElement != null && neighborElement.m_oid == oid)
            {
              if(!neighborElement.m_statusControl.toLowerCase().
                 equals("disconnect"))
                  found = true;

              break;
            }

        if(!found)
        {
            if(m_neighbors.get(oid) != null)
              m_neighbors.get(oid).abort();

            m_neighbors.remove(oid);
        }
      }
    }

  return neighbors;
}

public String remoteClientAddress(int position)
{
  ArrayList<String> arrayList = new ArrayList<>();

  m_listenersMutex.readLock().lock();

  try
  {
      int size = m_listeners.size();

      for(int i = 0; i < size; i++)
      {
        int j = m_listeners.keyAt(i);

        if(m_listeners.get(j) != null)
        {
            ArrayList<String> addresses =
              m_listeners.get(j).clientsAddresses();

            if(addresses != null)
            {
              arrayList.addAll(addresses);
              addresses.clear();
            }
```

```java
              }
          }
      }
    finally
    {
        m_listenersMutex.readLock().unlock();
    }

  Collections.sort(arrayList);
  return arrayList.get(position);
}

public boolean ourMessage(String buffer,
                          UUID clientIdentity,
                          boolean userDefined)
{
  /*
  ** false - echo
  ** true - do not echo
  */

  if(buffer == null)
      return true;

  try
  {
      long value = s_congestionSipHash.hmac
        (buffer.getBytes(), Cryptography.SIPHASH_OUTPUT_LENGTH / 2)[0];

      if(!userDefined)
        /*
        ** A server socket!
        */

        if(buffer.contains("type=0095a&content="))
        {
            s_databaseHelper.writeCongestionDigest(value);

            /*
            ** A client has shared an identity stream.
            */

            s_databaseHelper.writeIdentity
              (clientIdentity, Messages.stripMessage(buffer));

            /*
            ** Do not echo the identity stream to other neighbors.
            */

            return true;
        }
        else if(buffer.contains("type=0095b&content="))
        {
            /*
            ** We've received identities.
            */

            s_databaseHelper.writeCongestionDigest(value);
            s_databaseHelper.deleteRoutingEntry
              (clientIdentity.toString());

            byte bytes[] = Base64.decode
              (Messages.stripMessage(buffer), Base64.DEFAULT);
```

```java
        s_databaseHelper.writeIdentities(clientIdentity, bytes);
        return true;
      }
    else if(buffer.contains("type=0096&content="))
        return true;
    else if(buffer.contains("type=0097a&content="))
        return true;
    else if(buffer.contains("type=0097b&content="))
        return true;

    if(s_databaseHelper.containsCongestionDigest(value))
      return true;

    byte bytes[] =
      Base64.decode(Messages.stripMessage(buffer), Base64.DEFAULT);

    if(bytes == null || bytes.length < 128)
      return false;

    /*
    ** EPKS?
    */

    ArrayList<SipHashIdElement> arrayList1 = null;

    m_sipHashIdsMutex.readLock().lock();

    try
    {
      arrayList1 = m_sipHashIds;
    }
    finally
    {
      m_sipHashIdsMutex.readLock().unlock();
    }

    byte data[] = Arrays.copyOfRange // Blocks #1, #2, etc.
      (bytes, 0, bytes.length - 2 * Cryptography.HASH_KEY_LENGTH);
    byte hmac[] = Arrays.copyOfRange // Second to the last block.
      (bytes,
       bytes.length - 2 * Cryptography.HASH_KEY_LENGTH,
       bytes.length - Cryptography.HASH_KEY_LENGTH);

    if(arrayList1 != null && arrayList1.size() > 0)
    {
      byte destination[] = Arrays.copyOfRange
          (bytes,
           bytes.length - Cryptography.HASH_KEY_LENGTH,
           bytes.length);

      for(SipHashIdElement sipHashIdElement : arrayList1)
      {
          if(sipHashIdElement == null)
            continue;
          else if(sipHashIdElement.m_epksCompleted)
            continue;

          if(!(Cryptography.
            memcmp(hmac,
                 Cryptography.hmac(data, Arrays.
                            copyOfRange(sipHashIdElement.
                                 m_stream,
```

```java
                                           Cryptography.
                                           CIPHER_KEY_LENGTH,
                                           sipHashIdElement.
                                           m_stream.
                                           length))) &&
                 Cryptography.
                 memcmp(destination,
                     Cryptography.
                     hmac(Arrays.
                         copyOfRange(bytes,
                             0,
                             bytes.length -
                             Cryptography.HASH_KEY_LENGTH),
                         Cryptography.
                         sha512(sipHashIdElement.
                             m_sipHashId.
                             getBytes(StandardCharsets.
                                 UTF_8))))))
            continue;

        s_databaseHelper.writeCongestionDigest(value);

        byte aes256[] = Cryptography.decrypt
          (data,
           Arrays.copyOfRange(sipHashIdElement.m_stream,
                         0,
                         Cryptography.CIPHER_KEY_LENGTH));

        if(s_databaseHelper.
           writeParticipant(s_cryptography,
                     sipHashIdElement.
                     m_acceptWithoutSignatures,
                     aes256))
        {
          Intent intent = new Intent
              ("org.purple.smokestack.populate_participants");
          LocalBroadcastManager localBroadcastManager =
              LocalBroadcastManager.getInstance
              (SmokeStack.getApplication());

          localBroadcastManager.sendBroadcast(intent);
        }

        /*
        ** Echo the key bundle.
        */

        return false;
      }
    }

    /*
    ** Ozone-based messages.
    */

    ArrayList<OzoneElement> arrayList2 = null;

    m_ozonesMutex.readLock().lock();

    try
    {
      arrayList2 = m_ozones;
    }
```

```
  finally
  {
    m_ozonesMutex.readLock().unlock();
  }

if(arrayList2 == null || arrayList2.size() == 0)
  return false;

data = Arrays.copyOfRange
  (bytes, 0, bytes.length - Cryptography.HASH_KEY_LENGTH);
hmac = Arrays.copyOfRange
  (bytes,
   bytes.length - Cryptography.HASH_KEY_LENGTH,
   bytes.length);

for(OzoneElement ozoneElement : arrayList2)
{
  if(ozoneElement == null)
      continue;

  if(Cryptography.
     memcmp(hmac,
         Cryptography.
         hmac(data,
             Arrays.
             copyOfRange(ozoneElement.m_addressStream,
                     Cryptography.CIPHER_KEY_LENGTH,
                     ozoneElement.m_addressStream.
                     length))))
  {
     byte aes256[] = Cryptography.decrypt
       (data,
        Arrays.copyOfRange(ozoneElement.m_addressStream,
                     0,
                     Cryptography.CIPHER_KEY_LENGTH));

     if(aes256 == null)
       return true;

     if(aes256[0] == Messages.CHAT_MESSAGE_READ[0] ||
        aes256[0] == Messages.CHAT_MESSAGE_RETRIEVAL[0])
     {
       long current = System.currentTimeMillis();
       long timestamp = Miscellaneous.byteArrayToLong
          (Arrays.copyOfRange(aes256, 1, 9));

       if(current - timestamp < 0L)
       {
           if(timestamp - current >
             CHAT_MESSAGE_RETRIEVAL_WINDOW)
            return true;
       }
       else if(current - timestamp >
             CHAT_MESSAGE_RETRIEVAL_WINDOW)
           return true;

       byte identity[] = Arrays.copyOfRange(aes256, 9, 73);

       if(identity == null || identity.length != 64)
           return true;

       PublicKey signatureKey = s_databaseHelper.
           signatureKeyForDigest
```

```java
                        (s_cryptography,
                         Arrays.copyOfRange(aes256, 73, 137));

                if(signatureKey == null)
                    return true;

                if(!Cryptography.
                   verifySignature(signatureKey,
                                   Arrays.copyOfRange(aes256,
                                                      137,
                                                      aes256.length),
                                   Arrays.
                                   copyOfRange(aes256,
                                               0,
                                               137)))
                    return true;

                s_databaseHelper.writeCongestionDigest(value);

                String sipHashIdDigest = s_databaseHelper.
                    sipHashIdDigestFromDigest
                    (s_cryptography,
                     Arrays.copyOfRange(aes256, 73, 73 + 64));

                if(aes256[0] == Messages.CHAT_MESSAGE_READ[0])
                    s_databaseHelper.timestampReleasedMessage
                      (s_cryptography, identity);
                else
                {
                    /*
                    ** Tag all of sipHashIdDigest's messages for
                    ** release.
                    */

                    prepareReleaseMessagesScheduler
                      (sipHashIdDigest, identity);
                    s_databaseHelper.tagMessagesForRelease
                      (s_cryptography, sipHashIdDigest);
                }

                s_databaseHelper.updateSipHashIdTimestamp
                    (sipHashIdDigest.getBytes());
                return true;
            }
            else if(aes256[0] == Messages.PKP_MESSAGE_REQUEST[0])
            {
                /*
                ** Request a public key pair.
                */

                long current = System.currentTimeMillis();
                long timestamp = Miscellaneous.byteArrayToLong
                    (Arrays.copyOfRange(aes256, 1, 9));

                if(current - timestamp < 0L)
                {
                    if(timestamp - current >
                       PKP_MESSAGE_RETRIEVAL_WINDOW)
                      return true;
                }
                else if(current - timestamp >
                        PKP_MESSAGE_RETRIEVAL_WINDOW)
                    return true;
```

```java
            String sipHashId = new String
                (Arrays.copyOfRange(aes256,
                          9 +
                          Cryptography.
                          SIPHASH_IDENTITY_LENGTH,
                          aes256.length),
             StandardCharsets.UTF_8);
        String array[] = s_databaseHelper.readPublicKeyPair
            (s_cryptography, sipHashId);

        if(array == null)
            return true;

        sipHashId = new String
            (Arrays.
             copyOfRange(aes256,
                    9,
                    9 +
                    Cryptography.SIPHASH_IDENTITY_LENGTH));

        String message = Messages.bytesToMessageString
            (Messages.epksMessage(sipHashId, array));

        enqueueMessage(message);
        return true;
    }
    else if(aes256[0] == Messages.SHARE_SIPHASH_ID[0])
    {
      long current = System.currentTimeMillis();
      long timestamp = Miscellaneous.byteArrayToLong
          (Arrays.copyOfRange(aes256, 1, 9));

      if(current - timestamp < 0L)
      {
          if(timestamp - current >
             SHARE_SIPHASH_IDENTITY_WINDOW)
           return true;
      }
      else if(current - timestamp >
           SHARE_SIPHASH_IDENTITY_WINDOW)
          return true;

      String name = "";
      String sipHashId = new String
          (Arrays.
           copyOfRange(aes256,
                  9,
                  9 +
                  Cryptography.SIPHASH_IDENTITY_LENGTH),
           StandardCharsets.UTF_8);

      name = sipHashId.toUpperCase().trim();

      if(s_databaseHelper.
         writeSipHashParticipant(s_cryptography,
                        name,
                        sipHashId,
                        true))
      {
          if((bytes = Cryptography.
            generateOzone(name)) != null)
            if(s_databaseHelper.
```

```java
                       writeOzone(s_cryptography, name, bytes))
                        populateOzones();

                populateSipHashIds();

                Intent intent = new Intent
                  ("org.purple.smokestack." +
                   "populate_ozones_participants");
                LocalBroadcastManager localBroadcastManager =
                  LocalBroadcastManager.getInstance
                  (SmokeStack.getApplication());

                localBroadcastManager.sendBroadcast(intent);
            }

            byte identity[] = Arrays.copyOfRange
                (aes256,
                 9 + Cryptography.SIPHASH_IDENTITY_LENGTH,
                 9 + Cryptography.SIPHASH_IDENTITY_LENGTH + 8);

            bytes = Messages.shareSipHashIdMessageConfirmation
                (s_cryptography,
                 sipHashId,
                 identity,
                 ozoneElement.m_addressStream);
            enqueueMessage(Messages.bytesToMessageString(bytes));

            /*
            ** Echo the shared Smoke identity.
            */

            return false;
            }
          else
            return true;
        }

        if(arrayList1 != null && arrayList1.size() > 0)
            for(SipHashIdElement sipHashIdElement : arrayList1)
            {
              if(sipHashIdElement == null)
                  continue;

              long minutes = TimeUnit.MILLISECONDS.toMinutes
                  (System.currentTimeMillis());

              for(int i = 0; i < 2; i++)
                  if(Cryptography.
                     memcmp(hmac,
                         Cryptography.
                         hmac(Miscellaneous.
                            joinByteArrays
                            (data,
                             sipHashIdElement.
                             m_sipHashId.
                             getBytes(StandardCharsets.UTF_8),
                             Miscellaneous.
                             longToByteArray
                             (i + minutes)),
                           Arrays.copyOfRange(ozoneElement.
                                     m_addressStream,
                                     32,
                                     ozoneElement.
```

```java
                                         m_addressStream.
                                         length))))
                    {
                        /*
                        ** Discovered.
                        */

                        s_databaseHelper.writeCongestionDigest(value);
                        s_databaseHelper.writeMessage
                            (s_cryptography,
                             sipHashIdElement.m_sipHashId,
                             data);
                        return true;
                    }
                }
            }
        }
    catch(Exception exception)
    {
        return false;
    }

    return false;
}

public int listenersCount()
{
  m_listenersMutex.readLock().lock();

  try
  {
      return m_listeners.size();
  }
  finally
  {
      m_listenersMutex.readLock().unlock();
  }
}

public int neighborsCount()
{
  synchronized(m_neighbors)
  {
      return m_neighbors.size();
  }
}

public int remoteClientsCount()
{
  int count = 0;

  m_listenersMutex.readLock().lock();

  try
  {
      int size = m_listeners.size();

      for(int i = 0; i < size; i++)
      {
        int j = m_listeners.keyAt(i);

        if(m_listeners.get(j) != null)
            count += m_listeners.get(j).clientsCount();
```

```java
                }
        }
        finally
        {
            m_listenersMutex.readLock().unlock();
        }

        return count;
    }

    public static synchronized Kernel getInstance()
    {
      if(s_instance == null)
          s_instance = new Kernel();

      return s_instance;
    }

    public static void writeCongestionDigest(String message)
    {
      if(message != null)
          try
          {
            s_databaseHelper.writeCongestionDigest
                (s_congestionSipHash.
                 hmac(message.getBytes(),
                   Cryptography.SIPHASH_OUTPUT_LENGTH)[0]);
          }
          catch(Exception exception)
          {
          }
    }

    public static void writeCongestionDigest(byte data[])
    {
      if(data != null)
          try
          {
            s_databaseHelper.writeCongestionDigest
                (s_congestionSipHash.
                 hmac(data, Cryptography.SIPHASH_OUTPUT_LENGTH)[0]);
          }
          catch(Exception exception)
          {
          }
    }

    public void clearNeighborQueues()
    {
      synchronized(m_neighbors)
      {
          int size = m_neighbors.size();

          for(int i = 0; i < size; i++)
          {
            int j = m_neighbors.keyAt(i);

            if(m_neighbors.get(j) != null)
            {
                m_neighbors.get(j).clearEchoQueue();
                m_neighbors.get(j).clearQueue();
            }
          }
```

```java
    }
  }

  public void echo(String message, int oid)
  {
    if(message == null || message.trim().isEmpty())
        return;

    m_listenersMutex.readLock().lock();

    try
    {
        int size = m_listeners.size();

        for(int i = 0; i < size; i++)
        {
          int j = m_listeners.keyAt(i);

          if(m_listeners.get(j) != null)
              m_listeners.get(j).scheduleEchoSend(message, oid);
        }
    }
    finally
    {
        m_listenersMutex.readLock().unlock();
    }

    synchronized(m_neighbors)
    {
        int size = m_neighbors.size();

        for(int i = 0; i < size; i++)
        {
          int j = m_neighbors.keyAt(i);

          if(m_neighbors.get(j) != null &&
             m_neighbors.get(j).getOid() != oid)
              m_neighbors.get(j).scheduleEchoSend(message);
        }
    }
  }

  public void enqueueMessage(String message)
  {
    if(!isNetworkAvailable() || message == null || message.trim().isEmpty())
        return;

    m_listenersMutex.readLock().lock();

    try
    {
        int size = m_listeners.size();

        for(int i = 0; i < size; i++)
        {
          int j = m_listeners.keyAt(i);

          if(m_listeners.get(j) != null)
              m_listeners.get(j).scheduleSend(message);
        }
    }
    finally
    {
```

```java
            m_listenersMutex.readLock().unlock();
    }

    ArrayList<NeighborElement> arrayList =
        s_databaseHelper.readNeighborOids(s_cryptography);

    if(arrayList != null && arrayList.size() > 0)
    {
        int size = arrayList.size();

        for(int i = 0; i < size; i++)
          if(arrayList.get(i) != null &&
             arrayList.get(i).m_statusControl.toLowerCase().
             equals("connect"))
              s_databaseHelper.enqueueOutboundMessage
                (s_cryptography,
                 message,
                 false,
                 arrayList.get(i).m_oid);

        arrayList.clear();
    }
}

public void populateOzones()
{
  m_ozonesMutex.writeLock().lock();

  try
  {
      m_ozones = s_databaseHelper.readOzones(s_cryptography);
  }
  catch(Exception exception)
  {
  }
  finally
  {
      m_ozonesMutex.writeLock().unlock();
  }
}

public void populateSipHashIds()
{
  m_sipHashIdsMutex.writeLock().lock();

  try
  {
      m_sipHashIds = s_databaseHelper.readSipHashIds(s_cryptography);
  }
  catch(Exception exception)
  {
  }
  finally
  {
      m_sipHashIdsMutex.writeLock().unlock();
  }
}

public void toggleListenerPrivacy(int oid)
{
  m_listenersMutex.readLock().lock();

  try
```

```java
        {
            int size = m_listeners.size();

            for(int i = 0; i < size; i++)
            {
              int j = m_listeners.keyAt(i);

              if(m_listeners.get(j) != null &&
                 m_listeners.get(j).oid() == oid)
              {
                  m_listeners.get(j).togglePrivacy();
                  break;
              }
            }
        }
        finally
        {
            m_listenersMutex.readLock().unlock();
        }
    }
}
```

/* ListenerElement.java

```
https://github.com/textbrowser/smokestack/blob/master/SmokeStack/app/src/main/
java/org/purple/smokestack/ListenerElement.java
** Copyright (c) Alexis Megas.
** All rights reserved.
**
** Redistribution and use in source and binary forms, with or without
** modification, are permitted provided that the following conditions
** are met:
** 1. Redistributions of source code must retain the above copyright
**    notice, this list of conditions and the following disclaimer.
** 2. Redistributions in binary form must reproduce the above copyright
**    notice, this list of conditions and the following disclaimer in the
**    documentation and/or other materials provided with the distribution.
** 3. The name of the author may not be used to endorse or promote products
**    derived from SmokeStack without specific prior written permission.
**
** SMOKESTACK IS PROVIDED BY THE AUTHOR ``AS IS'' AND ANY EXPRESS OR
** IMPLIED WARRANTIES, INCLUDING, BUT NOT LIMITED TO, THE IMPLIED WARRANTIES
** OF MERCHANTABILITY AND FITNESS FOR A PARTICULAR PURPOSE ARE DISCLAIMED.
** IN NO EVENT SHALL THE AUTHOR BE LIABLE FOR ANY DIRECT, INDIRECT,
** INCIDENTAL, SPECIAL, EXEMPLARY, OR CONSEQUENTIAL DAMAGES (INCLUDING, BUT
** NOT LIMITED TO, PROCUREMENT OF SUBSTITUTE GOODS OR SERVICES; LOSS OF USE,
** DATA, OR PROFITS; OR BUSINESS INTERRUPTION) HOWEVER CAUSED AND ON ANY
** THEORY OF LIABILITY, WHETHER IN CONTRACT, STRICT LIABILITY, OR TORT
** (INCLUDING NEGLIGENCE OR OTHERWISE) ARISING IN ANY WAY OUT OF THE USE OF
** SMOKESTACK, EVEN IF ADVISED OF THE POSSIBILITY OF SUCH DAMAGE.
*/

package org.purple.smokestack;

public class ListenerElement
{
    public String m_error = "";
    public String m_ipVersion = "";
    public String m_localIpAddress = "";
    public String m_localPort = "";
```

```java
    public String m_localScopeId = "";
    public String m_status = "";
    public String m_statusControl = "";
    public String m_uptime = "";
    public boolean m_isPrivate = false;
    public byte m_certificate[] = null;
    public byte m_privateKey[] = null;
    public byte m_publicKey[] = null;
    public int m_oid = -1;
    public long m_peersCount = 0L;

    public ListenerElement()
    {
    }
}



/* ListenersAdapter.java

https://raw.githubusercontent.com/textbrowser/smokestack/master/SmokeStack/app
/src/main/java/org/purple/smokestack/ListenersAdapter.java
** Copyright (c) Alexis Megas.
** All rights reserved.
**
** Redistribution and use in source and binary forms, with or without
** modification, are permitted provided that the following conditions
** are met:
** 1. Redistributions of source code must retain the above copyright
**    notice, this list of conditions and the following disclaimer.
** 2. Redistributions in binary form must reproduce the above copyright
**    notice, this list of conditions and the following disclaimer in the
**    documentation and/or other materials provided with the distribution.
** 3. The name of the author may not be used to endorse or promote products
**    derived from Smoke without specific prior written permission.
**
** SMOKESTACK IS PROVIDED BY THE AUTHOR ``AS IS'' AND ANY EXPRESS OR
** IMPLIED WARRANTIES, INCLUDING, BUT NOT LIMITED TO, THE IMPLIED WARRANTIES
** OF MERCHANTABILITY AND FITNESS FOR A PARTICULAR PURPOSE ARE DISCLAIMED.
** IN NO EVENT SHALL THE AUTHOR BE LIABLE FOR ANY DIRECT, INDIRECT,
** INCIDENTAL, SPECIAL, EXEMPLARY, OR CONSEQUENTIAL DAMAGES (INCLUDING, BUT
** NOT LIMITED TO, PROCUREMENT OF SUBSTITUTE GOODS OR SERVICES; LOSS OF USE,
** DATA, OR PROFITS; OR BUSINESS INTERRUPTION) HOWEVER CAUSED AND ON ANY
** THEORY OF LIABILITY, WHETHER IN CONTRACT, STRICT LIABILITY, OR TORT
** (INCLUDING NEGLIGENCE OR OTHERWISE) ARISING IN ANY WAY OUT OF THE USE OF
** SMOKESTACK, EVEN IF ADVISED OF THE POSSIBILITY OF SUCH DAMAGE.
*/

package org.purple.smokestack;

import android.support.v7.widget.RecyclerView;
import android.view.ContextMenu;
import android.view.ContextMenu.ContextMenuInfo;
import android.view.View;
import android.view.View.OnCreateContextMenuListener;
import android.view.ViewGroup;

public class ListenersAdapter extends RecyclerView.Adapter
                              <ListenersAdapter.ViewHolder>
{
    private Settings m_settings = null;

    public static class ViewHolder extends RecyclerView.ViewHolder
```

```java
  implements OnCreateContextMenuListener
{
 ClientBubble m_clientBubble = null;

    public ViewHolder(ClientBubble clientBubble)
  {
      super(clientBubble.view());
      clientBubble.view().setOnCreateContextMenuListener(this);
      m_clientBubble = clientBubble;
    }

 public void onCreateContextMenu(ContextMenu menu,
                      View view,
                      ContextMenuInfo menuInfo)
  {
  }

 public void setData(ClientElement clientElement, int position)
   {
      if(clientElement == null)
      {
        if(m_clientBubble != null)
           m_clientBubble.setAddress("");

        return;
      }
      else if(m_clientBubble == null)
        return;

      m_clientBubble.setAddress(clientElement.m_address);
   }
}

public ListenersAdapter(Settings settings)
{
 m_settings = settings;
}

@Override
public ListenersAdapter.ViewHolder onCreateViewHolder
 (ViewGroup parent, int viewType)
{
 return new ViewHolder
     (new ClientBubble(parent.getContext(), m_settings, parent));
}

@Override
public int getItemCount()
{
 return Kernel.getInstance().remoteClientsCount();
}

@Override
public void onBindViewHolder(ViewHolder viewHolder, int position)
{
 if(viewHolder == null)
     return;

 ClientElement clientElement = new ClientElement();

 clientElement.m_address = Kernel.getInstance().
     remoteClientAddress(position);
 viewHolder.setData(clientElement, position);
```

```
	}
}




```
/* MessageTotals.java


```java
package org.purple.smokestack;

public class MessageTotals
{
    public long m_inMessages = 0L;
    public long m_outMessages = 0L;
    public long m_totalMessages = 0L;

    public MessageTotals()
    {
    }
}
```

/* Messages.java

```
https://raw.githubusercontent.com/textbrowser/smokestack/master/SmokeStack/app
/src/main/java/org/purple/smokestack/Messages.java
** Copyright (c) Alexis Megas.
** All rights reserved.
**
** Redistribution and use in source and binary forms, with or without
** modification, are permitted provided that the following conditions
** are met:
** 1. Redistributions of source code must retain the above copyright
**    notice, this list of conditions and the following disclaimer.
** 2. Redistributions in binary form must reproduce the above copyright
**    notice, this list of conditions and the following disclaimer in the
**    documentation and/or other materials provided with the distribution.
** 3. The name of the author may not be used to endorse or promote products
**    derived from SmokeStack without specific prior written permission.
**
** SMOKESTACK IS PROVIDED BY THE AUTHOR ``AS IS'' AND ANY EXPRESS OR
** IMPLIED WARRANTIES, INCLUDING, BUT NOT LIMITED TO, THE IMPLIED WARRANTIES
** OF MERCHANTABILITY AND FITNESS FOR A PARTICULAR PURPOSE ARE DISCLAIMED.
** IN NO EVENT SHALL THE AUTHOR BE LIABLE FOR ANY DIRECT, INDIRECT,
** INCIDENTAL, SPECIAL, EXEMPLARY, OR CONSEQUENTIAL DAMAGES (INCLUDING, BUT
** NOT LIMITED TO, PROCUREMENT OF SUBSTITUTE GOODS OR SERVICES; LOSS OF USE,
** DATA, OR PROFITS; OR BUSINESS INTERRUPTION) HOWEVER CAUSED AND ON ANY
** THEORY OF LIABILITY, WHETHER IN CONTRACT, STRICT LIABILITY, OR TORT
** (INCLUDING NEGLIGENCE OR OTHERWISE) ARISING IN ANY WAY OUT OF THE USE OF
** SMOKESTACK, EVEN IF ADVISED OF THE POSSIBILITY OF SUCH DAMAGE.
*/

package org.purple.smokestack;

import android.util.Base64;
import java.nio.charset.StandardCharsets;
import java.util.Arrays;

public class Messages
{
    public final static String EOM = "\r\n\r\n\r\n";
    public final static byte CHAT_KEY_TYPE[] = new byte[] {0x00};
    public final static byte CHAT_MESSAGE_READ[] = new byte[] {0x04};
    public final static byte CHAT_MESSAGE_RETRIEVAL[] = new byte[] {0x00};
    public final static byte PKP_MESSAGE_REQUEST[] = new byte[] {0x01};
    public final static byte SHARE_SIPHASH_ID[] = new byte[] {0x02};
    public final static byte SHARE_SIPHASH_IDENTITY_CONFIRIMATION[] =
      new byte[] {0x03};
    public final static int EPKS_GROUP_ONE_ELEMENT_COUNT = 7;

    public static String bytesToMessageString(byte bytes[])
    {
      if(bytes == null || bytes.length == 0)
          return "";

      try
      {
          StringBuilder results = new StringBuilder();

          results.append("POST HTTP/1.1\r\n");
          results.append
            ("Content-Type: application/x-www-form-urlencoded\r\n");
          results.append("Content-Length: %1\r\n");
          results.append("\r\n");
          results.append("content=%2");
```

```java
        results.append(EOM);

        String base64 = Base64.encodeToString(bytes, Base64.NO_WRAP);
        int indexOf = results.indexOf("%1");
        int length = EOM.length() + base64.length() + "content=".length();

        results = results.replace
          (indexOf, indexOf + 2, String.valueOf(length));
        indexOf = results.indexOf("%2");
        results = results.replace(indexOf, indexOf + 2, base64);
        return results.toString();
    }
  catch(Exception exception)
    {
    }

    return "";
  }

  public static String identitiesMessage(byte bytes[])
  {
    if(bytes == null || bytes.length == 0)
        return "";

    try
    {
        StringBuilder results = new StringBuilder();

        results.append("POST HTTP/1.1\r\n");
        results.append
          ("Content-Type: application/x-www-form-urlencoded\r\n");
        results.append("Content-Length: %1\r\n");
        results.append("\r\n");
        results.append("type=0095b&content=%2");
        results.append(EOM);

        String base64 = Base64.encodeToString(bytes, Base64.NO_WRAP);
        int indexOf = results.indexOf("%1");
        int length = EOM.length() +
          base64.length() +
          "type=0095b&content=".length();

        results = results.replace
          (indexOf, indexOf + 2, String.valueOf(length));
        indexOf = results.indexOf("%2");
        results = results.replace(indexOf, indexOf + 2, base64);
        return results.toString();
    }
  catch(Exception exception)
    {
    }

    return "";
  }

  public static String requestAuthentication(StringBuffer stringBuffer)
  {
    if(stringBuffer == null || stringBuffer.length() == 0)
        return "";

    try
    {
        StringBuilder results = new StringBuilder();
```

```java
        results.append("POST HTTP/1.1\r\n");
        results.append
          ("Content-Type: application/x-www-form-urlencoded\r\n");
        results.append("Content-Length: %1\r\n");
        results.append("\r\n");
        results.append("type=0097a&content=%2");
        results.append(EOM);

        int indexOf = results.indexOf("%1");
        int length = EOM.length() +
          stringBuffer.length() +
          "type=0097a&content=".length();

        results = results.replace
          (indexOf, indexOf + 2, String.valueOf(length));
        indexOf = results.indexOf("%2");
        results = results.replace
          (indexOf, indexOf + 2, stringBuffer.toString());
        return results.toString();
      }
    catch(Exception exception)
      {
      }

    return "";
  }

  public static String requestUnsolicited()
  {
    try
      {
        StringBuilder results = new StringBuilder();

        results.append("POST HTTP/1.1\r\n");
        results.append
          ("Content-Type: application/x-www-form-urlencoded\r\n");
        results.append("Content-Length: %1\r\n");
        results.append("\r\n");
        results.append("type=0096&content=%2");
        results.append(EOM);

        String base64 = Base64.encodeToString
          ("true".getBytes(), Base64.NO_WRAP);
        int indexOf = results.indexOf("%1");
        int length = EOM.length() +
          base64.length() +
          "type=0096&content=".length();

        results = results.replace
          (indexOf, indexOf + 2, String.valueOf(length));
        indexOf = results.indexOf("%2");
        results = results.replace(indexOf, indexOf + 2, base64);
        return results.toString();
      }
    catch(Exception exception)
      {
      }

    return "";
  }

  public static String stripMessage(String message)
```

```java
   {
     if(message == null)
        return "";

      /*
      ** Remove SmokeStack-specific leading and trailing data.
      */

      int indexOf = message.indexOf("content=");

      if(indexOf >= 0)
         message = message.substring(indexOf + 8);

      return message.trim();
   }

   public static byte[] epksMessage(String sipHashId,
                                    String strings[])
   {
     if(strings == null ||
        strings.length != EPKS_GROUP_ONE_ELEMENT_COUNT - 1)
         return null;

      /*
      ** keyStream
      ** [0 ... 31] - AES-256 Encryption Key
      ** [32 ... 95] - SHA-512 HMAC Key
      */

      try
      {
         byte keyStream[] = Cryptography.sipHashIdStream(sipHashId);

         if(keyStream == null)
           return null;

         StringBuilder stringBuilder = new StringBuilder();

         /*
         ** [ A Timestamp ]
         */

         stringBuilder.append
           (Base64.encodeToString(Miscellaneous.
                           longToByteArray(System.
                                    currentTimeMillis()),
                           Base64.NO_WRAP));
         stringBuilder.append("\n");

         /*
         ** [ Key Type ]
         */

         stringBuilder.append(strings[0]);
         stringBuilder.append("\n");

         /*
         ** [ Sender's Smoke Identity ]
         */

         stringBuilder.append(strings[5]);
         stringBuilder.append("\n");
```

```java
        /*
        ** [ Encryption Public Key ]
        */

      stringBuilder.append(strings[1]);
      stringBuilder.append("\n");

        /*
        ** [ Encryption Public Key Signature ]
        */

      stringBuilder.append(strings[2]);
      stringBuilder.append("\n");

        /*
        ** [ Signature Public Key ]
        */

      stringBuilder.append(strings[3]);
      stringBuilder.append("\n");

        /*
        ** [ Signature Public Key Signature ]
        */

      stringBuilder.append(strings[4]);

      byte aes256[] = Cryptography.encrypt
        (stringBuilder.toString().getBytes(),
         Arrays.copyOfRange(keyStream, 0, 32));

      stringBuilder.delete(0, stringBuilder.length());

      if(aes256 == null)
        return null;

        /*
        ** [ SHA-512 HMAC ]
        */

      byte sha512[] = Cryptography.hmac
        (aes256,
         Arrays.copyOfRange(keyStream, 32, keyStream.length));

      if(sha512 == null)
        return null;

        /*
        ** [ Destination ]
        */

      byte destination[] = Cryptography.hmac
        (Miscellaneous.joinByteArrays(aes256, sha512),
         Cryptography.
         sha512(sipHashId.getBytes(StandardCharsets.UTF_8)));

      return Miscellaneous.joinByteArrays(aes256, sha512, destination);
    }
    catch(Exception exception)
    {
    }

    return null;
```

```java
      }

      public static byte[] shareSipHashIdMessageConfirmation
        (Cryptography cryptography,
         String sipHashId,
         byte identity[],
         byte keyStream[])
      {
        if(cryptography == null)
            return null;

        try
        {
            byte bytes[] = Miscellaneous.joinByteArrays
              (
               /*
               ** [ A Byte ]
               */

               SHARE_SIPHASH_IDENTITY_CONFIRIMATION,

               /*
               ** [ A Timestamp ]
               */

               Miscellaneous.longToByteArray(System.currentTimeMillis()),

               /*
               ** [ SipHash Identity ]
               */

               sipHashId.getBytes(StandardCharsets.UTF_8),

               /*
               ** [ Temporary Identity ]
               */

               identity);

            /*
            ** [ AES-256 ]
            */

            byte aes256[] = Cryptography.encrypt
              (bytes, Arrays.copyOfRange(keyStream, 0, 32));

            if(aes256 == null)
              return null;

            /*
            ** [ SHA-512 HMAC ]
            */

            byte sha512[] = Cryptography.hmac
              (aes256, Arrays.copyOfRange(keyStream, 32, keyStream.length));

            if(sha512 == null)
              return null;

            /*
            ** [ Destination ]
            */

```

```java
          byte destination[] = Cryptography.hmac
            (Miscellaneous.joinByteArrays(aes256, sha512),
             Cryptography.
             sha512(sipHashId.getBytes(StandardCharsets.UTF_8)));

          return Miscellaneous.joinByteArrays(aes256, sha512, destination);
      }
    catch(Exception exception)
      {
      }

    return null;
    }
}
```

/* Miscellaneous.java

```
https://raw.githubusercontent.com/textbrowser/smokestack/master/SmokeStack/app
/src/main/java/org/purple/smokestack/Miscellaneous.java
** Copyright (c) Alexis Megas.
** All rights reserved.
**
** Redistribution and use in source and binary forms, with or without
** modification, are permitted provided that the following conditions
** are met:
** 1. Redistributions of source code must retain the above copyright
**    notice, this list of conditions and the following disclaimer.
** 2. Redistributions in binary form must reproduce the above copyright
**    notice, this list of conditions and the following disclaimer in the
**    documentation and/or other materials provided with the distribution.
** 3. The name of the author may not be used to endorse or promote products
**    derived from SmokeStack without specific prior written permission.
**
** SMOKESTACK IS PROVIDED BY THE AUTHOR ``AS IS'' AND ANY EXPRESS OR
** IMPLIED WARRANTIES, INCLUDING, BUT NOT LIMITED TO, THE IMPLIED WARRANTIES
** OF MERCHANTABILITY AND FITNESS FOR A PARTICULAR PURPOSE ARE DISCLAIMED.
** IN NO EVENT SHALL THE AUTHOR BE LIABLE FOR ANY DIRECT, INDIRECT,
** INCIDENTAL, SPECIAL, EXEMPLARY, OR CONSEQUENTIAL DAMAGES (INCLUDING, BUT
** NOT LIMITED TO, PROCUREMENT OF SUBSTITUTE GOODS OR SERVICES; LOSS OF USE,
** DATA, OR PROFITS; OR BUSINESS INTERRUPTION) HOWEVER CAUSED AND ON ANY
** THEORY OF LIABILITY, WHETHER IN CONTRACT, STRICT LIABILITY, OR TORT
** (INCLUDING NEGLIGENCE OR OTHERWISE) ARISING IN ANY WAY OUT OF THE USE OF
** SMOKESTACK, EVEN IF ADVISED OF THE POSSIBILITY OF SUCH DAMAGE.
*/

package org.purple.smokestack;

import android.app.Activity;
import android.app.AlertDialog;
import android.content.Context;
import android.content.DialogInterface;
import android.text.InputType;
import android.util.Base64;
import android.widget.Button;
import android.widget.CheckBox;
import android.widget.CompoundButton;
import android.widget.EditText;
import java.nio.ByteBuffer;
import java.text.DecimalFormat;

public abstract class Miscellaneous
```

```java
{
    public static final int INTEGER_BYTES = 4;
    public static final int LONG_BYTES = 8;
    public static final long LONG_LONG_BYTES = 8L;

    public static String byteArrayAsHexString(byte bytes[])
    {
      if(bytes == null || bytes.length == 0)
          return "";

      try
      {
          StringBuilder stringBuilder = new StringBuilder();

          for(byte b : bytes)
            stringBuilder.append(String.format("%02x", b));

          return stringBuilder.toString();
      }
      catch(Exception exception)
      {
          return "";
      }
    }

    public static String byteArrayAsHexStringDelimited(byte bytes[],
                                       char delimiter,
                                       int offset)
    {
      if(bytes == null || bytes.length == 0 || offset < 0)
          return "";

      String string = byteArrayAsHexString(bytes);

      try
      {
          StringBuilder stringBuilder = new StringBuilder();
          int length = string.length();

          for(int i = 0; i < length; i += offset)
          {
            if(i < length - offset)
                stringBuilder.append(string, i, i + offset);
            else
                stringBuilder.append(string.substring(i));

            stringBuilder.append(delimiter);
          }

          if(stringBuilder.length() > 0 &&
             stringBuilder.charAt(stringBuilder.length() - 1) == delimiter)
            return stringBuilder.substring(0, stringBuilder.length() - 1);
          else
            return stringBuilder.toString();
      }
      catch(Exception exception)
      {
          return "";
      }
    }

    public static String delimitString(String string,
                            char delimiter,
```

```java
                             int offset)
    {
      if(offset < 0)
          return "";

      try
      {
          StringBuilder stringBuilder = new StringBuilder();
          int length = string.length();

          for(int i = 0; i < length; i += offset)
          {
            if(i < length - offset)
                stringBuilder.append(string, i, i + offset);
            else
                stringBuilder.append(string.substring(i));

            stringBuilder.append(delimiter);
          }

          if(stringBuilder.length() > 0 &&
              stringBuilder.charAt(stringBuilder.length() - 1) == delimiter)
            return stringBuilder.substring(0, stringBuilder.length() - 1);
          else
            return stringBuilder.toString();
      }
      catch(Exception exception)
      {
          return "";
      }
    }

    public static String formattedDigitalInformation(String bytes)
    {
      try
      {
          DecimalFormat decimalFormat = new DecimalFormat("0.00");
          StringBuilder stringBuilder = new StringBuilder();
          long v = Integer.decode(bytes).longValue();

          if(v < 1024L)
          {
            stringBuilder.append(decimalFormat.format(v));
            stringBuilder.append(" B");
          }
          else if(v < 1048576L)
          {
            stringBuilder.append(decimalFormat.format(v / 1024.0));
            stringBuilder.append(" KiB");
          }
          else if(v < 1073741824L)
          {
            stringBuilder.append(decimalFormat.format(v / 1048576.0));
            stringBuilder.append(" MiB");
          }
          else
          {
            stringBuilder.append(decimalFormat.format(v / 1073741824.0));
            stringBuilder.append(" GiB");
          }

          return stringBuilder.toString();
      }
```

```java
      catch(Exception exception)
      {
          return "";
      }
  }

  public static String pemFormat(byte bytes[])
  {
    if(bytes == null || bytes.length == 0)
        return "";

    try
    {
        String string = Base64.encodeToString(bytes, Base64.NO_WRAP);
        StringBuilder stringBuilder = new StringBuilder();

        stringBuilder.append("-----BEGIN CERTIFICATE-----\n");

        int length = string.length();

        for(int i = 0; i < length; i += 64)
          if(i < length - 64)
            {
                stringBuilder.append(string, i, i + 64);
                stringBuilder.append("\n");
            }
          else
            {
                stringBuilder.append(string.substring(i));
                stringBuilder.append("\n");
                break;
            }

        stringBuilder.append("-----END CERTIFICATE-----\n");
        return stringBuilder.toString();
    }
    catch(Exception exception)
    {
        return "";
    }
  }

  public static String sipHashIdFromData(byte bytes[])
  {
    SipHash sipHash = new SipHash();

    return byteArrayAsHexStringDelimited
        (longArrayToByteArray(sipHash.
                      hmac(bytes,
                           Cryptography.keyForSipHash(bytes),
                           Cryptography.SIPHASH_OUTPUT_LENGTH)),
          '-', 4);
  }

  public static byte[] intToByteArray(int value)
  {
    try
    {
        return ByteBuffer.allocate(INTEGER_BYTES).putInt(value).array();
    }
    catch(Exception exception)
    {
        return null;
```

```java
    }
  }

  public static byte[] joinByteArrays(byte[] ... data)
  {
    if(data == null)
        return null;

    try
    {
        int length = 0;

        for(byte b[] : data)
          if(b != null && b.length > 0)
              length += b.length;

        if(length == 0)
          return null;

        byte bytes[] = new byte[length];
        int i = 0;

        for(byte b[] : data)
          if(b != null && b.length > 0)
          {
              System.arraycopy(b, 0, bytes, i, b.length);
              i += b.length;
          }

        return bytes; // data[0] + data[1] + ... + data[n - 1]
    }
    catch(Exception exception)
    {
        return null;
    }
  }

  public static byte[] longArrayToByteArray(long value[])
  {
    try
    {
        ByteBuffer byteBuffer = ByteBuffer.allocate
          (LONG_BYTES * value.length);

        for(long l : value)
          byteBuffer.putLong(l);

        return byteBuffer.array();
    }
    catch(Exception exception)
    {
        return null;
    }
  }

  public static byte[] longToByteArray(long value)
  {
    try
    {
        return ByteBuffer.allocate(LONG_BYTES).putLong(value).array();
    }
    catch(Exception exception)
    {
```

```java
            return null;
        }
    }

    public static int countOf(StringBuilder stringBuilder, char character)
    {
      if(stringBuilder == null || stringBuilder.length() == 0)
          return 0;

      int count = 0;
      int length = stringBuilder.length();

      for(int i = 0; i < length; i++)
          if(character == stringBuilder.charAt(i))
            count += 1;

      return count;
    }

    public static int byteArrayToInt(byte bytes[])
    {
      if(bytes == null || bytes.length != INTEGER_BYTES)
          return 0;

      try
      {
          ByteBuffer byteBuffer = ByteBuffer.allocate(INTEGER_BYTES);

          byteBuffer.put(bytes);
          byteBuffer.flip();
          return byteBuffer.getInt();
      }
      catch(Exception exception)
      {
          return 0;
      }
    }

    public static long byteArrayToLong(byte bytes[])
    {
      if(bytes == null || bytes.length != LONG_BYTES)
          return 0L;

      try
      {
          ByteBuffer byteBuffer = ByteBuffer.allocate(LONG_BYTES);

          byteBuffer.put(bytes);
          byteBuffer.flip();
          return byteBuffer.getLong();
      }
      catch(Exception exception)
      {
          return 0L;
      }
    }

    public static void showErrorDialog(Context context, String error)
    {
      if(((Activity) context).isFinishing())
          return;

      AlertDialog alertDialog = new AlertDialog.Builder(context).create();
```

```java
    alertDialog.setButton
        (AlertDialog.BUTTON_NEUTRAL, "Dismiss",
         new DialogInterface.OnClickListener()
          {
            public void onClick(DialogInterface dialog, int which)
             {
                dialog.dismiss();
             }
          });
    alertDialog.setMessage(error);
    alertDialog.setTitle("Error");
    alertDialog.show();
  }

  public static void showPromptDialog
    (Context context,
     DialogInterface.OnCancelListener cancelListener,
     String prompt)
  {
    if(((Activity) context).isFinishing())
        return;

    AlertDialog alertDialog = new AlertDialog.Builder(context).create();
    CheckBox checkBox = new CheckBox(context);

    State.getInstance().removeKey("dialog_accepted");
    alertDialog.setButton
        (AlertDialog.BUTTON_NEGATIVE, "No",
         new DialogInterface.OnClickListener()
          {
            public void onClick(DialogInterface dialog, int which)
             {
                State.getInstance().removeKey("dialog_accepted");
                dialog.dismiss();
             }
          });
    alertDialog.setButton
        (AlertDialog.BUTTON_POSITIVE, "Yes",
         new DialogInterface.OnClickListener()
          {
            public void onClick(DialogInterface dialog, int which)
             {
                State.getInstance().setString("dialog_accepted", "true");
                dialog.cancel();
             }
          });
    alertDialog.setMessage(prompt);
    alertDialog.setOnCancelListener(cancelListener); /*
                                      ** We cannot wait
                                      ** for a response.
                                      */
    alertDialog.setTitle("Confirmation");
    alertDialog.setView(checkBox);
    alertDialog.show();

    final Button button = alertDialog.getButton
        (AlertDialog.BUTTON_POSITIVE);

    button.setEnabled(false);
    checkBox.setOnCheckedChangeListener
        (new CompoundButton.OnCheckedChangeListener()
         {
```

```java
        @Override
        public void onCheckedChanged
            (CompoundButton buttonView, boolean isChecked)
        {
            button.setEnabled(isChecked);
        }
      });
   checkBox.setText("Confirm");
 }

  public static void showTextInputDialog
    (Context context,
     DialogInterface.OnCancelListener cancelListener,
     String prompt,
     String title)
  {
    if(((Activity) context).isFinishing())
        return;

    AlertDialog alertDialog = new AlertDialog.Builder(context).create();
    final EditText editText = new EditText(context);
    final boolean contextIsSettings = context instanceof Settings;

    alertDialog.setButton
        (AlertDialog.BUTTON_NEGATIVE, "Cancel",
         new DialogInterface.OnClickListener()
         {
           public void onClick(DialogInterface dialog, int which)
           {
               if(contextIsSettings)
                 State.getInstance().removeKey
                     ("settings_participant_name_input");

               dialog.dismiss();
           }
        });
    alertDialog.setButton
        (AlertDialog.BUTTON_POSITIVE, "Accept",
         new DialogInterface.OnClickListener()
         {
           public void onClick(DialogInterface dialog, int which)
           {
               if(contextIsSettings)
                 State.getInstance().setString
                     ("settings_participant_name_input",
                      editText.getText().toString());

               dialog.cancel();
           }
        });
    alertDialog.setMessage(prompt);
    alertDialog.setOnCancelListener(cancelListener); /*
                                    ** We cannot wait
                                    ** for a response.
                                    */
    alertDialog.setTitle(title);
    editText.setInputType(InputType.TYPE_CLASS_TEXT);
    alertDialog.setView(editText);
    alertDialog.show();
  }
}
```

```java
/* Neighbor.java
https://raw.githubusercontent.com/textbrowser/smokestack/master/SmokeStack/app
/src/main/java/org/purple/smokestack/Neighbor.java
** Copyright (c) Alexis Megas.
** All rights reserved.
**
** Redistribution and use in source and binary forms, with or without
** modification, are permitted provided that the following conditions
** are met:
** 1. Redistributions of source code must retain the above copyright
**    notice, this list of conditions and the following disclaimer.
** 2. Redistributions in binary form must reproduce the above copyright
**    notice, this list of conditions and the following disclaimer in the
**    documentation and/or other materials provided with the distribution.
** 3. The name of the author may not be used to endorse or promote products
**    derived from SmokeStack without specific prior written permission.
**
** SMOKESTACK IS PROVIDED BY THE AUTHOR ``AS IS'' AND ANY EXPRESS OR
** IMPLIED WARRANTIES, INCLUDING, BUT NOT LIMITED TO, THE IMPLIED WARRANTIES
** OF MERCHANTABILITY AND FITNESS FOR A PARTICULAR PURPOSE ARE DISCLAIMED.
** IN NO EVENT SHALL THE AUTHOR BE LIABLE FOR ANY DIRECT, INDIRECT,
** INCIDENTAL, SPECIAL, EXEMPLARY, OR CONSEQUENTIAL DAMAGES (INCLUDING, BUT
** NOT LIMITED TO, PROCUREMENT OF SUBSTITUTE GOODS OR SERVICES; LOSS OF USE,
** DATA, OR PROFITS; OR BUSINESS INTERRUPTION) HOWEVER CAUSED AND ON ANY
** THEORY OF LIABILITY, WHETHER IN CONTRACT, STRICT LIABILITY, OR TORT
** (INCLUDING NEGLIGENCE OR OTHERWISE) ARISING IN ANY WAY OUT OF THE USE OF
** SMOKESTACK, EVEN IF ADVISED OF THE POSSIBILITY OF SUCH DAMAGE.
*/

package org.purple.smokestack;

import android.content.Context;
import android.net.ConnectivityManager;
import android.net.NetworkInfo;
import android.util.Base64;
import java.util.ArrayList;
import java.util.UUID;
import java.util.concurrent.Executors;
import java.util.concurrent.ScheduledExecutorService;
import java.util.concurrent.TimeUnit;
import java.util.concurrent.atomic.AtomicBoolean;
import java.util.concurrent.atomic.AtomicInteger;
import java.util.concurrent.atomic.AtomicLong;

public abstract class Neighbor
{
    private ArrayList<String> m_queue = null;
    private final Object m_queueMutex = new Object();
    private final ScheduledExecutorService m_parsingScheduler =
      Executors.newSingleThreadScheduledExecutor();
    private final ScheduledExecutorService m_scheduler =
      Executors.newSingleThreadScheduledExecutor();
    private final ScheduledExecutorService m_sendOutboundScheduler =
      Executors.newSingleThreadScheduledExecutor();
    private final static int LANE_WIDTH = 8 * 1024 * 1024; // 8 MiB
    private final static long DATA_LIFETIME = 15000L; // 15 Seconds
    private final static long PARSING_INTERVAL = 100L; // Milliseconds
    private final static long SEND_OUTBOUND_TIMER_INTERVAL =
      25L; // Milliseconds
    private final static long SILENCE = 90000L; // 90 Seconds
    private final static long TIMER_INTERVAL = 2500L; // 2.5 Seconds
    protected AtomicBoolean m_aborted = null;
```

```java
    protected AtomicBoolean m_allowUnsolicited = null;
    protected AtomicBoolean m_clientSupportsCryptographicDiscovery = null;
    protected AtomicBoolean m_isPrivateServer = null;
    protected AtomicBoolean m_remoteUserAuthenticated = null;
    protected AtomicBoolean m_requestUnsolicitedSent = null;
    protected AtomicBoolean m_userDefined = null;
    protected AtomicInteger m_oid = null;
    protected AtomicLong m_bytesRead = null;
    protected AtomicLong m_bytesWritten = null;
    protected AtomicLong m_lastParsed = null;
    protected AtomicLong m_lastTimeRead = null;
    protected AtomicLong m_startTime = null;
    protected Cryptography m_cryptography = null;
    protected Database m_databaseHelper = null;
    protected String m_ipAddress = "";
    protected String m_ipPort = "";
    protected String m_version = "";
    protected UUID m_uuid = null;
    protected final Object m_mutex = new Object();
    protected final Object m_parsingSchedulerObject = new Object();
    protected final ScheduledExecutorService m_readSocketScheduler =
      Executors.newSingleThreadScheduledExecutor();
    protected final StringBuffer m_error = new StringBuffer();
    protected final StringBuffer m_randomBuffer = new StringBuffer();
    protected final StringBuffer m_stringBuffer = new StringBuffer();
    protected final static int BYTES_PER_READ = 1024 * 1024; // 1 MiB
    protected final static int MAXIMUM_BYTES = LANE_WIDTH;
    protected final static int SO_SNDBUF = 32 * 1024; // 32 KiB
    protected final static int SO_TIMEOUT = 0; // 0 Seconds
    protected final static long READ_SOCKET_INTERVAL = 50L; // 50 Milliseconds
    protected final static long WAIT_TIMEOUT = 10000L; // 10 Seconds
    public final static int SO_RCVBUF = 32 * 1024; // 32 KiB

    private void saveStatistics()
    {
      String localIp = getLocalIp();
      String localPort = String.valueOf(getLocalPort());
      String queueSize = "";
      String sessionCiper = getSessionCipher();
      boolean connected = connected();
      long uptime = System.nanoTime() - m_startTime.get();

      synchronized(m_queueMutex)
      {
          queueSize = String.valueOf(m_queue.size());
      }

      m_databaseHelper.saveNeighborInformation
          (m_cryptography,
           String.valueOf(m_stringBuffer.length()),
           String.valueOf(m_bytesRead.get()),
           String.valueOf(m_bytesWritten.get()),
           m_error.toString(),
           localIp,
           localPort,
           queueSize,
           sessionCiper,
           connected ? "connected" : "disconnected",
           String.valueOf(uptime),
           String.valueOf(m_oid.get()));
    }

    private void terminateOnSilence()
```

```java
    {
      if((System.nanoTime() - m_lastTimeRead.get()) / 1000000L > SILENCE)
          disconnect();
    }

    protected Neighbor(String ipAddress,
                       String ipPort,
                       String scopeId,
                       String transport,
                       String version,
                       boolean isPrivateServer,
                       boolean userDefined,
                       int oid)
    {
      m_aborted = new AtomicBoolean(false);
      m_allowUnsolicited = new AtomicBoolean(false);
      m_bytesRead = new AtomicLong(0L);
      m_bytesWritten = new AtomicLong(0L);
      m_clientSupportsCryptographicDiscovery = new AtomicBoolean(false);
      m_cryptography = Cryptography.getInstance();
      m_databaseHelper = Database.getInstance();
      m_ipAddress = ipAddress;
      m_ipPort = ipPort;
      m_isPrivateServer = new AtomicBoolean(isPrivateServer);
      m_lastParsed = new AtomicLong(System.currentTimeMillis());
      m_lastTimeRead = new AtomicLong(System.nanoTime());
      m_oid = new AtomicInteger(oid);
      m_queue = new ArrayList<> ();
      m_remoteUserAuthenticated = new AtomicBoolean(userDefined);
      m_requestUnsolicitedSent = new AtomicBoolean(false);
      m_startTime = new AtomicLong(System.nanoTime());
      m_userDefined = new AtomicBoolean(userDefined);
      m_uuid = UUID.randomUUID();
      m_version = version;

      /*
      ** Start the schedules.
      */

      m_parsingScheduler.scheduleAtFixedRate(new Runnable()
      {
          @Override
          public void run()
          {
            try
            {
                if(!connected() && !m_aborted.get())
                  synchronized(m_mutex)
                  {
                      try
                      {
                        m_mutex.wait(WAIT_TIMEOUT);
                      }
                      catch(Exception exception)
                      {
                      }
                  }

                if(!connected() || m_aborted.get())
                  return;

                /*
                ** Await new data.
```

```java
*/

synchronized(m_parsingSchedulerObject)
{
  try
  {
      m_parsingSchedulerObject.wait(WAIT_TIMEOUT);
  }
  catch(Exception exception)
  {
  }
}

/*
** Detect our end-of-message delimiter.
** If the end-of-message marker has not been detected
** for some period of time, purge m_stringBuffer.
*/

int indexOf = -1;

while((indexOf = m_stringBuffer.indexOf(Messages.EOM)) >= 0)
{
  if(m_aborted.get())
      break;

  m_lastParsed.set(System.currentTimeMillis());

  String buffer = m_stringBuffer.
      substring(0, indexOf + Messages.EOM.length());

  m_stringBuffer.delete(0, buffer.length());
  m_stringBuffer.trimToSize();

  if(m_isPrivateServer.get())
      if(!m_remoteUserAuthenticated.get())
      {
        if(buffer.contains("type=0097b&content="))
            /*
            ** A response to an authentication request.
            */

                m_remoteUserAuthenticated.set
                  (m_databaseHelper.
                   authenticate(m_cryptography,
                        Messages.
                        stripMessage(buffer),
                        m_randomBuffer));

            if(!m_remoteUserAuthenticated.get())
                continue;
            else
            {
                m_randomBuffer.delete
                  (0, m_randomBuffer.length());
                m_randomBuffer.trimToSize();
            }
      }

  if(!Kernel.getInstance().
     ourMessage(buffer,
            m_uuid,
            m_userDefined.get()))
```

```java
                    echo(buffer);
                else if(!m_userDefined.get())
                {
                    if(buffer.contains("type=0095a&content="))
                      m_clientSupportsCryptographicDiscovery.
                            set(true);

                    /*
                    ** The client is allowing unsolicited data.
                    */

                    else if(buffer.contains("type=0096&content="))
                      m_allowUnsolicited.set(true);
                }
                }

            if(System.currentTimeMillis() - m_lastParsed.get() >
               DATA_LIFETIME ||
               m_stringBuffer.length() > MAXIMUM_BYTES)
              m_stringBuffer.delete(0, m_stringBuffer.length());

            m_stringBuffer.trimToSize();
        }
        catch(Exception exception)
        {
        }
    }
}, 0L, PARSING_INTERVAL, TimeUnit.MILLISECONDS);
m_scheduler.scheduleAtFixedRate(new Runnable()
{
    @Override
    public void run()
    {
      try
      {
            if(m_oid.get() >= 0)
            {
              String statusControl = m_databaseHelper.
                  readListenerNeighborStatusControl
                  (m_cryptography, "neighbors", m_oid.get());

              switch(statusControl)
              {
              case "connect":
                  connect();
                  break;
              case "disconnect":
                  disconnect();
                  setError("");
                  break;
              default:
                  /*
                  ** Abort!
                  */

                  disconnect();
                  return;
              }

              saveStatistics();
            }

            terminateOnSilence();
```

```java
                }
            catch(Exception exception)
                {
                }
            }
    }, 0L, TIMER_INTERVAL, TimeUnit.MILLISECONDS);
    m_sendOutboundScheduler.scheduleAtFixedRate(new Runnable()
    {
        private long m_accumulatedTime = System.nanoTime();

        @Override
        public void run()
        {
          try
            {
                if(!connected() && !m_aborted.get())
                  synchronized(m_mutex)
                    {
                        try
                        {
                          m_mutex.wait(WAIT_TIMEOUT);
                        }
                        catch(Exception exception)
                        {
                        }
                    }

                if(!connected() || m_aborted.get())
                  return;

                if(System.nanoTime() - m_accumulatedTime >= 30000000000L)
                {
                  m_accumulatedTime = System.nanoTime();
                  send(getCapabilities());

                  if(m_userDefined.get())
                      if(!m_requestUnsolicitedSent.get())
                        m_requestUnsolicitedSent.set
                            (send(Messages.requestUnsolicited()));
                }

                if(m_oid.get() >= 0)
                {
                  /*
                  ** Retrieve the first database message.
                  */

                  String array[] = m_databaseHelper.readOutboundMessage
                      (false, m_oid.get());

                  /*
                  ** If the message is sent successfully, remove it.
                  */

                  if(array != null && array.length == 2)
                      if(send(array[0]))
                        m_databaseHelper.deleteEntry
                            (array[1], "outbound_queue");
                }

            /*
            ** Echo packets.
            */
```

```java
            String array[] = m_databaseHelper.readOutboundMessage
              (true, m_oid.get());

            if(array != null && array.length == 2)
            {
              m_databaseHelper.deleteEntry
                  (array[1], "outbound_queue");

              if(!m_userDefined.get()) // A server.
              {
                  if(m_allowUnsolicited.get() ||
                    !m_clientSupportsCryptographicDiscovery.get())
                    send(array[0]);
                  else
                    try
                    {
                        /*
                        ** Determine if the message's destination
                        ** is correct.
                        */

                        if(m_databaseHelper.
                          containsRoutingIdentity(m_uuid.
                                        toString(),
                                        array[0]))
                          send(array[0]); // Ignore the results.
                    }
                    catch(Exception exception)
                    {
                    }
              }
              else
                  send(array[0]); // Ignore the results.
            }

            /*
            ** Transfer real-time packets.
            */

            synchronized(m_queueMutex)
            {
              if(!m_queue.isEmpty())
                  send(m_queue.remove(0)); // Ignore the results.
            }
          }
        catch(Exception exception)
          {
          }
        }
    }, 0L, SEND_OUTBOUND_TIMER_INTERVAL, TimeUnit.MILLISECONDS);
}

protected String getCapabilities()
{
  try
  {
      StringBuilder message = new StringBuilder();

      message.append(m_uuid.toString());
      message.append("\n");
      message.append(LANE_WIDTH);
      message.append("\n");
```

```java
            message.append("full"); // Echo Mode

            StringBuilder results = new StringBuilder();

            results.append("POST HTTP/1.1\r\n");
            results.append
              ("Content-Type: application/x-www-form-urlencoded\r\n");
            results.append("Content-Length: %1\r\n");
            results.append("\r\n");
            results.append("type=0014&content=%2\r\n");
            results.append("\r\n\r\n");

            String base64 = Base64.encodeToString
              (message.toString().getBytes(), Base64.DEFAULT);
            int indexOf = results.indexOf("%1");
            int length = base64.length() +
              "type=0014&content=\r\n\r\n\r\n".length();

            results = results.replace
              (indexOf, indexOf + 2, String.valueOf(length));
            indexOf = results.indexOf("%2");
            results = results.replace(indexOf, indexOf + 2, base64);
            return results.toString();
      }
    catch(Exception exception)
    {
        return "";
    }
  }

    protected String getSessionCipher()
    {
      return "";
    }

    protected abstract String getLocalIp();
    protected abstract String getRemoteIp();
    protected abstract boolean connected();
    protected abstract boolean send(String message);
    protected abstract int getLocalPort();
    protected abstract int getRemotePort();
    protected abstract void connect();

    protected boolean isNetworkConnected()
    {
      try
      {
          ConnectivityManager connectivityManager = (ConnectivityManager)
            SmokeStack.getApplication().getApplicationContext().
            getSystemService(Context.CONNECTIVITY_SERVICE);
          NetworkInfo networkInfo = connectivityManager.
            getActiveNetworkInfo();

          return networkInfo != null && networkInfo.isConnected();
      }
    catch(Exception exception)
      {
      }

      return false;
    }

    protected void abort()
```

```java
{
  m_aborted.set(true);

  synchronized(m_mutex)
  {
      m_mutex.notifyAll();
  }

  synchronized(m_parsingScheduler)
  {
      try
      {
        m_parsingScheduler.shutdown();
      }
      catch(Exception exception)
      {
      }
  }

  synchronized(m_parsingSchedulerObject)
  {
      m_parsingSchedulerObject.notify();
  }

  synchronized(m_parsingScheduler)
  {
      try
      {
        if(!m_parsingScheduler.awaitTermination(60L, TimeUnit.SECONDS))
            m_parsingScheduler.shutdownNow();
      }
      catch(Exception exception)
      {
      }
  }

  synchronized(m_scheduler)
  {
      try
      {
        m_scheduler.shutdown();
      }
      catch(Exception exception)
      {
      }

      try
      {
        if(!m_scheduler.awaitTermination(60L, TimeUnit.SECONDS))
            m_scheduler.shutdownNow();
      }
      catch(Exception exception)
      {
      }
  }

  synchronized(m_sendOutboundScheduler)
  {
      try
      {
        m_sendOutboundScheduler.shutdown();
      }
      catch(Exception exception)
```

```java
        {
        }

        try
        {
          if(!m_sendOutboundScheduler.
              awaitTermination(60L, TimeUnit.SECONDS))
                m_sendOutboundScheduler.shutdownNow();
        }
        catch(Exception exception)
        {
        }
      }
    }

    protected void disconnect()
    {
      m_databaseHelper.deleteEchoQueue(m_oid.get());

      synchronized(m_mutex)
      {
          m_mutex.notifyAll();
      }

      synchronized(m_parsingSchedulerObject)
      {
          m_parsingSchedulerObject.notify();
      }

      synchronized(m_queueMutex)
      {
          m_queue.clear();
      }

      m_stringBuffer.delete(0, m_stringBuffer.length());
      m_stringBuffer.trimToSize();
    }

    protected void echo(String message)
    {
      Kernel.getInstance().echo(message, m_oid.get());
    }

    protected void reset()
    {
      m_allowUnsolicited.set(false);
      m_bytesRead.set(0);
      m_bytesWritten.set(0);
      m_clientSupportsCryptographicDiscovery.set(false);
      m_lastParsed.set(0);
      m_remoteUserAuthenticated.set(false);
      m_requestUnsolicitedSent.set(false);
      m_startTime.set(System.nanoTime());
      m_stringBuffer.delete(0, m_stringBuffer.length());
      m_stringBuffer.trimToSize();
    }

    protected void setError(String error)
    {
      m_error.delete(0, m_error.length());
      m_error.trimToSize();
      m_error.append(error);
    }
```

```java
  public String address()
  {
    return "Local: " + getLocalIp() +
        ":" + getLocalPort() +
        "\nRemote: " + getRemoteIp() +
        ":" + getRemotePort();
  }

  public int getOid()
  {
    return m_oid.get();
  }

  public void clearEchoQueue()
  {
    m_databaseHelper.deleteEchoQueue(m_oid.get());
  }

  public void clearQueue()
  {
    synchronized(m_queueMutex)
    {
        m_queue.clear();
    }
  }

  public void scheduleEchoSend(String message)
  {
    if(!connected() || message == null || message.trim().isEmpty())
        return;

    m_databaseHelper.enqueueOutboundMessage
        (m_cryptography, message, true, m_oid.get());
  }

  public void scheduleSend(String message)
  {
    if(!connected() || message == null || message.trim().isEmpty())
        return;

    synchronized(m_queueMutex)
    {
        m_queue.add(message);
    }
  }
}
```

/* NeighborElement.java

```
https://raw.githubusercontent.com/textbrowser/smokestack/master/SmokeStack/app
/src/main/java/org/purple/smokestack/NeighborElement.java
** Copyright (c) Alexis Megas.
** All rights reserved.
**
** Redistribution and use in source and binary forms, with or without
** modification, are permitted provided that the following conditions
** are met:
** 1. Redistributions of source code must retain the above copyright
**    notice, this list of conditions and the following disclaimer.
** 2. Redistributions in binary form must reproduce the above copyright
```

```java
**     notice, this list of conditions and the following disclaimer in the
**     documentation and/or other materials provided with the distribution.
** 3. The name of the author may not be used to endorse or promote products
**     derived from SmokeStack without specific prior written permission.
**
** SMOKESTACK IS PROVIDED BY THE AUTHOR ``AS IS'' AND ANY EXPRESS OR
** IMPLIED WARRANTIES, INCLUDING, BUT NOT LIMITED TO, THE IMPLIED WARRANTIES
** OF MERCHANTABILITY AND FITNESS FOR A PARTICULAR PURPOSE ARE DISCLAIMED.
** IN NO EVENT SHALL THE AUTHOR BE LIABLE FOR ANY DIRECT, INDIRECT,
** INCIDENTAL, SPECIAL, EXEMPLARY, OR CONSEQUENTIAL DAMAGES (INCLUDING, BUT
** NOT LIMITED TO, PROCUREMENT OF SUBSTITUTE GOODS OR SERVICES; LOSS OF USE,
** DATA, OR PROFITS; OR BUSINESS INTERRUPTION) HOWEVER CAUSED AND ON ANY
** THEORY OF LIABILITY, WHETHER IN CONTRACT, STRICT LIABILITY, OR TORT
** (INCLUDING NEGLIGENCE OR OTHERWISE) ARISING IN ANY WAY OUT OF THE USE OF
** SMOKESTACK, EVEN IF ADVISED OF THE POSSIBILITY OF SUCH DAMAGE.
*/

package org.purple.smokestack;

public class NeighborElement
{
    public String m_bytesBuffered = "";
    public String m_bytesRead = "";
    public String m_bytesWritten = "";
    public String m_error = "";
    public String m_ipVersion = "";
    public String m_localIpAddress = "";
    public String m_localPort = "";
    public String m_proxyIpAddress = "";
    public String m_proxyPort = "";
    public String m_proxyType = "";
    public String m_queueSize = "";
    public String m_remoteIpAddress = "";
    public String m_remotePort = "";
    public String m_remoteScopeId = "";
    public String m_sessionCipher = "";
    public String m_status = "";
    public String m_statusControl = "";
    public String m_transport = "";
    public String m_uptime = "";
    public byte m_remoteCertificate[] = null;
    public int m_oid = -1;
    public long m_outboundEchoQueued = 0L;
    public long m_outboundQueued = 0L;

    public NeighborElement()
    {
    }
}
```

/* OzoneElement.java

```
https://raw.githubusercontent.com/textbrowser/smokestack/master/SmokeStack/app
/src/main/java/org/purple/smokestack/OzoneElement.java
** Copyright (c) Alexis Megas.
** All rights reserved.
**
** Redistribution and use in source and binary forms, with or without
** modification, are permitted provided that the following conditions
** are met:
** 1. Redistributions of source code must retain the above copyright
**    notice, this list of conditions and the following disclaimer.
** 2. Redistributions in binary form must reproduce the above copyright
**    notice, this list of conditions and the following disclaimer in the
**    documentation and/or other materials provided with the distribution.
** 3. The name of the author may not be used to endorse or promote products
**    derived from SmokeStack without specific prior written permission.
**
** SMOKESTACK IS PROVIDED BY THE AUTHOR ``AS IS'' AND ANY EXPRESS OR
** IMPLIED WARRANTIES, INCLUDING, BUT NOT LIMITED TO, THE IMPLIED WARRANTIES
** OF MERCHANTABILITY AND FITNESS FOR A PARTICULAR PURPOSE ARE DISCLAIMED.
** IN NO EVENT SHALL THE AUTHOR BE LIABLE FOR ANY DIRECT, INDIRECT,
** INCIDENTAL, SPECIAL, EXEMPLARY, OR CONSEQUENTIAL DAMAGES (INCLUDING, BUT
** NOT LIMITED TO, PROCUREMENT OF SUBSTITUTE GOODS OR SERVICES; LOSS OF USE,
** DATA, OR PROFITS; OR BUSINESS INTERRUPTION) HOWEVER CAUSED AND ON ANY
** THEORY OF LIABILITY, WHETHER IN CONTRACT, STRICT LIABILITY, OR TORT
** (INCLUDING NEGLIGENCE OR OTHERWISE) ARISING IN ANY WAY OUT OF THE USE OF
** SMOKESTACK, EVEN IF ADVISED OF THE POSSIBILITY OF SUCH DAMAGE.
*/

package org.purple.smokestack;

public class OzoneElement
{
    public String m_address = "";
    public byte m_addressStream[] = null;
    public int m_oid = -1;

    public OzoneElement()
    {
    }
}
```

/* Settings.java


```java
package org.purple.smokestack;

import android.app.ProgressDialog;
import android.content.BroadcastReceiver;
import android.content.Context;
import android.content.DialogInterface;
import android.content.Intent;
import android.content.IntentFilter;
import android.graphics.Color;
import android.os.Build;
import android.os.Bundle;
import android.support.v4.content.LocalBroadcastManager;
import android.support.v7.app.AppCompatActivity;
import android.support.v7.widget.LinearLayoutManager;
import android.support.v7.widget.RecyclerView;
import android.text.InputFilter;
import android.text.InputType;
import android.text.Spanned;
import android.util.Base64;
import android.view.ContextMenu.ContextMenuInfo;
import android.view.ContextMenu;
import android.view.Gravity;
import android.view.Menu;
import android.view.MenuItem;
import android.view.View;
import android.widget.AdapterView.OnItemSelectedListener;
import android.widget.AdapterView;
import android.gid.widget.ArrayAdapter;
import android.widget.Button;
import android.widget.CheckBox;
import android.widget.CompoundButton;
import android.widget.LinearLayout.LayoutParams;
import android.widget.PopupWindow;
```

```java
import android.widget.RadioButton;
import android.widget.RadioGroup;
import android.widget.Spinner;
import android.widget.TableLayout;
import android.widget.TableRow;
import android.widget.TextView;
import java.net.Inet4Address;
import java.net.Inet6Address;
import java.net.InetAddress;
import java.net.NetworkInterface;
import java.util.ArrayList;
import java.util.Enumeration;
import java.util.Locale;
import java.util.concurrent.Executors;
import java.util.concurrent.ScheduledExecutorService;
import java.util.concurrent.TimeUnit;
import javax.crypto.SecretKey;

public class Settings extends AppCompatActivity
{
    static private abstract class ContextMenuEnumerator
    {
      public final static int DELETE_ALL_MESSAGES = 0;
      public final static int DELETE_LISTENER = 1;
      public final static int DELETE_MESSAGES = 2;
      public final static int DELETE_OZONE = 3;
      public final static int DELETE_PARTICIPANT = 4;
      public final static int NEW_NAME = 5;
      public final static int RESET_RETRIEVAL_STATE = 6;
      public final static int TOGGLE_LISTENER_PRIVACY = 7;
    }

    private static class ListenersLinearLayoutManager
      extends LinearLayoutManager
    {
      ListenersLinearLayoutManager(Context context)
      {
          super(context);
      }

      @Override
      public void onLayoutChildren(RecyclerView.Recycler recycler,
                          RecyclerView.State state)
      {
          /*
          ** Android may terminate!
          */

          try
          {
            super.onLayoutChildren(recycler, state);
          }
          catch(Exception exception)
          {
          }
      }
    }

    private class PopulateListeners implements Runnable
    {
      private ArrayList<ListenerElement> m_arrayList = null;

      public PopulateListeners(ArrayList<ListenerElement> arrayList)
```

```java
    {
        m_arrayList = arrayList;
    }

    @Override
    public void run()
    {
        try
        {
          populateListeners(m_arrayList);
        }
        catch(Exception exception)
        {
        }

        if(m_arrayList != null)
          m_arrayList.clear();
    }
}

private class PopulateNeighbors implements Runnable
{
  private ArrayList<NeighborElement> m_arrayList = null;

  public PopulateNeighbors(ArrayList<NeighborElement> arrayList)
  {
      m_arrayList = arrayList;
  }

  @Override
  public void run()
  {
      try
      {
        populateNeighbors(m_arrayList);
      }
      catch(Exception exception)
      {
      }

      if(m_arrayList != null)
        m_arrayList.clear();
  }
}

private class SettingsBroadcastReceiver extends BroadcastReceiver
{
  public SettingsBroadcastReceiver()
  {
  }

  @Override
  public void onReceive(Context context, Intent intent)
  {
      if(intent == null || intent.getAction() == null)
        return;

      if(intent.getAction().
         equals("org.purple.smokestack.populate_participants"))
        populateParticipants();
      else if(intent.getAction().
            equals("org.purple.smokestack.populate_" +
                "ozones_participants"))
```

```java
          {
            populateOzoneAddresses();
            populateParticipants();
          }
      }
  }

    private Database m_databaseHelper = null;
    private ListenersLinearLayoutManager m_listenersLayoutManager = null;
    private RecyclerView m_listenersRecyclerView = null;
    private RecyclerView.Adapter<?> m_listenersAdapter = null;
    private ScheduledExecutorService m_generalScheduler = null;
    private ScheduledExecutorService m_listenersScheduler = null;
    private ScheduledExecutorService m_neighborsScheduler = null;
    private SettingsBroadcastReceiver m_receiver = null;
    private boolean m_receiverRegistered = false;
    private final static Cryptography s_cryptography =
      Cryptography.getInstance();
    private final static InputFilter s_portFilter = new InputFilter()
    {
      public CharSequence filter(CharSequence source,
                                 int start,
                                 int end,
                                 Spanned dest,
                                 int dstart,
                                 int dend)
      {
          try
          {
            int port = Integer.parseInt
                (dest.toString() + source.toString());

            if(port >= 0 && port <= 65535)
                return null;
          }
          catch(Exception exception)
          {
          }

          return "";
      }
    };
    private final static InputFilter s_sipHashInputFilter = new InputFilter()
    {
      public CharSequence filter(CharSequence source,
                                 int start,
                                 int end,
                                 Spanned dest,
                                 int dstart,
                                 int dend)
      {
          for(int i = start; i < end; i++)
            /*
            ** Allow hexadecimal characters only.
            */

            if(!((source.charAt(i) == ' ' || source.charAt(i) == '-') ||
                 (source.charAt(i) >= '0' && source.charAt(i) <= '9') ||
                 (source.charAt(i) >= 'A' && source.charAt(i) <= 'F') ||
                 (source.charAt(i) >= 'a' && source.charAt(i) <= 'f')))
                return source.subSequence(start, i);

          return null;
```

```java
    }
};
private final static String MINIMUM_PASSWORD_LENGTH_TEXT = "three";
private final static int CHECKBOX_TEXT_SIZE = 13;
private final static int CHECKBOX_WIDTH = 500;
private final static int MINIMUM_PASSWORD_LENGTH = 3;
private final static int TEXTVIEW_TEXT_SIZE = 13;
private final static int TEXTVIEW_WIDTH = 500;
private final static long REFRESH_INTERVAL = 2500L; // 2.5 Seconds
private final static long TIMER_INTERVAL = 2500L; // 2.5 Seconds

private boolean generateOzone(String string)
{
  byte bytes[] = Cryptography.generateOzone(string);

  if(bytes != null)
      return m_databaseHelper.writeOzone
        (s_cryptography, string.trim(), bytes);
  else
      return false;
}

private void addListener()
{
  if(Settings.this.isFinishing())
      return;

  CheckBox checkBox1 = (CheckBox) findViewById
      (R.id.automatic_refresh_listeners);
  CheckBox checkBox2 = (CheckBox) findViewById(R.id.private_server);
  RadioGroup radioGroup1 = (RadioGroup) findViewById
      (R.id.listeners_ipv_radio_group);
  String ipVersion = "";
  TextView textView1 = (TextView) findViewById(R.id.listeners_ip_address);
  TextView textView2 = (TextView) findViewById(R.id.listeners_port);
  TextView textView3 = (TextView) findViewById(R.id.listeners_scope_id);

  if(radioGroup1.getCheckedRadioButtonId() == R.id.listeners_ipv4)
      ipVersion = "IPv4";
  else
      ipVersion = "IPv6";

  if(textView1.getText().toString().trim().isEmpty())
      Miscellaneous.showErrorDialog
        (Settings.this, "Please provide a listener IP address.");
  else if(!m_databaseHelper.
          writeListener(s_cryptography,
                  textView1.getText().toString(),
                  textView2.getText().toString(),
                  textView3.getText().toString(),
                  ipVersion,
                  checkBox2.isChecked()))
      Miscellaneous.showErrorDialog
        (Settings.this,
          "An error occurred while saving the listener information.");
  else
  {
      if(generateOzone(textView1.getText().toString() +
              ":" +
              textView2.getText().toString() +
              ":TCP"))
      {
        Kernel.getInstance().populateOzones();
```

```java
            populateOzoneAddresses();
        }

        if(!checkBox1.isChecked())
          populateListeners(null);
    }
  }

  private void addNeighbor()
  {
    if(Settings.this.isFinishing())
        return;

    CheckBox checkBox1 = (CheckBox) findViewById
        (R.id.automatic_refresh_neighbors);
    RadioGroup radioGroup1 = (RadioGroup) findViewById
        (R.id.neighbors_ipv_radio_group);
    Spinner spinner1 = (Spinner) findViewById(R.id.neighbors_transport);
    Spinner spinner2 = (Spinner) findViewById(R.id.proxy_type);
    String ipVersion = "";
    TextView proxyIpAddress = (TextView) findViewById
        (R.id.proxy_ip_address);
    TextView proxyPort = (TextView) findViewById(R.id.proxy_port);
    TextView textView1 = (TextView) findViewById(R.id.neighbors_ip_address);
    TextView textView2 = (TextView) findViewById(R.id.neighbors_port);
    TextView textView3 = (TextView) findViewById(R.id.neighbors_scope_id);

    if(radioGroup1.getCheckedRadioButtonId() == R.id.neighbors_ipv4)
        ipVersion = "IPv4";
    else
        ipVersion = "IPv6";

    if(textView1.getText().toString().trim().isEmpty())
        Miscellaneous.showErrorDialog
          (Settings.this, "Please provide a neighbor IP address.");
    else if(!m_databaseHelper.
          writeNeighbor(s_cryptography,
                        proxyIpAddress.getText().toString(),
                        proxyPort.getText().toString(),
                        spinner2.getSelectedItem().toString(),
                        textView1.getText().toString(),
                        textView2.getText().toString(),
                        textView3.getText().toString(),
                        spinner1.getSelectedItem().toString(),
                        ipVersion))
      Miscellaneous.showErrorDialog
          (Settings.this,
           "An error occurred while saving the neighbor information.");
    else if(!checkBox1.isChecked())
        populateNeighbors(null);
  }


  private void addParticipant()
  {
    if(Settings.this.isFinishing())
        return;

    String string = "";
    TextView textView1 = (TextView) findViewById
        (R.id.participant_siphash_id);

    string = Miscellaneous.delimitString
        (textView1.getText().toString().
```

```java
            replace(" ", "").replace("-", "").replace(":", "").trim(),
            '-', 4);

    if(string.length() != Cryptography.SIPHASH_IDENTITY_LENGTH)
    {
        Miscellaneous.showErrorDialog
          (Settings.this,
           "A Smoke ID must be of the form " +
           "HHHH-HHHH-HHHH-HHHH-HHHH-HHHH-HHHH-HHHH.");
        return;
    }

    final ProgressDialog dialog = new ProgressDialog(Settings.this);

    dialog.setCancelable(false);
    dialog.setIndeterminate(true);
    dialog.setMessage("Generating key material. Please be patient and " +
                "do not rotate the device while the process " +
                "executes.");
    dialog.show();

    class SingleShot implements Runnable
    {
        private String m_name = "";
        private String m_sipHashId = "";
        private boolean m_acceptWithoutSignatures = false;
        private boolean m_error = false;

        SingleShot(String name,
                   String sipHashId,
                   boolean acceptWithoutSignatures)
        {
          m_acceptWithoutSignatures = acceptWithoutSignatures;
          m_name = name;
          m_sipHashId = sipHashId.toUpperCase();
        }

        @Override
        public void run()
        {
          try
          {
              if(!m_databaseHelper.
                writeSipHashParticipant(s_cryptography,
                                        m_name,
                                        m_sipHashId,
                                        m_acceptWithoutSignatures))
                m_error = true;
              else
                generateOzone(m_sipHashId);

              Settings.this.runOnUiThread(new Runnable()
              {
                @Override
                public void run()
                {
                    dialog.dismiss();

                    if(m_error)
                      Miscellaneous.showErrorDialog
                          (Settings.this,
                           "An error occurred while attempting " +
                           "to save the specified Smoke ID.");
```

```java
                      else
                      {
                        Kernel.getInstance().populateOzones();
                        Kernel.getInstance().populateSipHashIds();
                        populateOzoneAddresses();
                        populateParticipants();
                      }
                }
              });
          }
        catch(Exception exception)
          {
          }
        }
     }

   Thread thread = new Thread
        (new
         SingleShot(((TextView) findViewById(R.id.participant_name)).
                getText().toString(), string,
                ((CheckBox) findViewById(R.id.
                                  accept_without_signatures)).
                isChecked()));

   thread.start();
 }

 private void enableWidgets(boolean state)
 {
   Button button1 = null;

   button1 = (Button) findViewById(R.id.add_listener);
   button1.setEnabled(state);
   button1 = (Button) findViewById(R.id.add_neighbor);
   button1.setEnabled(state);
   button1 = (Button) findViewById(R.id.add_participant);
   button1.setEnabled(state);
   button1 = (Button) findViewById(R.id.refresh_listeners);
   button1.setEnabled(state);
     button1 = (Button) findViewById(R.id.refresh_neighbors);
     button1.setEnabled(state);
   button1 = (Button) findViewById(R.id.refresh_ozones);
     button1.setEnabled(state);
   button1 = (Button) findViewById(R.id.refresh_participants);
   button1.setEnabled(state);
   button1 = (Button) findViewById(R.id.reset_listener_fields);
   button1.setEnabled(state);
   button1 = (Button) findViewById(R.id.reset_neighbor_fields);
   button1.setEnabled(state);
   button1 = (Button) findViewById(R.id.reset_participants_fields);
   button1.setEnabled(state);
   button1 = (Button) findViewById(R.id.save_ozone);
   button1.setEnabled(state);


   CheckBox checkBox1 = null;

   checkBox1 = (CheckBox) findViewById(R.id.accept_without_signatures);
   checkBox1.setChecked(!state);
   checkBox1.setEnabled(state);
   checkBox1 = (CheckBox) findViewById(R.id.overwrite);
   checkBox1.setChecked(!state);
   checkBox1.setEnabled(state);
   button1 = (Button) findViewById(R.id.set_password);
```

```java
        button1.setEnabled(checkBox1.isChecked());
        checkBox1 = (CheckBox) findViewById(R.id.private_server);
        checkBox1.setChecked(!state);
        checkBox1.setEnabled(state);

    RadioButton radioButton1 = null;

    radioButton1 = (RadioButton) findViewById(R.id.listeners_ipv4);
    radioButton1.setEnabled(state);
    radioButton1 = (RadioButton) findViewById(R.id.listeners_ipv6);
    radioButton1.setEnabled(state);
    radioButton1 = (RadioButton) findViewById(R.id.neighbors_ipv4);
    radioButton1.setEnabled(state);
    radioButton1 = (RadioButton) findViewById(R.id.neighbors_ipv6);
    radioButton1.setEnabled(state);

    Spinner spinner1 = null;

    spinner1 = (Spinner) findViewById(R.id.neighbors_transport);
    spinner1.setEnabled(state);
    spinner1 = (Spinner) findViewById(R.id.proxy_type);
    spinner1.setEnabled(state);

    TextView textView1 = null;

    textView1 = (TextView) findViewById(R.id.listeners_ip_address);
    textView1.setEnabled(state);
      textView1 = (TextView) findViewById(R.id.listeners_port);
    textView1.setEnabled(state);
    textView1 = (TextView) findViewById(R.id.listeners_scope_id);
      textView1.setEnabled(state);
    textView1 = (TextView) findViewById(R.id.neighbors_ip_address);
    textView1.setEnabled(state);
      textView1 = (TextView) findViewById(R.id.neighbors_port);
    textView1.setEnabled(state);
    textView1 = (TextView) findViewById(R.id.neighbors_scope_id);
      textView1.setEnabled(state);
    textView1 = (TextView) findViewById(R.id.ozone);
    textView1.setEnabled(state);
    textView1 = (TextView) findViewById(R.id.participant_name);
    textView1.setEnabled(state);
    textView1 = (TextView) findViewById(R.id.participant_siphash_id);
    textView1.setEnabled(state);
    textView1 = (TextView) findViewById(R.id.proxy_ip_address);
    textView1.setEnabled(state);
    textView1 = (TextView) findViewById(R.id.proxy_port);
    textView1.setEnabled(state);
    }

    private void populateListeners(ArrayList<ListenerElement> arrayList)
    {
      ((TextView) findViewById(R.id.internal_listeners)).setText
          ("Internal Listeners Container Size: " +
           Kernel.getInstance().listenersCount());

      if(arrayList == null)
          arrayList = m_databaseHelper.readListeners(s_cryptography, -1);

      final TableLayout tableLayout = (TableLayout)
          findViewById(R.id.listeners);

      if(arrayList == null || arrayList.size() == 0)
      {
```

```java
        tableLayout.removeAllViews();
        return;
    }

    StringBuilder stringBuilder = new StringBuilder();
    int i = 0;

    /*
    ** Remove table entries which do not exist in smokestack.db.
    */

    for(i = tableLayout.getChildCount() - 1; i >= 0; i--)
    {
        TableRow row = (TableRow) tableLayout.getChildAt(i);

        if(row == null)
          continue;

        CheckBox checkBox = (CheckBox) row.getChildAt(0);

        if(checkBox == null)
        {
          tableLayout.removeView(row);
          continue;
        }

        boolean found = false;

        for(ListenerElement listenerElement : arrayList)
        {
          stringBuilder.delete(0, stringBuilder.length());
          stringBuilder.append(listenerElement.m_localIpAddress);

          if(listenerElement.m_ipVersion.equals("IPv6"))
              if(!listenerElement.m_localScopeId.isEmpty())
              {
                stringBuilder.append("-");
                stringBuilder.append(listenerElement.m_localScopeId);
              }

          stringBuilder.append(":");
          stringBuilder.append(listenerElement.m_localPort);

          if(checkBox.getText().toString().
             contains(stringBuilder.toString()))
          {
              found = true;
              break;
          }
        }

        if(!found)
          tableLayout.removeView(row);
    }

    i = 0;

    for(ListenerElement listenerElement : arrayList)
    {
        if(listenerElement == null)
          continue;

        CheckBox checkBox = null;
```

```java
TableRow row = null;
int count = tableLayout.getChildCount();

for(int j = 0; j < count; j++)
{
  TableRow r = (TableRow) tableLayout.getChildAt(j);

  if(r == null)
      continue;

  CheckBox c = (CheckBox) r.getChildAt(0);

  if(c == null)
      continue;

  stringBuilder.delete(0, stringBuilder.length());
  stringBuilder.append(listenerElement.m_localIpAddress);

  if(listenerElement.m_ipVersion.equals("IPv6"))
      if(!listenerElement.m_localScopeId.isEmpty())
      {
        stringBuilder.append("-");
        stringBuilder.append(listenerElement.m_localScopeId);
      }

  stringBuilder.append(":");
  stringBuilder.append(listenerElement.m_localPort);

  if(c.getText().toString().contains(stringBuilder.toString()))
  {
      checkBox = c;
      break;
  }
}

if(checkBox == null)
{
  TableRow.LayoutParams layoutParams = new
      TableRow.LayoutParams(TableRow.LayoutParams.WRAP_CONTENT);
  final String oid = String.valueOf(listenerElement.m_oid);

  row = new TableRow(Settings.this);
  row.setId(listenerElement.m_oid);
  row.setLayoutParams(layoutParams);
  checkBox = new CheckBox(Settings.this);
  checkBox.setOnCheckedChangeListener
      (new CompoundButton.OnCheckedChangeListener()
      {
        @Override
        public void onCheckedChanged
            (CompoundButton buttonView, boolean isChecked)
        {
            m_databaseHelper.listenerNeighborControlStatus
              (s_cryptography,
                isChecked ? "listen" : "disconnect",
                oid,
                "listeners");
        }
      });
}

registerForContextMenu(checkBox);
```

```java
if(listenerElement.m_status.equals("listening"))
  checkBox.setTextColor(Color.rgb(27, 94, 32)); // Dark Green
else
  checkBox.setTextColor(Color.rgb(183, 28, 28)); // Dark Red

stringBuilder.delete(0, stringBuilder.length());
stringBuilder.append("Control: ");

try
{
  stringBuilder.append
      (listenerElement.m_statusControl.substring(0, 1).
       toUpperCase());
  stringBuilder.append
      (listenerElement.m_statusControl.substring(1));
}
catch(Exception exception)
{
  stringBuilder.append("Disconnect");
}

stringBuilder.append("\n");
stringBuilder.append("Status: ");

try
{
  stringBuilder.append
      (listenerElement.m_status.substring(0, 1).toUpperCase());
  stringBuilder.append(listenerElement.m_status.substring(1));
}
catch(Exception exception)
{
  stringBuilder.append("Disconnected");
}

stringBuilder.append("\n");

if(!listenerElement.m_error.isEmpty())
{
  stringBuilder.append("Error: ");
  stringBuilder.append(listenerElement.m_error);
  stringBuilder.append("\n");
}

stringBuilder.append(listenerElement.m_localIpAddress);

if(listenerElement.m_ipVersion.equals("IPv6"))
  if(!listenerElement.m_localScopeId.isEmpty())
  {
      stringBuilder.append("-");
      stringBuilder.append(listenerElement.m_localScopeId);
  }

stringBuilder.append(":");
stringBuilder.append(listenerElement.m_localPort);

if(listenerElement.m_certificate != null)
{
  /*
  ** In PEM format.
  */

  stringBuilder.append("\nCertificate Fingerprint: ");
```

```java
          stringBuilder.append
              (Cryptography.
               fingerPrint(Miscellaneous.
                     pemFormat(listenerElement.m_certificate).
                     getBytes())));
        }

        stringBuilder.append("\nPeers Count: ");
        stringBuilder.append(listenerElement.m_peersCount);
        stringBuilder.append("\nPrivate: ");
        stringBuilder.append(listenerElement.m_isPrivate ? "Yes" : "No");
        stringBuilder.append("\nUptime: ");

        try
        {
          long uptime = Long.parseLong(listenerElement.m_uptime);

          stringBuilder.append
              (String.
               format(Locale.getDefault(),
                   "%d:%02d",
                   TimeUnit.NANOSECONDS.toMinutes(uptime),
                   TimeUnit.NANOSECONDS.toSeconds(uptime) -
                   TimeUnit.MINUTES.
                   toSeconds(TimeUnit.NANOSECONDS.
                         toMinutes(uptime))));
        }
        catch(Exception exception)
        {
          stringBuilder.append("0:00");
        }

        stringBuilder.append(" Min.\n");
        checkBox.setChecked
          (listenerElement.m_statusControl.toLowerCase().
           equals("listen"));
        checkBox.setGravity(Gravity.CENTER_VERTICAL);
        checkBox.setId(listenerElement.m_oid);
        checkBox.setLayoutParams
          (new TableRow.LayoutParams(0, LayoutParams.WRAP_CONTENT, 1));
        checkBox.setTag
          (listenerElement.m_localIpAddress + ":" +
           listenerElement.m_localPort);
        checkBox.setText(stringBuilder);
        checkBox.setTextSize(CHECKBOX_TEXT_SIZE);
        checkBox.setWidth(CHECKBOX_WIDTH);

        if(row != null)
        {
          row.addView(checkBox);
          tableLayout.addView(row, i);
        }

        i += 1;
      }

    arrayList.clear();
    }

    private void populateNeighbors(ArrayList<NeighborElement> arrayList)
    {
      ((TextView) findViewById(R.id.internal_neighbors)).setText
          ("Internal Neighbors Container Size: " +
```

```java
                Kernel.getInstance().neighborsCount());

        if(arrayList == null)
            arrayList = m_databaseHelper.readNeighbors(s_cryptography);

        final TableLayout tableLayout = (TableLayout)
            findViewById(R.id.neighbors);

        if(arrayList == null || arrayList.size() == 0)
        {
            tableLayout.removeAllViews();
            return;
        }

        StringBuilder stringBuilder = new StringBuilder();
        int i = 0;

        /*
        ** Remove table entries which do not exist in smokestack.db.
        */

        for(i = tableLayout.getChildCount() - 1; i >= 0; i--)
        {
            TableRow row = (TableRow) tableLayout.getChildAt(i);

            if(row == null)
              continue;

            TextView textView = (TextView) row.getChildAt(1);

            if(textView == null)
            {
              tableLayout.removeView(row);
              continue;
            }

            boolean found = false;

            for(NeighborElement neighborElement : arrayList)
            {
              stringBuilder.delete(0, stringBuilder.length());
              stringBuilder.append(neighborElement.m_remoteIpAddress);

              if(neighborElement.m_ipVersion.equals("IPv6"))
                  if(!neighborElement.m_remoteScopeId.isEmpty())
                  {
                    stringBuilder.append("-");
                    stringBuilder.append(neighborElement.m_remoteScopeId);
                  }

              stringBuilder.append(":");
              stringBuilder.append(neighborElement.m_remotePort);
              stringBuilder.append(":");
              stringBuilder.append(neighborElement.m_transport);

              if(textView.getText().toString().
                  contains(stringBuilder.toString()))
              {
                  found = true;
                  break;
              }
            }
```

```java
            if(!found)
              tableLayout.removeView(row);
        }

    CheckBox checkBox = (CheckBox) findViewById(R.id.neighbor_details);

    i = 0;

    for(NeighborElement neighborElement : arrayList)
    {
        if(neighborElement == null)
          continue;

        Spinner spinner = null;
        TableRow row = null;
        TextView textView = null;
        int count = tableLayout.getChildCount();

        for(int j = 0; j < count; j++)
        {
          TableRow r = (TableRow) tableLayout.getChildAt(j);

          if(r == null)
              continue;

          TextView t = (TextView) r.getChildAt(1);

          if(t == null)
              continue;

          stringBuilder.delete(0, stringBuilder.length());
          stringBuilder.append(neighborElement.m_remoteIpAddress);

          if(neighborElement.m_ipVersion.equals("IPv6"))
              if(!neighborElement.m_remoteScopeId.isEmpty())
              {
                stringBuilder.append("-");
                stringBuilder.append(neighborElement.m_remoteScopeId);
              }

          stringBuilder.append(":");
          stringBuilder.append(neighborElement.m_remotePort);
          stringBuilder.append(":");
          stringBuilder.append(neighborElement.m_transport);

          if(t.getText().toString().contains(stringBuilder.toString()))
          {
              textView = t;
              break;
          }
        }

        if(textView == null)
        {
          TableRow.LayoutParams layoutParams = new
              TableRow.LayoutParams(TableRow.LayoutParams.WRAP_CONTENT);

          row = new TableRow(Settings.this);
          row.setId(neighborElement.m_oid);
          row.setLayoutParams(layoutParams);
          spinner = new Spinner(Settings.this);

          ArrayAdapter<String> arrayAdapter = null;
```

```java
            String array[] = null;

            if(neighborElement.m_transport.equals("TCP"))
                array = new String[]
                {
                  "Action",
                  "Connect",
                  "Delete",
                  "Disconnect",
                  "Reset SSL/TLS Credentials"
                };
            else
                array = new String[]
                {
                  "Action",
                  "Connect",
                  "Delete",
                  "Disconnect"
                };

            arrayAdapter = new ArrayAdapter<>
                (Settings.this,
                 android.R.layout.simple_spinner_item,
                 array);
            spinner.setAdapter(arrayAdapter);
            spinner.setId(neighborElement.m_oid);
            spinner.setOnItemSelectedListener
                (new OnItemSelectedListener()
                {
                 @Override
                 public void onItemSelected(AdapterView<?> parent,
                                            View view,
                                            int position,
                                            long id)
                 {
                     if(position == 1) // Connect.
                       m_databaseHelper.listenerNeighborControlStatus
                           (s_cryptography,
                            "connect",
                            String.valueOf(parent.getId()),
                            "neighbors");
                     else if(position == 2 && // Delete.
                            m_databaseHelper.
                            deleteEntry(String.valueOf(parent.getId()),
                                 "neighbors"))
                     {
                       /*
                       ** Prepare the kernel's neighbors container
                       ** if a neighbor was deleted as the OID
                       ** field may represent a recycled value.
                       */

                       Kernel.getInstance().purgeDeletedNeighbors();

                       TableRow row = (TableRow) findViewById
                           (parent.getId());

                       tableLayout.removeView(row);
                     }
                     else if(position == 3) // Disconnect.
                       m_databaseHelper.listenerNeighborControlStatus
                           (s_cryptography,
                            "disconnect",
```

```java
                                String.valueOf(parent.getId()),
                                "neighbors");
                    else if(position == 4) // Reset SSL/TLS credentials.
                    {
                      m_databaseHelper.neighborRecordCertificate
                          (s_cryptography,
                           String.valueOf(parent.getId()),
                           null);
                      m_databaseHelper.listenerNeighborControlStatus
                          (s_cryptography,
                           "disconnect",
                           String.valueOf(parent.getId()),
                           "neighbors");
                    }

                    parent.setSelection(0);
                  }

                  @Override
                  public void onNothingSelected(AdapterView<?> parent)
                  {
                  }
                });

          textView = new TextView(Settings.this);
        }

        switch(neighborElement.m_status)
        {
        case "connected":
            textView.setTextColor(Color.rgb(27, 94, 32)); // Dark Green
            break;
          case "connecting":
            textView.setTextColor(Color.rgb(255, 111, 0)); // Dark Orange
            break;
          default:
            textView.setTextColor(Color.rgb(183, 28, 28)); // Dark Red
            break;
        }

        stringBuilder.delete(0, stringBuilder.length());
        stringBuilder.append("Control: ");

        try
        {
          stringBuilder.append
              (neighborElement.m_statusControl.substring(0, 1).
               toUpperCase());
          stringBuilder.append
              (neighborElement.m_statusControl.substring(1));
        }
        catch(Exception exception)
        {
          stringBuilder.append("Disconnect");
        }

        stringBuilder.append("\n");
        stringBuilder.append("Status: ");

        try
        {
          stringBuilder.append
              (neighborElement.m_status.substring(0, 1).toUpperCase());
```

```java
      stringBuilder.append(neighborElement.m_status.substring(1));
}
catch(Exception exception)
{
  stringBuilder.append("Disconnected");
}

stringBuilder.append("\n");

if(!neighborElement.m_error.isEmpty())
{
  stringBuilder.append("Error: ");
  stringBuilder.append(neighborElement.m_error);
  stringBuilder.append("\n");
}

stringBuilder.append(neighborElement.m_remoteIpAddress);

if(neighborElement.m_ipVersion.equals("IPv6"))
  if(!neighborElement.m_remoteScopeId.isEmpty())
  {
      stringBuilder.append("-");
      stringBuilder.append(neighborElement.m_remoteScopeId);
  }

stringBuilder.append(":");
stringBuilder.append(neighborElement.m_remotePort);
stringBuilder.append(":");
stringBuilder.append(neighborElement.m_transport);

if(!neighborElement.m_localIpAddress.isEmpty() &&
   !neighborElement.m_localPort.isEmpty())
{
  stringBuilder.append("\n");
  stringBuilder.append(neighborElement.m_localIpAddress);
  stringBuilder.append(":");
  stringBuilder.append(neighborElement.m_localPort);
}

stringBuilder.append("\nProxy: ");

if(!neighborElement.m_proxyIpAddress.isEmpty() &&
   !neighborElement.m_proxyPort.isEmpty())
{
  stringBuilder.append(neighborElement.m_proxyIpAddress);
  stringBuilder.append(":");
  stringBuilder.append(neighborElement.m_proxyPort);
  stringBuilder.append(":");
  stringBuilder.append(neighborElement.m_proxyType);
}

if(checkBox.isChecked())
{
  if(neighborElement.m_remoteCertificate != null &&
     neighborElement.m_remoteCertificate.length > 0)
  {
      stringBuilder.append("\n");
      stringBuilder.append
        ("Remote Certificate's Fingerprint: ");
      stringBuilder.append
        (Cryptography.
         fingerPrint(Miscellaneous.
                 pemFormat(neighborElement.
```

```java
                                m_remoteCertificate).
                        getBytes()));
        }

      if(!neighborElement.m_sessionCipher.isEmpty())
        {
            stringBuilder.append("\n");
            stringBuilder.append("Session Cipher: ");
            stringBuilder.append(neighborElement.m_sessionCipher);
        }
    }

        stringBuilder.append("\n");
        stringBuilder.append("Echo Queue Size: ");
        stringBuilder.append(neighborElement.m_outboundEchoQueued);
        stringBuilder.append("\n");
        stringBuilder.append("Queue Size: ");
        stringBuilder.append(neighborElement.m_queueSize);
        stringBuilder.append("\n");
        stringBuilder.append("Buffered: ");
        stringBuilder.append
          (Miscellaneous.
           formattedDigitalInformation(neighborElement.m_bytesBuffered));
        stringBuilder.append("\n");
        stringBuilder.append("In: ");
        stringBuilder.append
          (Miscellaneous.
           formattedDigitalInformation(neighborElement.m_bytesRead));
        stringBuilder.append("\n");
        stringBuilder.append("Out: ");
        stringBuilder.append
          (Miscellaneous.
           formattedDigitalInformation(neighborElement.m_bytesWritten));
        stringBuilder.append("\n");
        stringBuilder.append("Outbound Queued: ");
        stringBuilder.append(neighborElement.m_outboundQueued);
        stringBuilder.append("\n");
        stringBuilder.append("Uptime: ");

        try
        {
          long uptime = Long.parseLong(neighborElement.m_uptime);

          stringBuilder.append
              (String.
               format(Locale.getDefault(),
                    "%d:%02d",
                    TimeUnit.NANOSECONDS.toMinutes(uptime),
                    TimeUnit.NANOSECONDS.toSeconds(uptime) -
                    TimeUnit.MINUTES.
                    toSeconds(TimeUnit.NANOSECONDS.
                         toMinutes(uptime))));
        }
        catch(Exception exception)
        {
          stringBuilder.append("0:00");
        }

        stringBuilder.append(" Min.\n");
        textView.setGravity(Gravity.CENTER_VERTICAL);
        textView.setLayoutParams
          (new TableRow.LayoutParams(0, LayoutParams.WRAP_CONTENT, 1));
        textView.setText(stringBuilder);
```

```java
        textView.setTextSize(TEXTVIEW_TEXT_SIZE);
        textView.setWidth(TEXTVIEW_WIDTH);

        if(row != null)
        {
          row.addView(spinner);
          row.addView(textView);
          tableLayout.addView(row, i);
        }

        i += 1;
    }

    arrayList.clear();
}

private void populateOzoneAddresses()
{
  ArrayList<OzoneElement> arrayList =
      m_databaseHelper.readOzones(s_cryptography);
  TableLayout tableLayout = (TableLayout) findViewById
      (R.id.ozones);

  tableLayout.removeAllViews();

  if(arrayList == null || arrayList.size() == 0)
      return;

  int i = 0;

  for(OzoneElement ozoneElement : arrayList)
  {
      if(ozoneElement == null)
        continue;

      TableRow.LayoutParams layoutParams = new
        TableRow.LayoutParams(TableRow.LayoutParams.WRAP_CONTENT);
      TableRow row = new TableRow(Settings.this);

      row.setLayoutParams(layoutParams);

      TextView textView = new TextView(Settings.this);

      textView.setGravity(Gravity.CENTER_VERTICAL);
      textView.setId(ozoneElement.m_oid);
      textView.setLayoutParams
        (new TableRow.LayoutParams(0,
                            LayoutParams.WRAP_CONTENT,
                            1));
      textView.setTag(ozoneElement.m_address);
      textView.setText(ozoneElement.m_address);
      textView.setTextSize(TEXTVIEW_TEXT_SIZE);
      registerForContextMenu(textView);
      row.addView(textView);
      tableLayout.addView(row, i);
      i += 1;
    }

    arrayList.clear();
}

private void populateParticipants()
{
```

```java
ArrayList<SipHashIdElement> arrayList =
    m_databaseHelper.readSipHashIds(s_cryptography);
TableLayout tableLayout = (TableLayout) findViewById
    (R.id.participants);

tableLayout.removeAllViews();

if(arrayList == null || arrayList.size() == 0)
    return;

int i = 0;

for(SipHashIdElement sipHashIdElement : arrayList)
{
    if(sipHashIdElement == null)
      continue;

    TableRow row = new TableRow(Settings.this);
    TableRow.LayoutParams layoutParams = new
      TableRow.LayoutParams(TableRow.LayoutParams.WRAP_CONTENT);

    row.setLayoutParams(layoutParams);

    for(int j = 0; j < 4; j++)
    {
      TextView textView = new TextView(Settings.this);

      textView.setId(sipHashIdElement.m_oid);

      switch(j)
      {
          case 0:
            textView.setGravity(Gravity.CENTER_VERTICAL);
            textView.setLayoutParams
              (new TableRow.LayoutParams(0,
                              LayoutParams.MATCH_PARENT,
                              1));
                textView.setText(sipHashIdElement.m_name);
                break;
            case 1:
                if(sipHashIdElement.m_epksCompleted &&
              sipHashIdElement.m_keysSigned)
                    textView.setCompoundDrawablesWithIntrinsicBounds
                  (R.drawable.keys_signed, 0, 0, 0);
                else if(sipHashIdElement.m_epksCompleted)
                    textView.setCompoundDrawablesWithIntrinsicBounds
                  (R.drawable.keys_not_signed, 0, 0, 0);
                else
                    textView.setCompoundDrawablesWithIntrinsicBounds
                  (R.drawable.warning, 0, 0, 0);

                textView.setCompoundDrawablePadding(5);
            textView.setGravity(Gravity.CENTER_VERTICAL);
            textView.setLayoutParams
              (new TableRow.LayoutParams(0,
                              LayoutParams.WRAP_CONTENT,
                              1));
                textView.setText(sipHashIdElement.m_sipHashId);
                break;
            case 2:
                textView.append
              (String.valueOf(sipHashIdElement.m_outMessages));
                textView.append(" / ");
```

```java
                    textView.append
                  (String.valueOf(sipHashIdElement.m_inMessages));
                    textView.append(" / ");
                    textView.append
                  (String.valueOf(sipHashIdElement.m_totalMessages));
                textView.setGravity(Gravity.CENTER);
                textView.setLayoutParams
                  (new TableRow.LayoutParams(0,
                                    LayoutParams.MATCH_PARENT,
                                    1));
                    break;
          default:
                textView.setGravity(Gravity.CENTER_VERTICAL);
                textView.setLayoutParams
                  (new TableRow.LayoutParams(0,
                                    LayoutParams.MATCH_PARENT,
                                    1));
                textView.setText(sipHashIdElement.m_timestamp);
                break;
            }

            if(j == 0 || j == 1)
                textView.setTag(textView.getText());
            else
                textView.setTag(sipHashIdElement.m_name);

            textView.setTextSize(TEXTVIEW_TEXT_SIZE);
            registerForContextMenu(textView);
            row.addView(textView);
            }

        tableLayout.addView(row, i);
        i += 1;
    }

  arrayList.clear();
}

private void prepareCredentials()
{
  if(Settings.this.isFinishing())
      return;

  final ProgressDialog dialog = new ProgressDialog(Settings.this);
  final Spinner spinner1 = (Spinner) findViewById(R.id.iteration_count);
  final TextView textView1 = (TextView) findViewById
      (R.id.password1);
  final TextView textView2 = (TextView) findViewById
      (R.id.password2);
  int iterationCount = 1000;

  try
  {
      iterationCount = Integer.parseInt
        (spinner1.getSelectedItem().toString());
  }
  catch(Exception exception)
  {
      iterationCount = 1000;
  }

  dialog.setCancelable(false);
  dialog.setIndeterminate(true);
```

```java
dialog.setMessage
    ("Generating confidential material. Please be patient and " +
     "do not rotate the device while the process executes.");
dialog.show();

class SingleShot implements Runnable
{
    private String m_error = "";
    private String m_password = "";
    private int m_iterationCount = 1000;

    SingleShot(String password,
            int iterationCount)
    {
      m_iterationCount = iterationCount;
      m_password = password;
    }

    @Override
    public void run()
    {
      SecretKey encryptionKey = null;
      SecretKey macKey = null;
      byte encryptionSalt[] = null;
      byte macSalt[] = null;

      try
      {
          encryptionSalt = Cryptography.randomBytes(32);
          encryptionKey = Cryptography.
            generateEncryptionKey
            (encryptionSalt,
             m_password.toCharArray(),
             m_iterationCount);

          if(encryptionSalt == null)
          {
            m_error = "generateEncryptionKey() failure";
            s_cryptography.reset();
            return;
          }

          macSalt = Cryptography.randomBytes(64);
          macKey = Cryptography.generateMacKey
            (macSalt,
             m_password.toCharArray(),
             m_iterationCount);

          if(macKey == null)
          {
            m_error = "generateMacKey() failure";
            s_cryptography.reset();
            return;
          }

          /*
          ** Prepare the Cryptography object's data.
          */

          s_cryptography.setEncryptionKey
            (encryptionKey);
          s_cryptography.setMacKey(macKey);
```

```java
        /*
        ** Record the data.
        */

    m_databaseHelper.writeSetting
      (null,
       "encryptionSalt",
       Base64.encodeToString(encryptionSalt,
                         Base64.DEFAULT));
    m_databaseHelper.writeSetting
      (null,
       "iterationCount",
       String.valueOf(m_iterationCount));
    m_databaseHelper.writeSetting
      (null,
       "macSalt",
       Base64.encodeToString(macSalt,
                         Base64.DEFAULT));

    byte saltedPassword[] = Cryptography.
      sha512(m_password.getBytes(),
             encryptionSalt,
             macSalt);

    if(saltedPassword != null)
      m_databaseHelper.writeSetting
          (null,
           "saltedPassword",
           Base64.encodeToString(saltedPassword,
                         Base64.DEFAULT));
    else
    {
      m_error = "sha512() failure";
      s_cryptography.reset();
    }
}
catch(Exception exception)
{
    m_error = exception.getMessage().toLowerCase().trim();
    s_cryptography.reset();
}

Settings.this.runOnUiThread(new Runnable()
{
    @Override
    public void run()
    {
      try
      {
          dialog.dismiss();

          if(!m_error.isEmpty())
            Miscellaneous.showErrorDialog
                (Settings.this,
                 "An error (" + m_error +
                 ") occurred while " +
                 "generating the confidential " +
                 "data.");
          else
          {
            Settings.this.enableWidgets(true);
            State.getInstance().setAuthenticated(true);
            textView1.requestFocus();
```

```java
                    textView1.setText("");
                    textView2.setText("");
                    populateOzoneAddresses();
                    populateParticipants();
                    startKernel();

                    if(m_databaseHelper.
                        readSetting(null,
                                "automatic_listeners_refresh").
                        equals("true"))
                          startListenersTimers();
                      else
                          populateListeners(null);

                    if(m_databaseHelper.
                        readSetting(null,
                                "automatic_neighbors_refresh").
                        equals("true"))
                          startNeighborsTimers();
                      else
                          populateNeighbors(null);
                  }
              }
              catch(Exception exception)
              {
              }
            }
        });

        m_password = "";
      }
    }

    Thread thread = new Thread
        (new SingleShot(textView1.getText().toString(),
                iterationCount));

    thread.start();
  }

  private void prepareListenerIpAddress()
  {
    RadioGroup radioGroup1 = (RadioGroup) findViewById
        (R.id.listeners_ipv_radio_group);
    TextView textView1 = (TextView) findViewById(R.id.listeners_ip_address);

    try
    {
        boolean found = false;

        for(Enumeration<NetworkInterface> enumeration1 = NetworkInterface.
              getNetworkInterfaces(); enumeration1.hasMoreElements();)
        {
          if(found)
              break;

          NetworkInterface networkInterface = enumeration1.nextElement();

          for(Enumeration<InetAddress> enumeration2 = networkInterface.
              getInetAddresses(); enumeration2.hasMoreElements();)
          {
              InetAddress inetAddress = enumeration2.nextElement();
```

```java
                    if(!inetAddress.isLoopbackAddress())
                    {
                      if(radioGroup1.getCheckedRadioButtonId() ==
                          R.id.listeners_ipv4)
                      {
                          if(inetAddress instanceof Inet4Address)
                          {
                            found = true;
                            textView1.setText
                                (inetAddress.getHostAddress());
                            break;
                          }
                      }
                      else
                      {
                          if(inetAddress instanceof Inet6Address)
                          {
                            found = true;
                            textView1.setText
                                (inetAddress.getHostAddress());
                            break;
                          }
                      }
                    }
                }
            }
        }
      catch(Exception exception)
      {
          textView1.setText("");
      }
    }

    private void prepareListeners()
    {
      if(Settings.this.isFinishing())
          return;

      Button button1 = null;
      Spinner spinner1 = (Spinner) findViewById(R.id.neighbors_transport);

      button1 = (Button) findViewById(R.id.add_listener);
      button1.setOnClickListener(new View.OnClickListener()
      {
          public void onClick(View view)
          {
            if(Settings.this.isFinishing())
                return;

            addListener();
          }
      });

      button1 = (Button) findViewById(R.id.add_neighbor);
      button1.setOnClickListener(new View.OnClickListener()
      {
          public void onClick(View view)
          {
            if(Settings.this.isFinishing())
                return;

            addNeighbor();
          }
```

```java
        });

    button1 = (Button) findViewById(R.id.add_participant);
    button1.setOnClickListener(new View.OnClickListener()
    {
        public void onClick(View view)
        {
          if(Settings.this.isFinishing())
              return;

          addParticipant();
        }
    });

    button1 = (Button) findViewById(R.id.clear_log);
    button1.setOnClickListener(new View.OnClickListener()
    {
        public void onClick(View view)
        {
          if(Settings.this.isFinishing())
              return;

          m_databaseHelper.clearTable("log");
        }
    });

    button1 = (Button) findViewById(R.id.gc);
    button1.setOnClickListener(new View.OnClickListener()
    {
        public void onClick(View view)
        {
          if(Settings.this.isFinishing())
              return;

          Database.releaseMemory();
          System.gc();
        }
    });

    button1 = (Button) findViewById(R.id.refresh_listeners);
    button1.setOnClickListener(new View.OnClickListener()
    {
        public void onClick(View view)
        {
          if(Settings.this.isFinishing())
              return;

          populateListeners(null);
        }
    });

    button1 = (Button) findViewById(R.id.refresh_neighbors);
    button1.setOnClickListener(new View.OnClickListener()
    {
        public void onClick(View view)
        {
          if(Settings.this.isFinishing())
              return;

          populateNeighbors(null);
        }
    });
```

```java
button1 = (Button) findViewById(R.id.refresh_ozones);
button1.setOnClickListener(new View.OnClickListener()
{
    public void onClick(View view)
      {
        if(Settings.this.isFinishing())
            return;

        populateOzoneAddresses();
      }
  });

button1 = (Button) findViewById(R.id.refresh_participants);
button1.setOnClickListener(new View.OnClickListener()
{
    public void onClick(View view)
      {
        if(Settings.this.isFinishing())
            return;

        populateParticipants();
      }
  });

final DialogInterface.OnCancelListener listener1 =
    new DialogInterface.OnCancelListener()
{
    public void onCancel(DialogInterface dialog)
      {
        if(State.getInstance().getString("dialog_accepted").
            equals("true"))
        {
            State.getInstance().reset();
            m_databaseHelper.resetAndDrop();
            s_cryptography.reset();

            Intent intent = getIntent();

            startActivity(intent);
            finish();
        }
      }
};

button1 = (Button) findViewById(R.id.reset);
  button1.setOnClickListener(new View.OnClickListener()
{
    public void onClick(View view)
      {
        Miscellaneous.showPromptDialog
            (Settings.this,
             listener1,
             "Are you sure that you " +
             "wish to reset SmokeStack? All " +
             "of the data will be removed.");
      }
  });

button1 = (Button) findViewById(R.id.reset_listener_fields);
  button1.setOnClickListener(new View.OnClickListener()
{
    public void onClick(View view)
      {
```

```java
            if(Settings.this.isFinishing())
                return;

            CheckBox checkBox1 = (CheckBox) findViewById
                (R.id.private_server);
            RadioButton radioButton1 = (RadioButton) findViewById
                (R.id.listeners_ipv4);
            TextView textView1 = (TextView) findViewById
                (R.id.listeners_ip_address);
            TextView textView2 = (TextView) findViewById
                (R.id.listeners_port);
            TextView textView3 = (TextView) findViewById
                (R.id.listeners_scope_id);

            checkBox1.setChecked(false);
            radioButton1.setChecked(true);
            textView1.setText("");
            textView2.setText("4710");
            textView3.setText("");
            textView1.requestFocus();
            prepareListenerIpAddress();
        }
    });

    button1 = (Button) findViewById(R.id.reset_neighbor_fields);
      button1.setOnClickListener(new View.OnClickListener()
    {
        public void onClick(View view)
        {
            if(Settings.this.isFinishing())
                return;

            RadioButton radioButton1 = (RadioButton) findViewById
                (R.id.neighbors_ipv4);
            Spinner spinner1 = (Spinner) findViewById
                (R.id.neighbors_transport);
            Spinner spinner2 = (Spinner) findViewById
                (R.id.proxy_type);
            TextView proxyIpAddress = (TextView) findViewById
                (R.id.proxy_ip_address);
            TextView proxyPort = (TextView) findViewById
                (R.id.proxy_port);
            TextView textView1 = (TextView) findViewById
                (R.id.neighbors_ip_address);
            TextView textView2 = (TextView) findViewById
                (R.id.neighbors_port);
            TextView textView3 = (TextView) findViewById
                (R.id.neighbors_scope_id);

            proxyIpAddress.setText("");
            proxyPort.setText("");
            radioButton1.setChecked(true);
            spinner1.setSelection(0);
            spinner2.setSelection(0);
            textView1.setText("");
            textView2.setText("4710");
            textView3.setText("");
            textView1.requestFocus();
        }
    });

    button1 = (Button) findViewById(R.id.reset_participants_fields);
    button1.setOnClickListener(new View.OnClickListener()
```

```java
      {
          public void onClick(View view)
          {
            if(Settings.this.isFinishing())
                return;

            CheckBox checkBox1 = (CheckBox) findViewById
                (R.id.accept_without_signatures);
            TextView textView1 = (TextView) findViewById
                (R.id.participant_name);
            TextView textView2 = (TextView) findViewById
                (R.id.participant_siphash_id);

            checkBox1.setChecked(false);
            textView1.setText("");
            textView2.setText("");
            textView1.requestFocus();
          }
      });

      button1 = (Button) findViewById(R.id.save_ozone);
      button1.setOnClickListener(new View.OnClickListener()
      {
          public void onClick(View view)
          {
            if(Settings.this.isFinishing())
                return;

            TextView textView = (TextView) findViewById(R.id.ozone);

            if(!generateOzone(textView.getText().toString()))
            {
                Miscellaneous.showErrorDialog
                  (Settings.this,
                    "An error occurred while processing the " +
                    "Ozone data. Perhaps a value should be provided.");
                textView.requestFocus();
            }
            else
            {
                Kernel.getInstance().populateOzones();
                populateOzoneAddresses();
            }
          }
      });

      final DialogInterface.OnCancelListener listener2 =
          new DialogInterface.OnCancelListener()
      {
          public void onCancel(DialogInterface dialog)
          {
            if(State.getInstance().getString("dialog_accepted").
              equals("true"))
            {
                m_databaseHelper.reset();
                Kernel.getInstance().populateOzones();
                Kernel.getInstance().populateSipHashIds();
                populateListeners(null);
                populateNeighbors(null);
                populateOzoneAddresses();
                populateParticipants();
                prepareCredentials();
            }
```

```java
            }
        };

    button1 = (Button) findViewById(R.id.set_password);
      button1.setOnClickListener(new View.OnClickListener()
      {
          public void onClick(View view)
          {
            if(Settings.this.isFinishing())
                return;

            TextView textView1 = (TextView) findViewById(R.id.password1);
            TextView textView2 = (TextView) findViewById(R.id.password2);

            textView1.setSelectAllOnFocus(true);
            textView2.setSelectAllOnFocus(true);

            if(textView1.getText().length() < MINIMUM_PASSWORD_LENGTH ||
               !textView1.getText().toString().
               equals(textView2.getText().toString()))
            {
                String error = "";

                if(textView1.getText().length() < MINIMUM_PASSWORD_LENGTH)
                  error = "Each password must contain " +
                      "at least " +
                      MINIMUM_PASSWORD_LENGTH_TEXT +
                      " characters.";
                else
                  error = "The provided passwords are not identical.";

                Miscellaneous.showErrorDialog(Settings.this, error);
                textView1.requestFocus();
                return;
            }

            int iterationCount = 1000;

            try
            {
                final Spinner spinner1 = (Spinner) findViewById
                  (R.id.iteration_count);

                iterationCount = Integer.parseInt
                  (spinner1.getSelectedItem().toString());
            }
            catch(Exception exception)
            {
                iterationCount = 1000;
            }

            if(iterationCount > 7500)
                Miscellaneous.showPromptDialog
                  (Settings.this,
                   listener2,
                   "You have selected an elevated iteration count. " +
                   "If you proceed, the initialization process may " +
                   "require a significant amount of time to complete. " +
                   "Continue?");
            else
                prepareCredentials();
        }
    });
```

```java
button1 = (Button) findViewById(R.id.siphash_help);
button1.setOnClickListener(new View.OnClickListener()
{
    public void onClick(View view)
    {
      if(Settings.this.isFinishing())
          return;

      PopupWindow popupWindow = new PopupWindow(Settings.this);
      TextView textView = new TextView(Settings.this);
      float density = getApplicationContext().getResources().
          getDisplayMetrics().density;

      textView.setBackgroundColor(Color.rgb(232, 234, 246));
      textView.setPaddingRelative
          ((int) (10 * density),
           (int) (10 * density),
           (int) (10 * density),
           (int) (10 * density));
      textView.setText
          ("A Smoke ID is a sequence of hexadecimal characters " +
           "assigned to a specific subscriber " +
           "(public key pair). " +
           "The tokens allow participants to exchange public " +
           "key pairs via the EPKS protocol.");
      textView.setTextSize(16);
      popupWindow.setContentView(textView);
      popupWindow.setOutsideTouchable(true);

      if(Build.VERSION.SDK_INT < Build.VERSION_CODES.M)
      {
          popupWindow.setHeight(450);
          popupWindow.setWidth(700);
      }

      popupWindow.showAsDropDown(view);
    }
});

CheckBox checkBox1 = null;

checkBox1 = (CheckBox) findViewById(R.id.automatic_refresh_listeners);
checkBox1.setOnCheckedChangeListener
    (new CompoundButton.OnCheckedChangeListener()
    {
      @Override
      public void onCheckedChanged
          (CompoundButton buttonView, boolean isChecked)
      {
          if(isChecked)
          {
            m_databaseHelper.writeSetting
                (null, "automatic_listeners_refresh", "true");
            startListenersTimers();
          }
          else
          {
            m_databaseHelper.writeSetting
                (null, "automatic_listeners_refresh", "false");
            stopListenersTimers();
          }
      }
```

```java
        });

    checkBox1 = (CheckBox) findViewById(R.id.automatic_refresh_neighbors);
    checkBox1.setOnCheckedChangeListener
        (new CompoundButton.OnCheckedChangeListener()
        {
          @Override
          public void onCheckedChanged
              (CompoundButton buttonView, boolean isChecked)
          {
              if(isChecked)
              {
                m_databaseHelper.writeSetting
                    (null, "automatic_neighbors_refresh", "true");
                startNeighborsTimers();
              }
              else
              {
                m_databaseHelper.writeSetting
                    (null, "automatic_neighbors_refresh", "false");
                stopNeighborsTimers();
              }
          }
        });

    checkBox1 = (CheckBox) findViewById(R.id.neighbor_details);
    checkBox1.setOnCheckedChangeListener
        (new CompoundButton.OnCheckedChangeListener()
        {
          @Override
          public void onCheckedChanged
              (CompoundButton buttonView, boolean isChecked)
          {
              if(isChecked)
                m_databaseHelper.writeSetting
                    (null, "neighbors_details", "true");
              else
                m_databaseHelper.writeSetting
                    (null, "neighbors_details", "false");

              CheckBox checkBox = (CheckBox) findViewById
                (R.id.automatic_refresh_neighbors);

              if(!checkBox.isChecked())
                populateNeighbors(null);
          }
        });

    checkBox1 = (CheckBox) findViewById(R.id.overwrite);
    checkBox1.setOnCheckedChangeListener
        (new CompoundButton.OnCheckedChangeListener()
        {
          @Override
          public void onCheckedChanged
              (CompoundButton buttonView, boolean isChecked)
          {
              Button button = (Button) findViewById
                (R.id.set_password);

              button.setEnabled(isChecked);
          }
        });
```

```java
    spinner1.setOnItemSelectedListener
        (new OnItemSelectedListener()
        {
          @Override
          public void onItemSelected(AdapterView<?> parent,
                               View view,
                               int position,
                               long id)
          {
              Spinner proxyType = (Spinner)
                findViewById(R.id.proxy_type);
              TextView proxyIpAddress =
                (TextView) findViewById(R.id.proxy_ip_address);
              TextView proxyPort = (TextView) findViewById
                (R.id.proxy_port);

              if(position == 0)
              {
                /*
                ** Events may occur prematurely.
                */

                boolean isAuthenticated = State.getInstance().
                    isAuthenticated();

                proxyIpAddress.setEnabled(isAuthenticated);
                proxyPort.setEnabled(isAuthenticated);
                proxyType.setEnabled(isAuthenticated);
              }
              else
              {
                proxyIpAddress.setEnabled(false);
                proxyIpAddress.setText("");
                proxyPort.setEnabled(false);
                proxyPort.setText("");
                proxyType.setEnabled(false);
              }
          }

          @Override
          public void onNothingSelected(AdapterView<?> parent)
          {
          }
        });
    }

    private void releaseResources()
    {
      Database.releaseMemory();

      if(m_receiverRegistered)
      {
          LocalBroadcastManager.getInstance(getApplicationContext()).
            unregisterReceiver(m_receiver);
          m_receiverRegistered = false;
      }

      stopGeneralTimers();
      stopListenersTimers();
      stopNeighborsTimers();
    }

    private void showAuthenticateActivity()
```

```java
    {
      Intent intent = new Intent(Settings.this, Authenticate.class);

      startActivity(intent);
      finish();
    }

    private void startGeneralTimer()
    {
      if(m_generalScheduler == null)
      {
          m_generalScheduler = Executors.newSingleThreadScheduledExecutor();
          m_generalScheduler.scheduleAtFixedRate(new Runnable()
          {
            @Override
            public void run()
            {
                try
                {
                  m_databaseHelper.cleanDanglingMessages();
                  m_databaseHelper.cleanDanglingOutboundQueued();
                  m_databaseHelper.cleanDanglingParticipants();
                  m_databaseHelper.purgeReleasedMessages(s_cryptography);
                  Settings.this.runOnUiThread(new Runnable()
                  {
                      @Override
                      public void run()
                      {
                        Database.releaseMemory();

                        Runtime runtime = Runtime.getRuntime();
                        long memory = (runtime.totalMemory() -
                                    runtime.freeMemory()) / 1048576L;

                        ((TextView) findViewById
                          (R.id.database_cursors_closed)).setText
                            (m_databaseHelper.cursorsClosed() +
                              " Database Cursors Closed");
                        ((TextView) findViewById
                          (R.id.database_cursors_opened)).setText
                            (m_databaseHelper.cursorsOpened() +
                              " Database Cursors Opened");
                        ((TextView) findViewById(R.id.memory)).setText
                            (memory + " MiB Consumed (JVM)");
                        m_listenersAdapter.notifyDataSetChanged();
                      }
                  });
                }
                catch(Exception exception)
                {
                }
            }
          }, 0L, TIMER_INTERVAL, TimeUnit.MILLISECONDS);
        }
    }

    private void startKernel()
    {
      Kernel.getInstance().populateOzones();
      Kernel.getInstance().populateSipHashIds();
    }

    private void startListenersTimers()
```

```java
{
  if(m_listenersScheduler == null)
  {
      m_listenersScheduler = Executors.newSingleThreadScheduledExecutor();
      m_listenersScheduler.scheduleAtFixedRate(new Runnable()
      {
        @Override
        public void run()
        {
            try
            {
              Settings.this.runOnUiThread
                  (new
                   PopulateListeners(m_databaseHelper.
                          readListeners(s_cryptography,
                                  -1)));
            }
            catch(Exception exception)
            {
            }
        }
      }, 0L, REFRESH_INTERVAL, TimeUnit.MILLISECONDS);
    }
}

private void startNeighborsTimers()
{
  if(m_neighborsScheduler == null)
  {
      m_neighborsScheduler = Executors.newSingleThreadScheduledExecutor();
      m_neighborsScheduler.scheduleAtFixedRate(new Runnable()
      {
        @Override
        public void run()
        {
            try
            {
              Settings.this.runOnUiThread
                  (new
                   PopulateNeighbors(m_databaseHelper.
                          readNeighbors(s_cryptography)));
            }
            catch(Exception exception)
            {
            }
        }
      }, 0L, REFRESH_INTERVAL, TimeUnit.MILLISECONDS);
    }
}

private void stopGeneralTimers()
{
  if(m_generalScheduler == null)
      return;

  try
  {
      m_generalScheduler.shutdown();
  }
  catch(Exception exception)
  {
  }
```

```java
        try
        {
            if(!m_generalScheduler.awaitTermination(60L, TimeUnit.SECONDS))
              m_generalScheduler.shutdownNow();
        }
        catch(Exception exception)
        {
        }
        finally
        {
            m_generalScheduler = null;
        }
    }

    private void stopListenersTimers()
    {
      if(m_listenersScheduler == null)
          return;

      try
      {
          m_listenersScheduler.shutdown();
      }
      catch(Exception exception)
      {
      }

      try
      {
          if(!m_listenersScheduler.awaitTermination(60L, TimeUnit.SECONDS))
            m_listenersScheduler.shutdownNow();
      }
      catch(Exception exception)
      {
      }
      finally
      {
          m_listenersScheduler = null;
      }
    }

    private void stopNeighborsTimers()
    {
      if(m_neighborsScheduler == null)
          return;

      try
      {
          m_neighborsScheduler.shutdown();
      }
      catch(Exception exception)
      {
      }

      try
      {
          if(!m_neighborsScheduler.awaitTermination(60L, TimeUnit.SECONDS))
            m_neighborsScheduler.shutdownNow();
      }
      catch(Exception exception)
      {
      }
      finally
```

```java
    {
        m_neighborsScheduler = null;
    }
}

@Override
protected void onCreate(Bundle savedInstanceState)
{
  super.onCreate(savedInstanceState);
  SmokeStackService.startForegroundTask(getApplicationContext());
    setContentView(R.layout.activity_settings);
  m_listenersLayoutManager = new ListenersLinearLayoutManager
      (Settings.this);
  m_listenersLayoutManager.setOrientation(LinearLayoutManager.VERTICAL);
  m_listenersLayoutManager.setStackFromEnd(false);

  try
  {
      getSupportActionBar().setTitle("SmokeStack | Settings");
  }
  catch(Exception exception)
  {
  }

  m_listenersRecyclerView = (RecyclerView) findViewById
      (R.id.listeners_clients_recycler_view);
  m_listenersRecyclerView.setHasFixedSize(true);

  boolean isAuthenticated = State.getInstance().isAuthenticated();
    Button button1 = null;

  button1 = (Button) findViewById(R.id.add_listener);
  button1.setEnabled(isAuthenticated);
  button1 = (Button) findViewById(R.id.add_neighbor);
    button1.setEnabled(isAuthenticated);
  button1 = (Button) findViewById(R.id.add_participant);
  button1.setEnabled(isAuthenticated);
  button1 = (Button) findViewById(R.id.refresh_listeners);
  button1.setEnabled(isAuthenticated);
    button1 = (Button) findViewById(R.id.refresh_neighbors);
    button1.setEnabled(isAuthenticated);
  button1 = (Button) findViewById(R.id.refresh_ozones);
    button1.setEnabled(isAuthenticated);
  button1 = (Button) findViewById(R.id.refresh_participants);
  button1.setEnabled(isAuthenticated);
  button1 = (Button) findViewById(R.id.reset_listener_fields);
  button1.setEnabled(isAuthenticated);
  button1 = (Button) findViewById(R.id.reset_neighbor_fields);
  button1.setEnabled(isAuthenticated);
  button1 = (Button) findViewById(R.id.reset_participants_fields);
  button1.setEnabled(isAuthenticated);
  button1 = (Button) findViewById(R.id.save_ozone);
  button1.setEnabled(isAuthenticated);
  button1 = (Button) findViewById(R.id.siphash_help);
  button1.setCompoundDrawablesWithIntrinsicBounds
      (R.drawable.help, 0, 0, 0);

    RadioButton radioButton1 = null;

  radioButton1 = (RadioButton) findViewById(R.id.listeners_ipv4);
  radioButton1.setEnabled(isAuthenticated);
  radioButton1 = (RadioButton) findViewById(R.id.listeners_ipv6);
  radioButton1.setEnabled(isAuthenticated);
```

```java
radioButton1 = (RadioButton) findViewById(R.id.neighbors_ipv4);
  radioButton1.setEnabled(isAuthenticated);
  radioButton1 = (RadioButton) findViewById(R.id.neighbors_ipv6);
  radioButton1.setEnabled(isAuthenticated);

Spinner spinner1 = (Spinner) findViewById(R.id.proxy_type);
  String array[] = new String[]
{
    "HTTP", "SOCKS"
};

spinner1.setEnabled(isAuthenticated);

ArrayAdapter<String> arrayAdapter = new ArrayAdapter<>
    (Settings.this, android.R.layout.simple_spinner_item, array);

  spinner1.setAdapter(arrayAdapter);
  spinner1 = (Spinner) findViewById(R.id.neighbors_transport);
  array = new String[]
{
    "TCP", "UDP"
};
  spinner1.setEnabled(isAuthenticated);
  arrayAdapter = new ArrayAdapter<>
    (Settings.this, android.R.layout.simple_spinner_item, array);
  spinner1.setAdapter(arrayAdapter);
array = new String[]
{
    "1000", "2500", "5000", "7500", "10000", "12500",
    "15000", "17500", "20000", "25000", "30000", "35000",
    "40000", "45000", "50000", "55000", "60000", "65000",
    "70000", "75000", "85000", "100000", "150000", "250000",
    "500000", "1000000"
};
arrayAdapter = new ArrayAdapter<>
    (Settings.this, android.R.layout.simple_spinner_item, array);
spinner1 = (Spinner) findViewById(R.id.iteration_count);
spinner1.setAdapter(arrayAdapter);

  RadioGroup radioGroup1 = null;

radioGroup1 = (RadioGroup) findViewById(R.id.listeners_ipv_radio_group);
  radioGroup1.setOnCheckedChangeListener
    (new RadioGroup.OnCheckedChangeListener()
{
    public void onCheckedChanged(RadioGroup group,
                    int checkedId)
    {
      TextView textView1 = (TextView) findViewById
          (R.id.listeners_scope_id);

      if(checkedId == R.id.listeners_ipv4)
      {
          textView1.setEnabled(false);
          textView1.setText("");
          textView1 = (TextView) findViewById(R.id.listeners_port);
          textView1.setNextFocusDownId(R.id.neighbors_ip_address);
      }
      else
      {
          textView1.setEnabled(true);
          textView1 = (TextView) findViewById(R.id.listeners_port);
          textView1.setNextFocusDownId(R.id.listeners_scope_id);
```

```java
                }

            prepareListenerIpAddress();
          }
    });

    radioGroup1 = (RadioGroup) findViewById(R.id.neighbors_ipv_radio_group);
      radioGroup1.setOnCheckedChangeListener
        (new RadioGroup.OnCheckedChangeListener()
    {
        public void onCheckedChanged(RadioGroup group,
                            int checkedId)
        {
          TextView textView1 = (TextView) findViewById
              (R.id.neighbors_scope_id);

          if(checkedId == R.id.neighbors_ipv4)
          {
              textView1.setEnabled(false);
              textView1.setText("");
              textView1 = (TextView) findViewById(R.id.neighbors_port);
              textView1.setNextFocusDownId(R.id.proxy_ip_address);
          }
          else
          {
              textView1.setEnabled(true);
              textView1 = (TextView) findViewById(R.id.neighbors_port);
              textView1.setNextFocusDownId(R.id.neighbors_scope_id);
          }
        }
    });

    /*
    ** Enable widgets.
    */

    CheckBox checkBox1 = (CheckBox) findViewById
        (R.id.accept_without_signatures);

    checkBox1.setEnabled(isAuthenticated);
    checkBox1 = (CheckBox) findViewById(R.id.overwrite);
    checkBox1.setChecked(!isAuthenticated);
    checkBox1.setEnabled(isAuthenticated);
    button1 = (Button) findViewById(R.id.set_password);
    button1.setEnabled(checkBox1.isChecked());
    checkBox1 = (CheckBox) findViewById(R.id.private_server);
    checkBox1.setEnabled(isAuthenticated);

    TextView textView1 = null;

    textView1 = (TextView) findViewById(R.id.about);
    textView1.setText(About.about());
    textView1 = (TextView) findViewById(R.id.listeners_scope_id);
      textView1.setEnabled(false);
    textView1 = (TextView) findViewById(R.id.neighbors_scope_id);
      textView1.setEnabled(false);
      textView1 = (TextView) findViewById(R.id.listeners_port);
      textView1.setEnabled(isAuthenticated);
    textView1.setFilters(new InputFilter[] { s_portFilter });
      textView1.setText("4710");
      textView1 = (TextView) findViewById(R.id.neighbors_port);
    textView1.setNextFocusDownId(R.id.proxy_ip_address);
      textView1.setEnabled(isAuthenticated);
```

```java
    textView1.setFilters(new InputFilter[] { s_portFilter });
      textView1.setText("4710");
      textView1 = (TextView) findViewById(R.id.listeners_ip_address);

    if(isAuthenticated)
        textView1.requestFocus();

    textView1.setEnabled(isAuthenticated);
    textView1 = (TextView) findViewById(R.id.ozone);
    textView1.setEnabled(isAuthenticated);
    textView1 = (TextView) findViewById(R.id.participant_name);
    textView1.setEnabled(isAuthenticated);
    textView1 = (TextView) findViewById(R.id.participant_siphash_id);
    textView1.setEnabled(isAuthenticated);
    textView1.setFilters(new InputFilter[] { new InputFilter.AllCaps(),
                             s_sipHashInputFilter });
    textView1.setInputType(InputType.TYPE_TEXT_FLAG_NO_SUGGESTIONS |
                   InputType.TYPE_TEXT_VARIATION_VISIBLE_PASSWORD);
    textView1 = (TextView) findViewById(R.id.password1);

    if(!isAuthenticated)
        textView1.requestFocus();

    textView1.setText("");
      textView1 = (TextView) findViewById(R.id.password2);
      textView1.setText("");
    textView1 = (TextView) findViewById(R.id.proxy_ip_address);
    textView1.setEnabled(isAuthenticated);
    textView1 = (TextView) findViewById(R.id.proxy_port);
    textView1.setEnabled(isAuthenticated);
    textView1.setFilters(new InputFilter[] { s_portFilter });

    /*
    ** Prepare recycler views.
    */

    m_listenersAdapter = new ListenersAdapter(this);
    m_listenersAdapter.registerAdapterDataObserver
        (new RecyclerView.AdapterDataObserver()
        {
          @Override
          public void onItemRangeInserted
              (int positionStart, int itemCount)
          {
              m_listenersLayoutManager.smoothScrollToPosition
                (m_listenersRecyclerView, null, positionStart);
          }

          @Override
          public void onItemRangeRemoved
              (int positionStart, int itemCount)
          {
              m_listenersLayoutManager.smoothScrollToPosition
                (m_listenersRecyclerView,
                 null,
                 positionStart - itemCount);
          }
        });
    m_listenersRecyclerView.setAdapter(m_listenersAdapter);
    m_listenersRecyclerView.setLayoutManager(m_listenersLayoutManager);
    }


    @Override
```

```java
  protected void onPause()
  {
    super.onPause();
    releaseResources();
  }

  @Override
  protected void onResume()
  {
    super.onResume();

    if(!m_receiverRegistered)
    {
        IntentFilter intentFilter = new IntentFilter();

        intentFilter.addAction
          ("org.purple.smokestack.populate_ozones_participants");
        intentFilter.addAction
          ("org.purple.smokestack.populate_participants");
        LocalBroadcastManager.getInstance(getApplicationContext()).
          registerReceiver(m_receiver, intentFilter);
        m_receiverRegistered = true;
    }

    try
    {
        m_listenersAdapter.notifyDataSetChanged();
        m_listenersLayoutManager.smoothScrollToPosition
          (m_listenersRecyclerView,
           null,
           m_listenersAdapter.getItemCount() - 1);
    }
    catch(Exception exception)
    {
    }
  }

  @Override
  protected void onStart()
  {
    super.onStart();
    m_databaseHelper = Database.getInstance(getApplicationContext());
    m_databaseHelper.deleteSetting("prefer_active_screen");

    /*
    ** Show the Authenticate activity if an account is present.
    */

    if(!State.getInstance().isAuthenticated())
        if(m_databaseHelper.accountPrepared())
        {
          showAuthenticateActivity();
          return;
        }

    if(m_receiver == null)
        m_receiver = new SettingsBroadcastReceiver();

    CheckBox checkBox1 = null;

    checkBox1 = (CheckBox) findViewById(R.id.automatic_refresh_listeners);

    if(m_databaseHelper.
```

```java
          readSetting(null, "automatic_listeners_refresh").equals("true"))
            checkBox1.setChecked(true);
    else
          checkBox1.setChecked(false);

    checkBox1 = (CheckBox) findViewById(R.id.automatic_refresh_neighbors);

    if(m_databaseHelper.
        readSetting(null, "automatic_neighbors_refresh").equals("true"))
          checkBox1.setChecked(true);
    else
          checkBox1.setChecked(false);

    checkBox1 = (CheckBox) findViewById(R.id.neighbor_details);

    if(m_databaseHelper.
        readSetting(null, "neighbors_details").equals("true"))
          checkBox1.setChecked(true);
    else
          checkBox1.setChecked(false);

    Spinner spinner1 = (Spinner) findViewById(R.id.iteration_count);

    try
    {
        @SuppressWarnings("unchecked") ArrayAdapter<String>
          arrayAdapter = (ArrayAdapter<String>) spinner1.getAdapter();
        int index = arrayAdapter.getPosition
          (m_databaseHelper.readSetting(null, "iterationCount"));

        if(index >= 0)
          spinner1.setSelection(index);
        else
          spinner1.setSelection(0);
    }
    catch(Exception exception)
    {
        spinner1.setSelection(0);
    }

    if(!m_receiverRegistered)
    {
        IntentFilter intentFilter = new IntentFilter();

        intentFilter.addAction
          ("org.purple.smokestack.populate_ozones_participants");
        intentFilter.addAction
          ("org.purple.smokestack.populate_participants");
        LocalBroadcastManager.getInstance(getApplicationContext()).
          registerReceiver(m_receiver, intentFilter);
        m_receiverRegistered = true;
    }

    if(m_databaseHelper.
        readSetting(null, "automatic_listeners_refresh").equals("true"))
          startListenersTimers();
    else
        populateListeners(null);

    if(m_databaseHelper.
        readSetting(null, "automatic_neighbors_refresh").equals("true"))
          startNeighborsTimers();
    else
```

```java
        populateNeighbors(null);

    m_databaseHelper.deleteEchoQueue();
    prepareListenerIpAddress();
    prepareListeners();
    startGeneralTimer();

    boolean isAuthenticated = State.getInstance().isAuthenticated();

    if(isAuthenticated)
    {
        checkBox1 = (CheckBox) findViewById
          (R.id.automatic_refresh_listeners);

        if(checkBox1.isChecked())
          startListenersTimers();

        checkBox1 = (CheckBox) findViewById
          (R.id.automatic_refresh_neighbors);

        if(checkBox1.isChecked())
          startNeighborsTimers();

        populateListeners(null);
        populateNeighbors(null);
        populateOzoneAddresses();
        populateParticipants();
        startKernel();
    }
    else
        ((TextView) findViewById(R.id.internal_neighbors)).setText
          ("Internal Neighbors Container Size: 0");
}

@Override
public boolean onContextItemSelected(MenuItem menuItem)
{
    if(menuItem == null)
        return false;

    final int groupId = menuItem.getGroupId();
    final int itemId = menuItem.getItemId();

    /*
    ** Prepare a listener.
    */

    final DialogInterface.OnCancelListener listener =
        new DialogInterface.OnCancelListener()
    {
        public void onCancel(DialogInterface dialog)
        {
          switch(groupId)
            {
            case ContextMenuEnumerator.DELETE_ALL_MESSAGES:
                if(State.getInstance().getString("dialog_accepted").
                   equals("true"))
                  if(m_databaseHelper.removeMessages())
                      populateParticipants();

                break;
            case ContextMenuEnumerator.DELETE_MESSAGES:
                if(State.getInstance().getString("dialog_accepted").
```

```java
                        equals("true"))
                    if(m_databaseHelper.
                        removeMessages(String.valueOf(itemId)))
                    {
                        TableLayout tableLayout = (TableLayout)
                            findViewById(R.id.participants);
                        int count = tableLayout.getChildCount();

                        for(int i = 0; i < count; i++)
                        {
                            TableRow row = (TableRow) tableLayout.
                                getChildAt(i);

                            if(row == null)
                                continue;

                            TextView textView = (TextView)
                                row.getChildAt(2);

                            if(textView == null)
                                continue;

                            if(itemId != textView.getId())
                                continue;

                            textView.setText("0 / 0 / 0");
                            break;
                        }
                    }

            break;
        case ContextMenuEnumerator.DELETE_OZONE:
            if(State.getInstance().getString("dialog_accepted").
                equals("true"))
                if(m_databaseHelper.
                    deleteEntry(String.valueOf(itemId), "ozones"))
                {
                    Kernel.getInstance().populateOzones();
                    populateOzoneAddresses();
                }

            break;
        case ContextMenuEnumerator.DELETE_PARTICIPANT:
            if(State.getInstance().getString("dialog_accepted").
                equals("true"))
                if(m_databaseHelper.
                    deleteOzoneAndSipHashId(String.valueOf(itemId)))
                {
                    Kernel.getInstance().populateOzones();
                    Kernel.getInstance().populateSipHashIds();
                    populateOzoneAddresses();
                    populateParticipants();
                }

            break;
        case ContextMenuEnumerator.NEW_NAME:
            String string = State.getInstance().
                getString("settings_participant_name_input");

            if(m_databaseHelper.
                writeParticipantName(s_cryptography,
                            string,
                            itemId))
```

```java
                    populateParticipants();

                State.getInstance().removeKey
                  ("settings_participant_name_input");
                break;
            case ContextMenuEnumerator.RESET_RETRIEVAL_STATE:
                if(State.getInstance().getString("dialog_accepted").
                  equals("true"))
                  if(m_databaseHelper.
                    resetRetrievalState(s_cryptography,
                                        String.valueOf(itemId)))
                  {
                      MessageTotals messageTotals = m_databaseHelper.
                        readMessageTotals(String.valueOf(itemId));

                      if(messageTotals != null)
                      {
                        TableLayout tableLayout = (TableLayout)
                            findViewById(R.id.participants);
                        int count = tableLayout.getChildCount();

                        for(int i = 0; i < count; i++)
                        {
                            TableRow row = (TableRow) tableLayout.
                              getChildAt(i);

                            if(row == null)
                              continue;

                            TextView textView = (TextView) row.
                              getChildAt(2);

                            if(textView == null)
                              continue;

                            if(itemId != textView.getId())
                              continue;

                            textView.setText
                              (messageTotals.m_outMessages + " / " +
                               messageTotals.m_inMessages + " / " +
                               messageTotals.m_totalMessages);
                            break;
                        }
                      }
                  }

                break;
            }
        }
    };

    /*
    ** Regular expression?
    */

    switch(groupId)
    {
    case ContextMenuEnumerator.DELETE_ALL_MESSAGES:
        Miscellaneous.showPromptDialog
          (Settings.this,
           listener,
           "Are you sure that you wish to delete all messages?");
```

```java
        break;
    case ContextMenuEnumerator.DELETE_LISTENER:
        ArrayList<ListenerElement> arrayList = m_databaseHelper.
          readListeners(s_cryptography, itemId);

        if(m_databaseHelper.
          deleteEntry(String.valueOf(itemId), "listeners"))
        {
          /*
          ** Prepare the kernel's listeners container
          ** if a listener was deleted as the OID
          ** field may represent a recycled value.
          */

          if(arrayList != null && !arrayList.isEmpty())
              if(m_databaseHelper.deleteOzone(s_cryptography,
                                 arrayList.get(0)))
              {
                Kernel.getInstance().populateOzones();
                populateOzoneAddresses();
              }

          TableLayout tableLayout = (TableLayout)
              findViewById(R.id.listeners);
          TableRow row = (TableRow) findViewById(itemId);

          tableLayout.removeView(row);
        }

        break;
    case ContextMenuEnumerator.DELETE_MESSAGES:
        Miscellaneous.showPromptDialog
          (Settings.this,
           listener,
           "Are you sure that you " +
           "wish to delete the messages of participant " +
           menuItem.getTitle().toString().
           replace("Delete Messages (", "").
           replace(")", "") + "?");
        break;
    case ContextMenuEnumerator.DELETE_OZONE:
        Miscellaneous.showPromptDialog
          (Settings.this,
           listener,
           "Are you sure that you " +
           "wish to delete the Ozone " +
           menuItem.getTitle().toString().replace("Delete Ozone (", "").
           replace(")", "") + "?");
        break;
    case ContextMenuEnumerator.DELETE_PARTICIPANT:
        Miscellaneous.showPromptDialog
          (Settings.this,
           listener,
           "Are you sure that you " +
           "wish to delete the participant " +
           menuItem.getTitle().toString().
           replace("Delete Participant (", "").
           replace(")", "") + "? If confirmed, the associated Ozone " +
           "will also be deleted.");
        break;
    case ContextMenuEnumerator.NEW_NAME:
        Miscellaneous.showTextInputDialog
          (Settings.this,
```

```java
                listener,
                "Please provide a new name for " +
                menuItem.getTitle().toString().
                replace("New Name (", "").
                replace(")", "") + ".",
                "Name");
            break;
      case ContextMenuEnumerator.RESET_RETRIEVAL_STATE:
            Miscellaneous.showPromptDialog
              (Settings.this,
               listener,
               "Are you sure that you " +
               "wish to reset the messages retrieval state for " +
               menuItem.getTitle().toString().
               replace("Reset Retrieval State (", "").
               replace(")", "") + "?");
            break;
      case ContextMenuEnumerator.TOGGLE_LISTENER_PRIVACY:
            if(m_databaseHelper.toggleListenerPrivacy(s_cryptography, itemId))
            {
              Kernel.getInstance().toggleListenerPrivacy(itemId);

              CheckBox checkBox = (CheckBox) findViewById
                  (R.id.automatic_refresh_listeners);

              if(!checkBox.isChecked())
                  populateListeners(null);
            }

            break;
      default:
            break;
      }

    return true;
  }


  @Override
  public boolean onCreateOptionsMenu(Menu menu)
  {
      getMenuInflater().inflate(R.menu.settings_menu, menu);
      return true;
  }


  @Override
  public boolean onOptionsItemSelected(MenuItem item)
  {
    if(item != null)
        switch(item.getItemId())
          {
          case R.id.action_exit:
            SmokeStack.exit(Settings.this);
            return true;
          default:
            break;
          }

      return super.onOptionsItemSelected(item);
  }


  @Override
  public boolean onPrepareOptionsMenu(Menu menu)
  {
```

```java
        boolean isAuthenticated = State.getInstance().isAuthenticated();

    if(!m_databaseHelper.accountPrepared())
        /*
        ** The database may have been modified or removed.
        */

        isAuthenticated = true;

    menu.findItem(R.id.action_authenticate).setEnabled(!isAuthenticated);
    return true;
    }

    @Override
    public void onCreateContextMenu(ContextMenu menu,
                                    View v,
                                    ContextMenuInfo menuInfo)
    {
      if(v == null)
          return;

      Object tag = v.getTag();

      if(tag != null)
      {
          super.onCreateContextMenu(menu, v, menuInfo);

          try
          {
            if(v.getParent().getParent() == findViewById(R.id.listeners))
            {
                menu.add(ContextMenuEnumerator.DELETE_LISTENER,
                        v.getId(),
                        0,
                        "Delete Listener (" + tag + ")");
                menu.add(ContextMenuEnumerator.TOGGLE_LISTENER_PRIVACY,
                        v.getId(),
                        0,
                        "Toggle Privacy (" + tag + ")");
            }
            else if(v.getParent().getParent() == findViewById(R.id.ozones))
                menu.add(ContextMenuEnumerator.DELETE_OZONE,
                        v.getId(),
                        0,
                        "Delete Ozone (" + tag + ")");
            else
            {
                menu.add(ContextMenuEnumerator.DELETE_ALL_MESSAGES,
                        v.getId(),
                        0,
                        "Delete All Messages");
                menu.add(ContextMenuEnumerator.DELETE_MESSAGES,
                        v.getId(),
                        0,
                        "Delete Messages (" + tag + ")");
                menu.add(ContextMenuEnumerator.DELETE_PARTICIPANT,
                        v.getId(),
                        0,
                        "Delete Participant (" + tag + ")");
                menu.add(ContextMenuEnumerator.NEW_NAME,
                        v.getId(),
                        0,
                        "New Name (" + tag + ")");
```

```java
                menu.add(ContextMenuEnumerator.RESET_RETRIEVAL_STATE,
                         v.getId(),
                         0,
                         "Reset Retrieval State (" + tag + ")");
            }
        }
        catch(Exception exception)
        {
        }
    }
}

    @Override
    public void onRestoreInstanceState(Bundle savedInstanceState)
    {
      /*
      ** Empty.
      */
    }
}
```

/* SipHash.java

```java
https://raw.githubusercontent.com/textbrowser/smokestack/master/SmokeStack/app
/src/main/java/org/purple/smokestack/SipHash.java
** Copyright (c) Alexis Megas.
** All rights reserved.
**
** Redistribution and use in source and binary forms, with or without
** modification, are permitted provided that the following conditions
** are met:
** 1. Redistributions of source code must retain the above copyright
**    notice, this list of conditions and the following disclaimer.
** 2. Redistributions in binary form must reproduce the above copyright
**    notice, this list of conditions and the following disclaimer in the
**    documentation and/or other materials provided with the distribution.
** 3. The name of the author may not be used to endorse or promote products
**    derived from SmokeStack without specific prior written permission.
**
** SMOKESTACK IS PROVIDED BY THE AUTHOR ``AS IS'' AND ANY EXPRESS OR
** IMPLIED WARRANTIES, INCLUDING, BUT NOT LIMITED TO, THE IMPLIED WARRANTIES
** OF MERCHANTABILITY AND FITNESS FOR A PARTICULAR PURPOSE ARE DISCLAIMED.
** IN NO EVENT SHALL THE AUTHOR BE LIABLE FOR ANY DIRECT, INDIRECT,
** INCIDENTAL, SPECIAL, EXEMPLARY, OR CONSEQUENTIAL DAMAGES (INCLUDING, BUT
** NOT LIMITED TO, PROCUREMENT OF SUBSTITUTE GOODS OR SERVICES; LOSS OF USE,
** DATA, OR PROFITS; OR BUSINESS INTERRUPTION) HOWEVER CAUSED AND ON ANY
** THEORY OF LIABILITY, WHETHER IN CONTRACT, STRICT LIABILITY, OR TORT
** (INCLUDING NEGLIGENCE OR OTHERWISE) ARISING IN ANY WAY OUT OF THE USE OF
** SMOKESTACK, EVEN IF ADVISED OF THE POSSIBILITY OF SUCH DAMAGE.
*/

/*
** Implementation of https://131002.net/siphash.
*/

package org.purple.smokestack;

public class SipHash
{
    private final static int C_ROUNDS[] = {2, 4};
    private final static int D_ROUNDS[] = {4, 8};
```

```java
    private final static long C0 = 0x736f6d6570736575L;
    private final static long C1 = 0x646f72616e646f6dL;
    private final static long C2 = 0x6c7967656e657261L;
    private final static long C3 = 0x7465646279746573L;
    private byte m_key[] = null;
    private int m_c_rounds_index = 1;
    private int m_d_rounds_index = 1;
    private long m_v0 = 0L;
    private long m_v1 = 0L;
    private long m_v2 = 0L;
    private long m_v3 = 0L;
    public final static int KEY_LENGTH = 16; // Bytes.

    private long byteArrayToLong(byte bytes[], int offset)
    {
      if(bytes == null || (bytes.length - offset) < Miscellaneous.LONG_BYTES)
          return 0L;

      long value = 0L;

      value |= (((long) bytes[0 + offset]) & 0xffL) <<
          (Miscellaneous.LONG_LONG_BYTES * 0L);
      value |= (((long) bytes[1 + offset]) & 0xffL) <<
          (Miscellaneous.LONG_LONG_BYTES * 1L);
      value |= (((long) bytes[2 + offset]) & 0xffL) <<
          (Miscellaneous.LONG_LONG_BYTES * 2L);
      value |= (((long) bytes[3 + offset]) & 0xffL) <<
          (Miscellaneous.LONG_LONG_BYTES * 3L);
      value |= (((long) bytes[4 + offset]) & 0xffL) <<
          (Miscellaneous.LONG_LONG_BYTES * 4L);
      value |= (((long) bytes[5 + offset]) & 0xffL) <<
          (Miscellaneous.LONG_LONG_BYTES * 5L);
      value |= (((long) bytes[6 + offset]) & 0xffL) <<
          (Miscellaneous.LONG_LONG_BYTES * 6L);
      value |= (((long) bytes[7 + offset]) & 0xffL) <<
          (Miscellaneous.LONG_LONG_BYTES * 7L);
      return value;
    }

    private long rotl(long x, long b)
    {
      return (x << b) | (x >>> (64L - b));
    }

    private void round()
    {
      m_v0 += m_v1;
      m_v1 = rotl(m_v1, 13L);
      m_v1 ^= m_v0;
      m_v0 = rotl(m_v0, 32L);
      m_v2 += m_v3;
      m_v3 = rotl(m_v3, 16L);
      m_v3 ^= m_v2;
      m_v2 += m_v1;
      m_v1 = rotl(m_v1, 17L);
      m_v1 ^= m_v2;
      m_v2 = rotl(m_v2, 32L);
      m_v0 += m_v3;
      m_v3 = rotl(m_v3, 21L);
      m_v3 ^= m_v0;
    }

    public SipHash()
```

```java
    {
    }

    public SipHash(byte key[])
    {
      if(key == null || key.length != KEY_LENGTH)
          return;

      m_key = key;
    }

    public SipHash(byte key[], int c_rounds_index, int d_rounds_index)
    {
      if(key == null || key.length != KEY_LENGTH)
          return;

      if(c_rounds_index >= 0 && c_rounds_index < C_ROUNDS.length)
          m_c_rounds_index = c_rounds_index;

      if(d_rounds_index >= 0 && d_rounds_index < D_ROUNDS.length)
          m_d_rounds_index = d_rounds_index;

      m_key = key;
    }

    public long[] hmac(byte data[], int outputLength)
    {
      return hmac(data, m_key, outputLength);
    }

    @SuppressWarnings("fallthrough")
    public synchronized long[] hmac(byte data[], byte key[], int outputLength)
    {
      if(data == null || key == null || key.length != KEY_LENGTH)
          return new long[] {0L, 0L};

      /*
      ** Initialization
      */

      long k0 = byteArrayToLong(key, 0);
      long k1 = byteArrayToLong(key, Miscellaneous.LONG_BYTES);

      m_v0 = k0 ^ C0;
      m_v1 = k1 ^ C1;
      m_v2 = k0 ^ C2;
      m_v3 = k1 ^ C3;

      if(outputLength == 16)
          m_v1 ^= 0xeeL;

      /*
      ** Compression
      */

      int length1 = data.length / 8;
      int length2 = C_ROUNDS[m_c_rounds_index];

      for(int i = 0; i < length1; i++)
      {
          long m = byteArrayToLong(data, 8 * i);

          m_v3 ^= m;
```

```java
        switch(length2)
        {
        case 2:
          round();
          round();
          break;
        case 4:
          round();
          round();
          round();
          round();
          break;
        default:
          break;
        }

        m_v0 ^= m;
        m = 0L;
    }

    int offset = (data.length / 8) * 8;
    long b = ((long) data.length) << 56L;

    switch(data.length % 8)
    {
    case 7:
        b |= ((long) data[offset + 6]) << 48L;
    case 6:
        b |= ((long) data[offset + 5]) << 40L;
    case 5:
        b |= ((long) data[offset + 4]) << 32L;
    case 4:
        b |= ((long) data[offset + 3]) << 24L;
    case 3:
        b |= ((long) data[offset + 2]) << 16L;
    case 2:
        b |= ((long) data[offset + 1]) << 8L;
    case 1:
        b |= ((long) data[offset]);
        break;
    case 0:
        break;
    default:
        break;
    }

    m_v3 ^= b;

    switch(C_ROUNDS[m_c_rounds_index])
    {
    case 2:
        round();
        round();
        break;
    case 4:
        round();
        round();
        round();
        round();
        break;
    default:
        break;
```

```java
    }

m_v0 ^= b;

/*
** Finalization
*/

if(outputLength == 16)
    m_v2 ^= 0xeeL;
else
    m_v2 ^= 0xffL;

switch(D_ROUNDS[m_d_rounds_index])
{
case 4:
    round();
    round();
    round();
    round();
    break;
case 8:
    round();
    round();
    round();
    round();
    round();
    round();
    round();
    round();
    break;
default:
    break;
}

long output[] = new long[] {m_v0 ^ m_v1 ^ m_v2 ^ m_v3, 0};

if(outputLength == 8)
{
    k0 = k1 = m_v0 = m_v1 = m_v2 = m_v3 = 0L;
    return output;
}

m_v1 ^= 0xddL;

switch(D_ROUNDS[m_d_rounds_index])
{
case 4:
    round();
    round();
    round();
    round();
    break;
case 8:
    round();
    round();
    round();
    round();
    round();
    round();
    round();
    round();
    break;
```

```java
        default:
            break;
        }

    output[1] = m_v0 ^ m_v1 ^ m_v2 ^ m_v3;
    k0 = k1 = m_v0 = m_v1 = m_v2 = m_v3 = 0L;
    return output;
    }

    public static boolean test1()
    {
      /*
      ** Please read the Test Values section of
      ** https://131002.net/siphash/siphash.pdf.
      */

      SipHash s = new SipHash
          (new byte[] {(byte) 0x00, (byte) 0x01, (byte) 0x02, (byte) 0x03,
                  (byte) 0x04, (byte) 0x05, (byte) 0x06, (byte) 0x07,
                  (byte) 0x08, (byte) 0x09, (byte) 0x0a, (byte) 0x0b,
                  (byte) 0x0c, (byte) 0x0d, (byte) 0x0e, (byte) 0x0f},
            0, 0);
      long result = Miscellaneous.byteArrayToLong
          (new byte[] {(byte) 0xa1, (byte) 0x29, (byte) 0xca, (byte) 0x61,
                  (byte) 0x49, (byte) 0xbe, (byte) 0x45, (byte) 0xe5});
      long value[] = s.hmac
          (new byte[] {(byte) 0x00, (byte) 0x01, (byte) 0x02, (byte) 0x03,
                  (byte) 0x04, (byte) 0x05, (byte) 0x06, (byte) 0x07,
                  (byte) 0x08, (byte) 0x09, (byte) 0x0a, (byte) 0x0b,
                  (byte) 0x0c, (byte) 0x0d, (byte) 0x0e},
            Cryptography.SIPHASH_OUTPUT_LENGTH / 2);

      return result == value[0];
    }
}




```

/* SipHashIdElement.java

```java
package org.purple.smokestack;

public class SipHashIdElement
{
    public String m_name = "";
    public String m_sipHashId = "";
    public String m_timestamp = "";
    public boolean m_acceptWithoutSignatures = false;
    public boolean m_epksCompleted = false;
    public boolean m_keysSigned = false;
    public byte m_chatEncryptionKeyDigest[] = null;
    public byte m_stream[] = null;
    public int m_oid = -1;
    public long m_inMessages = 0L;
    public long m_outMessages = 0L;
    public long m_totalMessages = 0L;

    public SipHashIdElement()
    {
    }
}
```

/* SmokeStack.java

https://raw.githubusercontent.com/textbrowser/smokestack/master/SmokeStack/app
/src/main/java/org/purple/smokestack/SmokeStack.java


```java
package org.purple.smokestack;

import android.app.Activity;
import android.app.Application;
```

```java
import android.content.Context;
import android.os.Build;
import android.os.Process;

public class SmokeStack extends Application
{
    private static SmokeStack s_instance = null;

    public static synchronized SmokeStack getApplication()
    {
      /*
      ** An unpleasant and necessary solution.
      */

      return s_instance;
    }

    public static synchronized void exit(Context context)
    {
      SmokeStackService.stopForegroundTask(getApplication());

      if(Build.VERSION.SDK_INT >= Build.VERSION_CODES.LOLLIPOP)
          if(context instanceof Activity)
             ((Activity) context).finishAndRemoveTask();

      Process.killProcess(Process.myPid());
    }

    @Override
    public void onCreate()
    {
      super.onCreate();
      s_instance = this;
    }

    @Override
    public void onLowMemory()
    {
      super.onLowMemory();

      try
      {
          Kernel.getInstance().clearNeighborQueues();
      }
      catch(Exception exception)
      {
      }
    }
}
```

/* SmokeStackService.java

```java
/* SmokeStackService.java
https://raw.githubusercontent.com/textbrowser/smokestack/master/SmokeStack/app
/src/main/java/org/purple/smokestack/SmokeStackService.java
** Copyright (c) Alexis Megas.
** All rights reserved.
**
** Redistribution and use in source and binary forms, with or without
** modification, are permitted provided that the following conditions
** are met:
** 1. Redistributions of source code must retain the above copyright
**    notice, this list of conditions and the following disclaimer.
** 2. Redistributions in binary form must reproduce the above copyright
**    notice, this list of conditions and the following disclaimer in the
**    documentation and/or other materials provided with the distribution.
** 3. The name of the author may not be used to endorse or promote products
**    derived from Smoke without specific prior written permission.
**
** SMOKESTACK IS PROVIDED BY THE AUTHOR ``AS IS'' AND ANY EXPRESS OR
** IMPLIED WARRANTIES, INCLUDING, BUT NOT LIMITED TO, THE IMPLIED WARRANTIES
** OF MERCHANTABILITY AND FITNESS FOR A PARTICULAR PURPOSE ARE DISCLAIMED.
** IN NO EVENT SHALL THE AUTHOR BE LIABLE FOR ANY DIRECT, INDIRECT,
** INCIDENTAL, SPECIAL, EXEMPLARY, OR CONSEQUENTIAL DAMAGES (INCLUDING, BUT
** NOT LIMITED TO, PROCUREMENT OF SUBSTITUTE GOODS OR SERVICES; LOSS OF USE,
** DATA, OR PROFITS; OR BUSINESS INTERRUPTION) HOWEVER CAUSED AND ON ANY
** THEORY OF LIABILITY, WHETHER IN CONTRACT, STRICT LIABILITY, OR TORT
** (INCLUDING NEGLIGENCE OR OTHERWISE) ARISING IN ANY WAY OUT OF THE USE OF
** SMOKESTACK, EVEN IF ADVISED OF THE POSSIBILITY OF SUCH DAMAGE.
*/

package org.purple.smokestack;

import android.app.Notification;
import android.app.PendingIntent;
import android.app.Service;
import android.content.Context;
import android.content.Intent;
import android.graphics.drawable.Icon;
import android.os.IBinder;

public class SmokeStackService extends Service
{
    private boolean m_isRunning = false;
    private final static int NOTIFICATION_ID = 796325177;

    private void prepareNotification()
    {
      if(m_isRunning)
          return;
      else
          m_isRunning = true;

      Intent notificationIntent = new Intent(this, Settings.class);
      Notification.Builder builder = new Notification.Builder(this);
      PendingIntent pendingIntent = PendingIntent.getActivity
          (this, 0, notificationIntent, 0);

      builder.setContentIntent(pendingIntent);
      builder.setContentText("SmokeStack");
      builder.setContentTitle("SmokeStack");
      builder.setSmallIcon(R.drawable.smokestack);
      builder.setTicker("SmokeStack");
```

```java
    /*
    ** Stop!
    */

    Intent stopIntent = new Intent(this, SmokeStackService.class);

      stopIntent.setAction("stop");

    PendingIntent pendingStopIntent = PendingIntent.getService
        (this, 0, stopIntent, 0);

    builder.addAction
        (new Notification.Action.
          Builder(Icon.createWithResource(this, R.drawable.smokestack),
              "Stop SmokeStack Foreground Service",
              pendingStopIntent).build());
    startForeground(NOTIFICATION_ID, builder.build());
  }

  private void start()
  {
    prepareNotification();
  }

  private void stop()
  {
    m_isRunning = false;
    stopForeground(true);
    stopSelf();
  }

  @Override
  public IBinder onBind(Intent intent)
  {
    return null;
  }

  @Override
  public int onStartCommand(Intent intent, int flags, int startId)
  {
    if(intent != null && intent.getAction() != null)
        switch(intent.getAction())
        {
        case "start":
          start();
          break;
        case "stop":
          stop();
          break;
        default:
          break;
        }

    return START_STICKY;
  }

  public static void startForegroundTask(Context context)
  {
    if(context == null)
        return;

    Intent intent = new Intent(context, SmokeStackService.class);
```

```java
    intent.setAction("start");
    context.startService(intent);
  }

  public static void stopForegroundTask(Context context)
  {
    if(context == null)
        return;

    Intent intent = new Intent(context, SmokeStackService.class);

    intent.setAction("stop");
    context.startService(intent);
  }

  @Override
  public void onCreate()
  {
    super.onCreate();
    start();
  }

  @Override
  public void onDestroy()
  {
    m_isRunning = false;
    super.onDestroy();
  }
}
```

/* State.java

```
https://raw.githubusercontent.com/textbrowser/smokestack/master/SmokeStack/app
/src/main/java/org/purple/smokestack/State.java
** Copyright (c) Alexis Megas.
** All rights reserved.
**
** Redistribution and use in source and binary forms, with or without
** modification, are permitted provided that the following conditions
** are met:
** 1. Redistributions of source code must retain the above copyright
**    notice, this list of conditions and the following disclaimer.
** 2. Redistributions in binary form must reproduce the above copyright
**    notice, this list of conditions and the following disclaimer in the
**    documentation and/or other materials provided with the distribution.
** 3. The name of the author may not be used to endorse or promote products
**    derived from SmokeStack without specific prior written permission.
**
** SMOKESTACK IS PROVIDED BY THE AUTHOR ``AS IS'' AND ANY EXPRESS OR
** IMPLIED WARRANTIES, INCLUDING, BUT NOT LIMITED TO, THE IMPLIED WARRANTIES
** OF MERCHANTABILITY AND FITNESS FOR A PARTICULAR PURPOSE ARE DISCLAIMED.
** IN NO EVENT SHALL THE AUTHOR BE LIABLE FOR ANY DIRECT, INDIRECT,
** INCIDENTAL, SPECIAL, EXEMPLARY, OR CONSEQUENTIAL DAMAGES (INCLUDING, BUT
** NOT LIMITED TO, PROCUREMENT OF SUBSTITUTE GOODS OR SERVICES; LOSS OF USE,
** DATA, OR PROFITS; OR BUSINESS INTERRUPTION) HOWEVER CAUSED AND ON ANY
** THEORY OF LIABILITY, WHETHER IN CONTRACT, STRICT LIABILITY, OR TORT
** (INCLUDING NEGLIGENCE OR OTHERWISE) ARISING IN ANY WAY OUT OF THE USE OF
** SMOKESTACK, EVEN IF ADVISED OF THE POSSIBILITY OF SUCH DAMAGE.
*/

package org.purple.smokestack;
```

```java
import android.os.Bundle;
import java.util.concurrent.locks.ReentrantReadWriteLock;

public class State
{
    private Bundle m_bundle = null;
    private final ReentrantReadWriteLock m_bundleMutex =
      new ReentrantReadWriteLock();
    private static State s_instance = null;

    private State()
    {
      m_bundle = new Bundle();
      setAuthenticated(false);
    }

    public static synchronized State getInstance()
    {
      if(s_instance == null)
          s_instance = new State();

      return s_instance;
    }

    public CharSequence getCharSequence(String key)
    {
      m_bundleMutex.readLock().lock();

      try
      {
          return m_bundle.getCharSequence(key, "");
      }
      finally
      {
          m_bundleMutex.readLock().unlock();
      }
    }

    public String getString(String key)
    {
      m_bundleMutex.readLock().lock();

      try
      {
          return m_bundle.getString(key, "");
      }
      finally
      {
          m_bundleMutex.readLock().unlock();
      }
    }

    public boolean isAuthenticated()
    {
      m_bundleMutex.readLock().lock();

      try
      {
          return m_bundle.getChar("is_authenticated", '0') == '1';
      }
      finally
      {
```

```java
        m_bundleMutex.readLock().unlock();
    }
  }

  public void removeKey(String key)
  {
    m_bundleMutex.writeLock().lock();

    try
    {
        m_bundle.remove(key);
    }
    finally
    {
        m_bundleMutex.writeLock().unlock();
    }
  }

  public void reset()
  {
    m_bundleMutex.writeLock().lock();

    try
    {
        m_bundle.clear();
    }
    finally
    {
        m_bundleMutex.writeLock().unlock();
    }
  }

  public void setAuthenticated(boolean state)
  {
    m_bundleMutex.writeLock().lock();

    try
    {
        m_bundle.putChar("is_authenticated", state ? '1' : '0');
    }
    finally
    {
        m_bundleMutex.writeLock().unlock();
    }
  }

  public void setString(String key, String value)
  {
    m_bundleMutex.writeLock().lock();

    try
    {
        m_bundle.putString(key, value);
    }
    finally
    {
        m_bundleMutex.writeLock().unlock();
    }
  }

  public void writeCharSequence(String key, CharSequence text)
  {
    m_bundleMutex.writeLock().lock();
```

```java
        try
        {
            m_bundle.putCharSequence(key, text);
        }
        finally
        {
            m_bundleMutex.writeLock().unlock();
        }
    }
}
```

/* TcpListener.java


```java
package org.purple.smokestack;

import android.content.Context;
import android.net.ConnectivityManager;
import android.net.NetworkInfo;
import android.os.Build;
import java.io.ByteArrayInputStream;
import java.math.BigInteger;
import java.net.InetAddress;
import java.net.InetSocketAddress;
import java.security.KeyPair;
import java.security.KeyStore;
import java.security.Security;
import java.security.cert.CertificateFactory;
import java.security.cert.X509Certificate;
import java.util.ArrayList;
import java.util.Date;
import java.util.Random;
import java.util.concurrent.Executors;
```

```java
import java.util.concurrent.ScheduledExecutorService;
import java.util.concurrent.TimeUnit;
import java.util.concurrent.atomic.AtomicBoolean;
import java.util.concurrent.atomic.AtomicInteger;
import java.util.concurrent.atomic.AtomicLong;
import java.util.concurrent.locks.ReentrantReadWriteLock;
import javax.net.ssl.KeyManagerFactory;
import javax.net.ssl.SSLContext;
import javax.net.ssl.SSLServerSocket;
import javax.net.ssl.SSLSocket;
import org.bouncycastle.asn1.x500.X500Name;
import org.bouncycastle.asn1.x500.X500NameBuilder;
import org.bouncycastle.asn1.x500.style.BCStyle;
import org.bouncycastle.asn1.x509.SubjectPublicKeyInfo;
import org.bouncycastle.cert.X509CertificateHolder;
import org.bouncycastle.cert.X509v3CertificateBuilder;
import org.bouncycastle.cert.jcajce.JcaX509CertificateConverter;
import org.bouncycastle.jce.provider.BouncyCastleProvider;
import org.bouncycastle.operator.ContentSigner;
import org.bouncycastle.operator.jcajce.JcaContentSignerBuilder;

public class TcpListener
{
    static
    {
      Security.addProvider(new BouncyCastleProvider());
    }

    private AtomicBoolean m_isPrivateServer = null;
    private AtomicInteger m_oid;
    private KeyStore m_keyStore = null;
    private SSLServerSocket m_socket = null;
    private final ScheduledExecutorService m_acceptScheduler =
      Executors.newSingleThreadScheduledExecutor();
    private final ScheduledExecutorService m_scheduler =
      Executors.newSingleThreadScheduledExecutor();
    private String m_ipAddress = "";
    private String m_ipPort = "";
    private final ArrayList<TcpNeighbor> m_neighbors = new ArrayList<> ();
    private final AtomicBoolean m_listen = new AtomicBoolean(false);
    private final AtomicInteger m_neighborCounter = new AtomicInteger(0);
    private final AtomicLong m_startTime = new AtomicLong(System.nanoTime());
    private final Cryptography m_cryptography = Cryptography.getInstance();
    private final Database m_databaseHelper = Database.getInstance();
    private final Object m_socketMutex = new Object();
    private final ReentrantReadWriteLock m_neighborsMutex =
      new ReentrantReadWriteLock();
    private final StringBuilder m_error = new StringBuilder();
    private final static int RSA_KEY_SIZE = 3072;
    private final static int SO_TIMEOUT = 5000; // 5 Seconds
    private final static long ACCEPT_INTERVAL = 100L; // Milliseconds
    private final static long TIMER_INTERVAL = 2500L; // 2.5 Seconds

    public TcpListener(String ipAddress,
                       String ipPort,
                       String scopeId,
                       String version,
                       boolean isPrivateServer,
                       byte certificate[],
                       byte privateKey[],
                       byte publicKey[],
                       int oid)
    {
```

```java
        m_oid = new AtomicInteger(oid);
        prepareCertificate(certificate, privateKey, publicKey);
        m_ipAddress = ipAddress;
        m_ipPort = ipPort;
        m_isPrivateServer = new AtomicBoolean(isPrivateServer);

        /*
        ** Launch the schedulers.
        */

        m_acceptScheduler.scheduleAtFixedRate(new Runnable()
        {
            @Override
            public void run()
            {
              try
              {
                  saveStatistics();
              }
              catch(Exception exception)
              {
              }

              SSLSocket sslSocket = null;

              try
              {
                  if(!m_listen.get())
                    return;

                  synchronized(m_socketMutex)
                  {
                    if(m_socket == null)
                        return;

                    sslSocket = (SSLSocket) m_socket.accept();
                  }

                  if(sslSocket == null)
                    return;

                  TcpNeighbor neighbor = new TcpNeighbor
                    (sslSocket,
                     m_isPrivateServer.get(),
                     -m_neighborCounter.incrementAndGet());

                  m_neighborsMutex.writeLock().lock();

                  try
                  {
                    m_neighbors.add(neighbor);
                  }
                  catch(Exception exception)
                  {
                    m_neighbors.remove(neighbor);
                    neighbor.abort();
                    neighbor = null;
                  }
                  finally
                  {
                    m_neighborsMutex.writeLock().unlock();
                  }
              }
```

```java
        catch(Exception exception1)
        {
            try
            {
              if(sslSocket != null)
                  sslSocket.close();
            }
            catch(Exception exception2)
            {
            }
        }
    }
}, 0L, ACCEPT_INTERVAL, TimeUnit.MILLISECONDS);
m_scheduler.scheduleAtFixedRate(new Runnable()
{
    @Override
    public void run()
    {
      try
      {
          String statusControl = m_databaseHelper.
            readListenerNeighborStatusControl
            (m_cryptography, "listeners", m_oid.get());

          switch(statusControl)
          {
          case "disconnect":
            disconnect();
            break;
          case "listen":
            if(isNetworkConnected())
                listen();
            else
                disconnect();

            break;
          default:
            /*
            ** Abort!
            */

            disconnect();
            return;
          }

          m_neighborsMutex.writeLock().lock();

          try
          {
            for(int i = m_neighbors.size() - 1; i >= 0; i--)
            {
                TcpNeighbor neighbor = m_neighbors.get(i);

                if(neighbor == null)
                  m_neighbors.remove(i);
                else if(!neighbor.connected())
                {
                  m_neighbors.remove(i);
                  neighbor.abort();
                  neighbor = null;
                }
            }
          }
```

```java
                catch(Exception exception)
                {
                }
                finally
                {
                 m_neighborsMutex.writeLock().unlock();
                }

                saveStatistics();
            }
            catch(Exception exception)
            {
            }
         }
    }, 0L, TIMER_INTERVAL, TimeUnit.MILLISECONDS);
    }

    protected boolean isNetworkConnected()
    {
      try
      {
          ConnectivityManager connectivityManager = (ConnectivityManager)
            SmokeStack.getApplication().getApplicationContext().
            getSystemService(Context.CONNECTIVITY_SERVICE);
          NetworkInfo networkInfo = connectivityManager.
            getActiveNetworkInfo();

          return networkInfo.getState() ==
            android.net.NetworkInfo.State.CONNECTED;
      }
      catch(Exception exception)
      {
      }

      return false;
    }

    private boolean listening()
    {
      synchronized(m_socketMutex)
      {
          try
          {
            return m_socket != null && m_socket.isBound();
          }
          catch(Exception exception)
          {
          }
      }

      return false;
    }

    private void prepareCertificate(byte certificateBytes[],
                        byte privateKey[],
                        byte publicKey[])
    {
      if(m_keyStore != null)
          return;

      KeyPair keyPair = null;

      try
```

```java
{
    if(certificateBytes == null ||
       certificateBytes.length == 0 ||
       privateKey == null ||
       privateKey.length == 0 ||
       publicKey == null ||
       publicKey.length == 0)
      keyPair = Cryptography.generatePrivatePublicKeyPair
          ("RSA", RSA_KEY_SIZE);
    else
    {
      keyPair = Cryptography.generatePrivatePublicKeyPair
          ("RSA", privateKey, publicKey);

      if(keyPair != null)
      {
          ByteArrayInputStream byteArrayInputStream = null;

          try
          {
            byteArrayInputStream = new
                ByteArrayInputStream(certificateBytes);

            CertificateFactory certificateFactory =
                CertificateFactory.getInstance("X.509");
            X509Certificate certificate = (X509Certificate)
                certificateFactory.generateCertificate
                (byteArrayInputStream);

            m_keyStore = KeyStore.getInstance
                (KeyStore.getDefaultType());
            m_keyStore.load(null, null);
            m_keyStore.deleteEntry(m_ipAddress);
            m_keyStore.setKeyEntry
                (m_ipAddress,
                 keyPair.getPrivate(),
                 null,
                 new X509Certificate[] {certificate});
            return;
          }
          catch(Exception exception)
          {
            setError("An error (" +
                  exception.getMessage() +
                  ") occurred while preparing the key pair.");
          }
          finally
          {
            if(byteArrayInputStream != null)
                byteArrayInputStream.close();
          }
        }
      }
    }
    catch(Exception exception)
    {
        setError("An error (" +
              exception.getMessage() +
              ") occurred while preparing the key pair.");
        return;
    }

    try
```

```java
        {
            Date endDate = new Date
                (System.currentTimeMillis() + 24L * 60L * 60L * 365L * 1000L);
            Date startDate = new Date
                (System.currentTimeMillis() - 24L * 60L * 60L * 1000L);
            X500NameBuilder nameBuilder = new X500NameBuilder(BCStyle.INSTANCE);

            /*
            ** Prepare self-signing.
            */

            ContentSigner contentSigner = null;
            Random random = new Random();
            SubjectPublicKeyInfo subjectPublicKeyInfo = SubjectPublicKeyInfo.
                getInstance(keyPair.getPublic().getEncoded());
            X500Name name = nameBuilder.build();
            X509v3CertificateBuilder v3CertificateBuilder =
                new X509v3CertificateBuilder
                (name,
                 BigInteger.valueOf(random.nextLong()),
                 startDate,
                 endDate,
                 name,
                 subjectPublicKeyInfo);

            contentSigner = new JcaContentSignerBuilder
                ("SHA512WithRSAEncryption").setProvider("BC").build
                (keyPair.getPrivate());

            X509Certificate certificate = null;
            X509CertificateHolder certificateHolder = v3CertificateBuilder.
                build(contentSigner);

            certificate = new JcaX509CertificateConverter().setProvider("BC").
                getCertificate(certificateHolder);
            m_keyStore = KeyStore.getInstance(KeyStore.getDefaultType());
            m_keyStore.load(null, null);
            m_keyStore.deleteEntry(m_ipAddress);
            m_keyStore.setKeyEntry(m_ipAddress,
                                   keyPair.getPrivate(),
                                   null,
                                   new X509Certificate[] {certificate});
            m_databaseHelper.writeListenerCertificateDetails
                (m_cryptography,
                 certificate.getEncoded(),
                 keyPair.getPrivate().getEncoded(),
                 keyPair.getPublic().getEncoded(),
                 m_oid.get());
        }
    catch(Exception exception)
    {
        m_keyStore = null;
        setError("An error (" + exception.getMessage() +
                ") occurred while preparing the key store.");
    }
    }

    private void saveStatistics()
    {
      String error = "";
      String peersCount = "";
      long uptime = System.nanoTime() - m_startTime.get();
```

```java
    synchronized(m_error)
    {
        error = m_error.toString();
    }

  m_neighborsMutex.readLock().lock();

  try
  {
      peersCount = String.valueOf(m_neighbors.size());
  }
  finally
  {
      m_neighborsMutex.readLock().unlock();
  }

  m_databaseHelper.saveListenerInformation
      (m_cryptography,
       error,
       peersCount,
       listening() ? "listening" : "disconnected",
       String.valueOf(uptime),
       String.valueOf(m_oid.get()));
}

private void setError(String error)
{
  synchronized(m_error)
  {
      m_error.delete(0, m_error.length());
      m_error.trimToSize();
      m_error.append(error);
  }
}

public ArrayList<String> clientsAddresses()
{
  ArrayList<String> arrayList = new ArrayList<> ();

  m_neighborsMutex.readLock().lock();

  try
  {
      int size = m_neighbors.size();

      for(int i = 0; i < size; i++)
        if(m_neighbors.get(i) != null)
            arrayList.add(m_neighbors.get(i).address());
  }
  catch(Exception exception)
  {
  }
  finally
  {
      m_neighborsMutex.readLock().unlock();
  }

  return arrayList;
}

public int clientsCount()
{
  m_neighborsMutex.readLock().lock();
```

```java
        try
        {
            return m_neighbors.size();
        }
        catch(Exception exception)
        {
        }
        finally
        {
            m_neighborsMutex.readLock().unlock();
        }

        return 0;
    }

    public int oid()
    {
      return m_oid.get();
    }

    public void abort()
    {
      disconnect();

      synchronized(m_acceptScheduler)
      {
          try
          {
            m_acceptScheduler.shutdown();
          }
          catch(Exception exception)
          {
          }

          try
          {
            if(!m_acceptScheduler.awaitTermination(60L, TimeUnit.SECONDS))
                m_acceptScheduler.shutdownNow();
          }
          catch(Exception exception)
          {
          }
      }

      synchronized(m_scheduler)
      {
          try
          {
            m_scheduler.shutdown();
          }
          catch(Exception exception)
          {
          }

          try
          {
            if(!m_scheduler.awaitTermination(60L, TimeUnit.SECONDS))
                m_scheduler.shutdownNow();
          }
          catch(Exception exception)
          {
          }
```

```java
        }
    }

    public void disconnect()
    {
      m_listen.set(false);

      synchronized(m_socketMutex)
      {
          try
          {
            if(m_socket != null)
                m_socket.close();
          }
          catch(Exception exception)
          {
          }
          finally
          {
            m_socket = null;
          }
      }

      m_neighborsMutex.writeLock().lock();

      try
      {
          for(int i = m_neighbors.size() - 1; i >= 0; i--)
          {
            TcpNeighbor neighbor = m_neighbors.remove(i);

            if(neighbor != null)
                neighbor.abort();

            neighbor = null;
          }
      }
      catch(Exception exception)
      {
      }
      finally
      {
          m_neighborsMutex.writeLock().unlock();
      }

      m_startTime.set(System.nanoTime());
    }

    public void listen()
    {
      if(listening())
          return;

      m_listen.set(true);

      try
      {
          SSLContext sslContext = null;

          if(Build.VERSION.SDK_INT >= Build.VERSION_CODES.LOLLIPOP)
            sslContext = SSLContext.getInstance("TLS");
          else
            sslContext = SSLContext.getInstance("SSL");
```

```java
        KeyManagerFactory keyManagerFactory = KeyManagerFactory.
          getInstance("X509");

        keyManagerFactory.init(m_keyStore, null);
        sslContext.init(keyManagerFactory.getKeyManagers(),
                    null,
                    null);

        synchronized(m_socketMutex)
        {
          m_socket = (SSLServerSocket)
              sslContext.getServerSocketFactory().createServerSocket();
          m_socket.setReceiveBufferSize(Neighbor.SO_RCVBUF);
          m_socket.setReuseAddress(true);
          m_socket.bind
              (new InetSocketAddress(InetAddress.getByName(m_ipAddress),
                            Integer.parseInt(m_ipPort)),
              0);

          if(Build.VERSION.SDK_INT >= 29) // Android 10
              m_socket.setEnabledProtocols
                (new String[] {"TLSv1",
                            "TLSv1.1",
                            "TLSv1.2",
                            "TLSv1.3"});
          else if(Build.VERSION.SDK_INT >= Build.VERSION_CODES.LOLLIPOP)
              m_socket.setEnabledProtocols
                (new String[] {"TLSv1", "TLSv1.1", "TLSv1.2"});
          else
              m_socket.setEnabledProtocols
                (new String[] {"SSLv3", "TLSv1", "TLSv1.1", "TLSv1.2"});

          m_socket.setNeedClientAuth(false);
          m_socket.setSoTimeout(SO_TIMEOUT);
        }

        m_startTime.set(System.nanoTime());
      }
    catch(Exception exception)
    {
        setError("An error (" +
              exception.getMessage() +
              ") occurred while attempting to listen.");
        disconnect();
    }
  }

  public void scheduleEchoSend(String message, int oid)
  {
    m_neighborsMutex.readLock().lock();

    try
    {
        int size = m_neighbors.size();

        for(int i = 0; i < size; i++)
          if(m_neighbors.get(i) != null)
              if(m_neighbors.get(i).getOid() != oid)
                m_neighbors.get(i).scheduleEchoSend(message);
    }
    catch(Exception exception)
    {
```

```java
          }
        finally
        {
            m_neighborsMutex.readLock().unlock();
        }
    }

    public void scheduleSend(String message)
    {
      m_neighborsMutex.readLock().lock();

      try
      {
          int size = m_neighbors.size();

          for(int i = 0; i < size; i++)
            if(m_neighbors.get(i) != null)
                m_neighbors.get(i).scheduleSend(message);
      }
      catch(Exception exception)
      {
      }
      finally
      {
          m_neighborsMutex.readLock().unlock();
      }
    }

    public void togglePrivacy()
    {
      m_isPrivateServer.set(!m_isPrivateServer.get());
    }
}
```

/* TcpNeighbor.java

```java
** SMOKESTACK, EVEN IF ADVISED OF THE POSSIBILITY OF SUCH DAMAGE.
*/

package org.purple.smokestack;

import android.os.Build;
import android.util.Base64;
import java.net.InetSocketAddress;
import java.net.Proxy;
import java.net.Socket;
import java.security.SecureRandom;
import java.security.cert.X509Certificate;
import java.util.concurrent.Executors;
import java.util.concurrent.ScheduledExecutorService;
import java.util.concurrent.TimeUnit;
import java.util.concurrent.atomic.AtomicBoolean;
import javax.net.ssl.HandshakeCompletedEvent;
import javax.net.ssl.HandshakeCompletedListener;
import javax.net.ssl.SSLContext;
import javax.net.ssl.SSLSocket;
import javax.net.ssl.TrustManager;
import javax.net.ssl.X509TrustManager;

public class TcpNeighbor extends Neighbor
{
    private AtomicBoolean m_handshakeCompleted = null;
    private AtomicBoolean m_isValidCertificate = null;
    private InetSocketAddress m_proxyInetSocketAddress = null;
    private SSLSocket m_socket = null;
    private ScheduledExecutorService m_requestAuthenticationScheduler = null;
    private String m_protocols[] = null;
    private String m_proxyIpAddress = "";
    private String m_proxyType = "";
    private TrustManager m_trustManagers[] = null;
    private final static int CONNECTION_TIMEOUT = 10000; // 10 Seconds
    private final static int HANDSHAKE_TIMEOUT = 10000; // 10 Seconds
    private final static long REQUEST_AUTHENTICATION_INTERVAL =
      10000L; // 10 Seconds
    private int m_proxyPort = -1;

    private void prepareMRandom()
    {
      m_randomBuffer.delete(0, m_randomBuffer.length());
      m_randomBuffer.trimToSize();

      try
      {
          byte bytes[] = Miscellaneous.joinByteArrays
            (Cryptography.randomBytes(64),
             Miscellaneous.longToByteArray(System.currentTimeMillis()));

          m_randomBuffer.append
            (Base64.encodeToString(Cryptography.sha512(bytes),
                         Base64.NO_WRAP));
      }
      catch(Exception exception)
      {
          m_randomBuffer.delete(0, m_randomBuffer.length());
          m_randomBuffer.trimToSize();
      }
    }

    protected String getLocalIp()
```

```java
{
  try
  {
      if(m_socket != null && m_socket.getLocalAddress() != null)
        return m_socket.getLocalAddress().getHostAddress();
  }
  catch(Exception exception)
  {
  }

  if(m_version.equals("IPv4"))
      return "0.0.0.0";
  else
      return "::";
}

protected String getRemoteIp()
{
  try
  {
      if(m_socket != null && m_socket.getInetAddress() != null)
        return m_socket.getInetAddress().getHostAddress();
  }
  catch(Exception exception)
  {
  }

  if(m_version.equals("IPv4"))
      return "0.0.0.0";
  else
      return "::";
}

protected String getSessionCipher()
{
  try
  {
      if(m_socket != null &&
        m_socket.getSession() != null &&
        m_socket.getSession().isValid())
        return m_socket.getSession().getCipherSuite();
  }
  catch(Exception exception)
  {
  }

  return "";
}

protected boolean connected()
{
  try
  {
      return isNetworkConnected() &&
        m_handshakeCompleted.get() &&
        m_isValidCertificate.get() &&
        m_socket != null &&
        !m_socket.isClosed();
  }
  catch(Exception exception)
  {
      return false;
  }
```

```java
    }

    protected boolean send(String message)
    {
      if(!connected() || message == null || message.isEmpty())
          return false;

      try
      {
          if(m_isPrivateServer.get())
            if(!m_remoteUserAuthenticated.get())
                if(!message.contains("type=0097a&content="))
                  return false;

          m_socket.getOutputStream().write(message.getBytes());
          Kernel.writeCongestionDigest(message);
          m_bytesWritten.getAndAdd(message.length());
      }
      catch(Exception exception)
      {
          setError("A socket error occurred on send().");
          disconnect();
          return false;
      }

      return true;
    }

    protected int getLocalPort()
    {
      try
      {
          if(m_socket != null && !m_socket.isClosed())
            return m_socket.getLocalPort();
      }
      catch(Exception exception)
      {
      }

      return 0;
    }

    protected int getRemotePort()
    {
      try
      {
          if(m_socket != null)
            return m_socket.getPort();
      }
      catch(Exception exception)
      {
      }

      return 0;
    }

    protected void disconnect()
    {
      super.disconnect();
      m_databaseHelper.deleteRoutingEntry(m_uuid.toString());

      try
      {
```

```java
        if(m_socket != null)
          m_socket.close();
    }
    catch(Exception exception)
    {
    }
    finally
    {
        m_handshakeCompleted.set(false);

        if(m_oid.get() >= 0)
          m_isValidCertificate.set(false);

        m_randomBuffer.delete(0, m_randomBuffer.length());
        m_randomBuffer.trimToSize();
        m_socket = null;
        reset();
    }
}

public TcpNeighbor(SSLSocket socket, boolean isPrivateServer, int oid)
{
  /*
  ** We're a server socket.
  */

  super("", "", "", "TCP", "", isPrivateServer, false, oid);
  m_handshakeCompleted = new AtomicBoolean(true);
  m_isValidCertificate = new AtomicBoolean(true);
  m_socket = socket;
  m_userDefined.set(false);

  if(m_socket != null)
      try
      {
        if(m_isPrivateServer.get())
            m_socket.addHandshakeCompletedListener
              (new HandshakeCompletedListener()
                {
                  @Override
                  public void handshakeCompleted
                    (HandshakeCompletedEvent event)
                  {
                    m_handshakeCompleted.set(true);
                    prepareMRandom();
                    scheduleSend
                        (Messages.
                         requestAuthentication(m_randomBuffer));

                    synchronized(m_mutex)
                    {
                        m_mutex.notifyAll();
                    }
                  }
                });

        m_socket.setKeepAlive(false);
        m_socket.setSoLinger(true, 0);
        m_socket.setSoTimeout(HANDSHAKE_TIMEOUT);
        m_socket.setTcpNoDelay(true);
      }
      catch(Exception exception)
      {
```

```java
        }

    /*
    ** Launch the schedulers.
    */

    if(isPrivateServer)
    {
        m_requestAuthenticationScheduler = Executors.
         newSingleThreadScheduledExecutor();
        m_requestAuthenticationScheduler.scheduleAtFixedRate(new Runnable()
        {
          @Override
          public void run()
          {
              try
              {
                if(!connected() && !m_aborted.get())
                    synchronized(m_mutex)
                    {
                      try
                      {
                          m_mutex.wait(WAIT_TIMEOUT);
                      }
                      catch(Exception exception)
                      {
                      }
                    }

                if(connected() && !m_remoteUserAuthenticated.get())
                {
                    prepareMRandom();
                    scheduleSend
                      (Messages.
                       requestAuthentication(m_randomBuffer));
                }
              }
              catch(Exception exception)
              {
              }
          }
        }, REQUEST_AUTHENTICATION_INTERVAL,
          REQUEST_AUTHENTICATION_INTERVAL,
          TimeUnit.MILLISECONDS);
    }

    m_readSocketScheduler.scheduleAtFixedRate(new Runnable()
    {
        private boolean m_error = false;

        @Override
        public void run()
        {
          try
          {
              if(!connected() && !m_aborted.get())
                synchronized(m_mutex)
                {
                    try
                    {
                      m_mutex.wait(WAIT_TIMEOUT);
                    }
                    catch(Exception exception)
```

```java
              {
              }
          }

          if(!connected())
            return;
          else if(m_error)
          {
            if(connected())
                m_error = false;
            else
                return;
          }
          else if(m_socket == null ||
                m_socket.getInputStream() == null)
            return;
          else if(m_socket.getSoTimeout() == HANDSHAKE_TIMEOUT)
            /*
            ** Reset SO_TIMEOUT from HANDSHAKE_TIMEOUT.
            */

            m_socket.setSoTimeout(SO_TIMEOUT);

          byte bytes[] = new byte[BYTES_PER_READ];
          int i = 0;

          try
          {
            i = m_socket.getInputStream().read(bytes);
          }
          catch(Exception exception)
          {
            i = -1;
            m_error = true;
          }

          long bytesRead = 0L;

          if(i < 0)
            bytesRead = -1L;
          else if(i > 0)
            bytesRead += (long) i;

          if(bytesRead < 0L)
          {
            m_error = true;
            setError("A socket read() error occurred.");
            disconnect();
            return;
          }
          else if(bytesRead == 0L)
            return;

          m_bytesRead.getAndAdd(bytesRead);
          m_lastTimeRead.set(System.nanoTime());

          if(m_stringBuffer.length() < MAXIMUM_BYTES)
            m_stringBuffer.append
                (new String(bytes, 0, (int) bytesRead));

          synchronized(m_parsingSchedulerObject)
          {
            m_parsingSchedulerObject.notify();
```

```java
                }
            }
            catch(java.net.SocketException exception)
            {
                m_error = true;
                setError("A socket error occurred while reading data.");
                disconnect();
            }
            catch(Exception exception)
            {
            }
        }
    }, 0L, READ_SOCKET_INTERVAL, TimeUnit.MILLISECONDS);
}

public TcpNeighbor(String proxyIpAddress,
                   String proxyPort,
                   String proxyType,
                   String ipAddress,
                   String ipPort,
                   String scopeId,
                   String version,
                   int oid)
{
    super(ipAddress, ipPort, scopeId, "TCP", version, false, true, oid);
    m_handshakeCompleted = new AtomicBoolean(false);
    m_isValidCertificate = new AtomicBoolean(false);

    if(Build.VERSION.RELEASE.startsWith("10"))
        m_protocols = new String[]
          {"TLSv1", "TLSv1.1", "TLSv1.2", "TLSv1.3"};
    else if(Build.VERSION.SDK_INT >= Build.VERSION_CODES.LOLLIPOP)
        m_protocols = new String[] {"TLSv1", "TLSv1.1", "TLSv1.2"};
    else
        m_protocols = new String[]
          {"SSLv3", "TLSv1", "TLSv1.1", "TLSv1.2"};

    m_proxyIpAddress = proxyIpAddress;

    try
    {
        m_proxyPort = Integer.parseInt(proxyPort);
    }
    catch(Exception exception)
    {
        m_proxyPort = -1;
    }

    m_proxyType = proxyType;

    if(!m_proxyIpAddress.isEmpty() && m_proxyPort != -1 &&
       !m_proxyType.isEmpty())
        try
        {
          m_proxyInetSocketAddress = new InetSocketAddress
              (m_proxyIpAddress, m_proxyPort);
        }
        catch(Exception exception)
        {
          m_proxyInetSocketAddress = null;
        }

    m_readSocketScheduler.scheduleAtFixedRate(new Runnable()
```

```java
        {
    private boolean m_error = false;

    @Override
    public void run()
    {
      try
        {
            if(!connected() && !m_aborted.get())
              synchronized(m_mutex)
              {
                  try
                  {
                    m_mutex.wait(WAIT_TIMEOUT);
                  }
                  catch(Exception exception)
                  {
                  }
              }

            if(!connected())
              return;
            else if(m_error)
            {
              if(connected())
                  m_error = false;
              else
                  return;
            }
            else if(m_socket == null ||
                  m_socket.getInputStream() == null)
              return;
            else if(m_socket.getSoTimeout() == HANDSHAKE_TIMEOUT)
              /*
              ** Reset SO_TIMEOUT from HANDSHAKE_TIMEOUT.
              */

              m_socket.setSoTimeout(SO_TIMEOUT);

            byte bytes[] = new byte[BYTES_PER_READ];
            int i = 0;

            try
            {
              i = m_socket.getInputStream().read(bytes);
            }
            catch(Exception exception)
            {
              i = -1;
              m_error = true;
            }

            long bytesRead = 0L;

            if(i < 0)
              bytesRead = -1L;
            else if(i > 0)
              bytesRead += (long) i;

            if(bytesRead < 0L)
            {
              m_error = true;
              setError("A socket read() error occurred.");
```

```java
              disconnect();
              return;
            }
          else if(bytesRead == 0L)
            return;

          m_bytesRead.getAndAdd(bytesRead);
          m_lastTimeRead.set(System.nanoTime());

          if(m_stringBuffer.length() < MAXIMUM_BYTES)
            m_stringBuffer.append
                (new String(bytes, 0, (int) bytesRead));

          synchronized(m_parsingSchedulerObject)
          {
            m_parsingSchedulerObject.notify();
          }
        }
      catch(java.net.SocketException exception)
      {
          m_error = true;
          setError("A socket error occurred while reading data.");
          disconnect();
      }
      catch(Exception exception)
      {
      }
    }
}, 0L, READ_SOCKET_INTERVAL, TimeUnit.MILLISECONDS);

m_trustManagers = new TrustManager[]
{
    new X509TrustManager()
    {
      public X509Certificate[] getAcceptedIssuers()
      {
          return new X509Certificate[0];
      }

      public void checkClientTrusted
          (X509Certificate chain[], String authType)
      {
      }

      public void checkServerTrusted
          (X509Certificate chain[], String authType)
      {
          if(authType == null || authType.length() == 0)
            m_isValidCertificate.set(false);
          else if(chain == null || chain.length == 0)
            m_isValidCertificate.set(false);
          else
          {
            try
            {
                chain[0].checkValidity();

                byte bytes[] = m_databaseHelper.
                  neighborRemoteCertificate
                  (m_cryptography, m_oid.get());

                if(bytes == null || bytes.length == 0)
                {
```

```java
                    m_databaseHelper.neighborRecordCertificate
                        (m_cryptography,
                         String.valueOf(m_oid.get()),
                         chain[0].getEncoded());
                    m_isValidCertificate.set(true);
                  }
                  else if(!Cryptography.memcmp(bytes,
                                      chain[0].getEncoded()))
                  {
                    setError("The stored server's " +
                            "certificate does not match the " +
                            "certificate that was provided by " +
                            "the server.");
                    m_isValidCertificate.set(false);
                  }
                  else
                    m_isValidCertificate.set(true);
              }
              catch(Exception exception)
              {
                  setError("The server's certificate has expired.");
                  m_isValidCertificate.set(false);
              }
            }

            if(!m_isValidCertificate.get())
              if(m_error.length() == 0)
                  m_error.append
                    ("A generic certificate error occurred.");
          }
        }
      };
    }

  public void abort()
  {
    disconnect();
    super.abort();
    m_handshakeCompleted.set(false);

    if(m_oid.get() >= 0)
        m_isValidCertificate.set(false);

    if(m_requestAuthenticationScheduler != null)
        synchronized(m_requestAuthenticationScheduler)
        {
          try
          {
              m_requestAuthenticationScheduler.shutdown();
          }
          catch(Exception exception)
          {
          }

          try
          {
              if(!m_requestAuthenticationScheduler.
                awaitTermination(60L, TimeUnit.SECONDS))
              m_requestAuthenticationScheduler.shutdownNow();
          }
          catch(Exception exception)
          {
          }
```

```java
        }

    synchronized(m_readSocketScheduler)
    {
        try
        {
          m_readSocketScheduler.shutdown();
        }
        catch(Exception exception)
        {
        }

        try
        {
          if(!m_readSocketScheduler.
             awaitTermination(60L, TimeUnit.SECONDS))
             m_readSocketScheduler.shutdownNow();
        }
        catch(Exception exception)
        {
        }
    }
    }

    public void connect()
    {
      if(connected())
          return;
      else if(m_oid.get() < 0)
          return;

      try
      {
          m_bytesRead.set(0);
          m_bytesWritten.set(0);
          m_handshakeCompleted.set(false);
          m_lastParsed.set(System.currentTimeMillis());
          m_lastTimeRead.set(System.nanoTime());

          InetSocketAddress inetSocketAddress =
            new InetSocketAddress(m_ipAddress, Integer.parseInt(m_ipPort));
          SSLContext sslContext = null;

          if(Build.VERSION.SDK_INT >= Build.VERSION_CODES.LOLLIPOP)
            sslContext = SSLContext.getInstance("TLS");
          else
            sslContext = SSLContext.getInstance("SSL");

          sslContext.init
            (null, m_trustManagers, new SecureRandom());

          if(m_proxyInetSocketAddress == null)
          {
            m_socket = (SSLSocket) sslContext.getSocketFactory().
                createSocket();
            m_socket.setReceiveBufferSize(SO_RCVBUF);
            m_socket.setSendBufferSize(SO_SNDBUF);
            m_socket.connect(inetSocketAddress, CONNECTION_TIMEOUT);
          }
          else
          {
            Socket socket = null;
```

```java
        if(m_proxyType.equals("HTTP"))
            socket = new Socket
                (new Proxy(Proxy.Type.HTTP, m_proxyInetSocketAddress));
        else
            socket = new Socket
                (new Proxy(Proxy.Type.SOCKS, m_proxyInetSocketAddress));

        socket.setReceiveBufferSize(SO_RCVBUF);
        socket.setSendBufferSize(SO_SNDBUF);
        socket.connect(inetSocketAddress, CONNECTION_TIMEOUT);
        m_socket = (SSLSocket) sslContext.getSocketFactory().
            createSocket(socket, m_proxyIpAddress, m_proxyPort, true);
        }

    m_socket.addHandshakeCompletedListener
        (new HandshakeCompletedListener()
        {
            @Override
            public void handshakeCompleted
                (HandshakeCompletedEvent event)
            {
              m_handshakeCompleted.set(true);

              synchronized(m_mutex)
              {
                  m_mutex.notifyAll();
              }
            }
        });
    m_socket.setEnabledProtocols(m_protocols);
    m_socket.setKeepAlive(false);
    m_socket.setSoLinger(true, 0);
    m_socket.setSoTimeout(HANDSHAKE_TIMEOUT); // SSL/TLS process.
    m_socket.setTcpNoDelay(true);
    m_startTime.set(System.nanoTime());
    setError("");

    synchronized(m_mutex)
    {
      m_mutex.notifyAll();
    }
  }
  catch(Exception exception)
  {
      setError("An error (" +
            exception.getMessage() +
            ") occurred while attempting a connection.");
      disconnect();
  }
}

public void startHandshake()
{
  try
  {
      if(m_socket != null)
        m_socket.startHandshake();
  }
  catch(Exception exception)
  {
  }
}
}
```

```java
/* UdpMulticastNeighbor.java

https://github.com/textbrowser/smokestack/blob/master/SmokeStack/app/src/main/
java/org/purple/smokestack/UdpMulticastNeighbor.java
** Copyright (c) Alexis Megas.
** All rights reserved.
**
** Redistribution and use in source and binary forms, with or without
** modification, are permitted provided that the following conditions
** are met:
** 1. Redistributions of source code must retain the above copyright
**    notice, this list of conditions and the following disclaimer.
** 2. Redistributions in binary form must reproduce the above copyright
**    notice, this list of conditions and the following disclaimer in the
**    documentation and/or other materials provided with the distribution.
** 3. The name of the author may not be used to endorse or promote products
**    derived from SmokeStack without specific prior written permission.
**
** SMOKESTACK IS PROVIDED BY THE AUTHOR ``AS IS'' AND ANY EXPRESS OR
** IMPLIED WARRANTIES, INCLUDING, BUT NOT LIMITED TO, THE IMPLIED WARRANTIES
** OF MERCHANTABILITY AND FITNESS FOR A PARTICULAR PURPOSE ARE DISCLAIMED.
** IN NO EVENT SHALL THE AUTHOR BE LIABLE FOR ANY DIRECT, INDIRECT,
** INCIDENTAL, SPECIAL, EXEMPLARY, OR CONSEQUENTIAL DAMAGES (INCLUDING, BUT
** NOT LIMITED TO, PROCUREMENT OF SUBSTITUTE GOODS OR SERVICES; LOSS OF USE,
** DATA, OR PROFITS; OR BUSINESS INTERRUPTION) HOWEVER CAUSED AND ON ANY
** THEORY OF LIABILITY, WHETHER IN CONTRACT, STRICT LIABILITY, OR TORT
** (INCLUDING NEGLIGENCE OR OTHERWISE) ARISING IN ANY WAY OUT OF THE USE OF
** SMOKESTACK, EVEN IF ADVISED OF THE POSSIBILITY OF SUCH DAMAGE.
*/

package org.purple.smokestack;

import java.io.ByteArrayOutputStream;
import java.net.DatagramPacket;
import java.net.InetAddress;
import java.net.MulticastSocket;
import java.util.concurrent.TimeUnit;

public class UdpMulticastNeighbor extends Neighbor
{
    private MulticastSocket m_socket = null;
    private final static int TTL = 255;

    protected String getLocalIp()
    {
      return m_ipAddress;
    }

    protected String getRemoteIp()
    {
      return m_ipAddress;
    }

    protected boolean connected()
    {
      try
      {
          return isNetworkConnected() &&
            m_socket != null &&
            !m_socket.isClosed();
      }
      catch(Exception exception)
      {
```

```java
      return false;
    }
  }

  protected boolean send(String message)
  {
    if(!connected() || message == null || message.isEmpty())
        return false;

    try
    {
        StringBuilder stringBuilder = new StringBuilder(message);

        while(stringBuilder.length() > 0)
        {
          if(m_aborted.get())
              return false;

          byte bytes[] = stringBuilder.substring
              (0, Math.min(576, stringBuilder.length())).getBytes();

          m_socket.send
              (new DatagramPacket(bytes,
                            bytes.length,
                            InetAddress.getByName(m_ipAddress),
                            Integer.parseInt(m_ipPort)));
          stringBuilder.delete(0, bytes.length);
        }

        Kernel.writeCongestionDigest(message);
        m_bytesWritten.getAndAdd(message.length());
        setError("");
    }
    catch(Exception exception)
    {
        setError("A socket error occurred on send().");
        disconnect();
        return false;
    }

    return true;
  }

  protected int getLocalPort()
  {
    try
    {
        if(m_socket != null && !m_socket.isClosed())
          return m_socket.getLocalPort();
    }
    catch(Exception exception)
    {
    }

    return 0;
  }

  protected int getRemotePort()
  {
    return getLocalPort();
  }

  protected void disconnect()
```

```java
    {
      super.disconnect();
      m_databaseHelper.deleteRoutingEntry(m_uuid.toString());

      try
      {
          if(m_socket != null)
          {
            m_socket.leaveGroup(InetAddress.getByName(m_ipAddress));
            m_socket.close();
          }
      }
      catch(Exception exception)
      {
      }
      finally
      {
          m_socket = null;
          reset();
      }
    }

    public UdpMulticastNeighbor(String ipAddress,
                                String ipPort,
                                String scopeId,
                                String version,
                                int oid)
    {
      super(ipAddress, ipPort, scopeId, "UDP", version, false, true, oid);
      m_readSocketScheduler.scheduleAtFixedRate(new Runnable()
      {
          private boolean m_error = false;

          @Override
          public void run()
          {
            ByteArrayOutputStream byteArrayOutputStream = null;

            try
            {
                if(!connected() && !m_aborted.get())
                  synchronized(m_mutex)
                  {
                      try
                      {
                        m_mutex.wait(WAIT_TIMEOUT);
                      }
                      catch(Exception exception)
                      {
                      }
                  }

                if(!connected())
                  return;
                else if(m_error)
                {
                  if(connected())
                      m_error = false;
                  else
                      return;
                }

                DatagramPacket datagramPacket = null;
```

```java
        byte bytes[] = new byte[BYTES_PER_READ];

        datagramPacket = new DatagramPacket(bytes, bytes.length);

        try
        {
          m_socket.receive(datagramPacket);
        }
        catch(Exception exception)
        {
          m_error = true;
          setError("A socket receive() error occurred.");
          disconnect();
          return;
        }

        if(datagramPacket.getLength() > 0)
        {
          byteArrayOutputStream = new ByteArrayOutputStream();
          byteArrayOutputStream.write
              (datagramPacket.getData(),
               0,
               datagramPacket.getLength());
        }

        int bytesRead = datagramPacket.getLength();

        if(bytesRead < 0)
        {
          m_error = true;
          setError("A socket receive() error occurred.");
          disconnect();
          return;
        }
        else if(bytesRead == 0)
          return;

        m_bytesRead.getAndAdd(bytesRead);
        m_lastTimeRead.set(System.nanoTime());

        if(byteArrayOutputStream != null &&
           m_stringBuffer.length() < MAXIMUM_BYTES)
          m_stringBuffer.append
              (new String(byteArrayOutputStream.toByteArray()));
      }
      catch(Exception exception)
      {
      }
      finally
      {
          try
          {
            if(byteArrayOutputStream != null)
              byteArrayOutputStream.close();
          }
          catch(Exception exception)
          {
          }
      }
    }
  }, 0L, READ_SOCKET_INTERVAL, TimeUnit.MILLISECONDS);
}
```

```java
    public void abort()
    {
      disconnect();
      super.abort();

      synchronized(m_readSocketScheduler)
      {
          try
          {
            m_readSocketScheduler.shutdown();
          }
          catch(Exception exception)
          {
          }

          try
          {
            if(!m_readSocketScheduler.
                awaitTermination(60L, TimeUnit.SECONDS))
                 m_readSocketScheduler.shutdownNow();
          }
          catch(Exception exception)
          {
          }
      }
    }

    public void connect()
    {
      if(connected())
          return;

      try
      {
          m_bytesRead.set(0);
          m_bytesWritten.set(0);
          m_lastParsed.set(System.currentTimeMillis());
          m_lastTimeRead.set(System.nanoTime());
          m_socket = new MulticastSocket(Integer.parseInt(m_ipPort));
          m_socket.joinGroup(InetAddress.getByName(m_ipAddress));
          m_socket.setLoopbackMode(true);
          m_socket.setSoTimeout(SO_TIMEOUT);
          m_socket.setTimeToLive(TTL);
          m_startTime.set(System.nanoTime());
          setError("");

          synchronized(m_mutex)
          {
            m_mutex.notifyAll();
          }
      }
      catch(Exception exception)
      {
          setError("An error occurred while attempting a connection.");
          disconnect();
      }
    }
}
```

/* UdpNeighbor.java

```
https://github.com/textbrowser/smokestack/blob/master/SmokeStack/app/src/main/
java/org/purple/smokestack/UdpNeighbor.java
** Copyright (c) Alexis Megas.
** All rights reserved.
**
** Redistribution and use in source and binary forms, with or without
** modification, are permitted provided that the following conditions
** are met:
** 1. Redistributions of source code must retain the above copyright
**    notice, this list of conditions and the following disclaimer.
** 2. Redistributions in binary form must reproduce the above copyright
**    notice, this list of conditions and the following disclaimer in the
**    documentation and/or other materials provided with the distribution.
** 3. The name of the author may not be used to endorse or promote products
**    derived from SmokeStack without specific prior written permission.
**
** SMOKESTACK IS PROVIDED BY THE AUTHOR ``AS IS'' AND ANY EXPRESS OR
** IMPLIED WARRANTIES, INCLUDING, BUT NOT LIMITED TO, THE IMPLIED WARRANTIES
** OF MERCHANTABILITY AND FITNESS FOR A PARTICULAR PURPOSE ARE DISCLAIMED.
** IN NO EVENT SHALL THE AUTHOR BE LIABLE FOR ANY DIRECT, INDIRECT,
** INCIDENTAL, SPECIAL, EXEMPLARY, OR CONSEQUENTIAL DAMAGES (INCLUDING, BUT
** NOT LIMITED TO, PROCUREMENT OF SUBSTITUTE GOODS OR SERVICES; LOSS OF USE,
** DATA, OR PROFITS; OR BUSINESS INTERRUPTION) HOWEVER CAUSED AND ON ANY
** THEORY OF LIABILITY, WHETHER IN CONTRACT, STRICT LIABILITY, OR TORT
** (INCLUDING NEGLIGENCE OR OTHERWISE) ARISING IN ANY WAY OUT OF THE USE OF
** SMOKESTACK, EVEN IF ADVISED OF THE POSSIBILITY OF SUCH DAMAGE.
*/
```

```java
package org.purple.smokestack;

import java.io.ByteArrayOutputStream;
import java.net.DatagramPacket;
import java.net.DatagramSocket;
import java.net.InetAddress;
import java.util.concurrent.TimeUnit;

public class UdpNeighbor extends Neighbor
{
    private DatagramSocket m_socket = null;

    protected String getLocalIp()
    {
        try
        {
            if(m_socket != null && m_socket.getLocalAddress() != null)
                return m_socket.getLocalAddress().getHostAddress();
        }
        catch(Exception exception)
        {
        }

        if(m_version.equals("IPv4"))
            return "0.0.0.0";
        else
            return "::";
    }

    protected String getRemoteIp()
    {
        return m_ipAddress;
    }

    protected boolean connected()
    {
```

```java
        try
        {
            return isNetworkConnected() &&
                m_socket != null &&
                !m_socket.isClosed();
        }
        catch(Exception exception)
        {
            return false;
        }
    }

    protected boolean send(String message)
    {
        if(!connected() || message == null || message.isEmpty())
            return false;

        try
        {
            StringBuilder stringBuilder = new StringBuilder(message);

            while(stringBuilder.length() > 0)
            {
                if(m_aborted.get())
                    return false;

                byte bytes[] = stringBuilder.substring
                    (0, Math.min(576, stringBuilder.length())).getBytes();

                m_socket.send
                    (new DatagramPacket(bytes,
                                        bytes.length,
                                        InetAddress.getByName(m_ipAddress),
                                        Integer.parseInt(m_ipPort)));
                stringBuilder.delete(0, bytes.length);
            }

            Kernel.writeCongestionDigest(message);
            m_bytesWritten.getAndAdd(message.length());
            setError("");
        }
        catch(Exception exception)
        {
            setError("A socket error occurred on send().");
            disconnect();
            return false;
        }

        return false;
    }

    protected int getLocalPort()
    {
        try
        {
            if(m_socket != null && !m_socket.isClosed())
                return m_socket.getLocalPort();
        }
        catch(Exception exception)
        {
        }

        return 0;
    }

    protected int getRemotePort()
```

```java
    {
        try
        {
            return Integer.parseInt(m_ipPort);
        }
        catch(Exception exception)
        {
        }

        return 0;
    }

    protected void disconnect()
    {
        super.disconnect();
        m_databaseHelper.deleteRoutingEntry(m_uuid.toString());

        try
        {
            if(m_socket != null)
                m_socket.close();
        }
        catch(Exception exception)
        {
        }
        finally
        {
            m_socket = null;
            reset();
        }
    }

    public UdpNeighbor(String ipAddress,
                       String ipPort,
                       String scopeId,
                       String version,
                       int oid)
    {
        super(ipAddress, ipPort, scopeId, "UDP", version, false, true, oid);
        m_readSocketScheduler.scheduleAtFixedRate(new Runnable()
        {
            private boolean m_error = false;

            @Override
            public void run()
            {
                ByteArrayOutputStream byteArrayOutputStream = null;

                try
                {
                    if(!connected() && !m_aborted.get())
                        synchronized(m_mutex)
                        {
                            try
                            {
                                m_mutex.wait(WAIT_TIMEOUT);
                            }
                            catch(Exception exception)
                            {
                            }
                        }

                    if(!connected())
                        return;
                    else if(m_error)
                    {
```

```java
            if(connected())
                m_error = false;
            else
                return;
        }

        DatagramPacket datagramPacket = null;
        byte bytes[] = new byte[BYTES_PER_READ];

        datagramPacket = new DatagramPacket(bytes, bytes.length);

        try
        {
            m_socket.receive(datagramPacket);
        }
        catch(Exception exception)
        {
            m_error = true;
            setError("A socket receive() error occurred.");
            disconnect();
            return;
        }

        if(datagramPacket.getLength() > 0)
        {
            byteArrayOutputStream = new ByteArrayOutputStream();
            byteArrayOutputStream.write
                (datagramPacket.getData(),
                 0,
                 datagramPacket.getLength());
        }

        int bytesRead = datagramPacket.getLength();

        if(bytesRead < 0)
        {
            m_error = true;
            setError("A socket receive() error occurred.");
            disconnect();
            return;
        }
        else if(bytesRead == 0)
            return;

        m_bytesRead.getAndAdd(bytesRead);
        m_lastTimeRead.set(System.nanoTime());

        if(byteArrayOutputStream != null &&
           m_stringBuffer.length() < MAXIMUM_BYTES)
            m_stringBuffer.append
                (new String(byteArrayOutputStream.toByteArray()));
    }
    catch(Exception exception)
    {
    }
    finally
    {
        try
        {
            if(byteArrayOutputStream != null)
                byteArrayOutputStream.close();
        }
        catch(Exception exception)
        {
        }
    }
```

```java
            }
        }, 0L, READ_SOCKET_INTERVAL, TimeUnit.MILLISECONDS);
    }

    public void abort()
    {
        disconnect();
        super.abort();

        synchronized(m_readSocketScheduler)
        {
            try
            {
                m_readSocketScheduler.shutdown();
            }
            catch(Exception exception)
            {
            }

            try
            {
                if(!m_readSocketScheduler.
                    awaitTermination(60L, TimeUnit.SECONDS))
                     m_readSocketScheduler.shutdownNow();
            }
            catch(Exception exception)
            {
            }
        }
    }

    public void connect()
    {
        if(connected())
            return;

        try
        {
            m_bytesRead.set(0);
            m_bytesWritten.set(0);
            m_lastParsed.set(System.currentTimeMillis());
            m_lastTimeRead.set(System.nanoTime());
            m_socket = new DatagramSocket();
            m_socket.connect
                (InetAddress.getByName(m_ipAddress),
                 Integer.parseInt(m_ipPort));
            m_socket.setSoTimeout(SO_TIMEOUT);
            m_startTime.set(System.nanoTime());
            setError("");

            synchronized(m_mutex)
            {
                m_mutex.notifyAll();
            }
        }
        catch(Exception exception)
        {
            setError("An error occurred while attempting a connection.");
            disconnect();
        }
    }
}
```

Drawable

https://github.com/textbrowser/smokestack/tree/master/SmokeStack/app/src/main/res/drawable

```
Directory of C:\smokestack-2020.11.15\SmokeStack\app\src\main\res\drawable

12.11.2020  14:09    <DIR>          .
12.11.2020  14:09    <DIR>          ..
12.11.2020  14:09             1.100 help.png
12.11.2020  14:09               832 keys_not_signed.png
12.11.2020  14:09               933 keys_signed.png
12.11.2020  14:09               295 sectiongradient.xml
12.11.2020  14:09             4.174 smokestack.png
12.11.2020  14:09               937 warning.png
               6 File(s),          8.271 Bytes
```

sectiongradient.xml

https://raw.githubusercontent.com/textbrowser/smokestack/master/SmokeStack/app/src/main/res/drawable/sectiongradient.xml

```xml
<?xml version="1.0" encoding="UTF-8"?>
<shape xmlns:android="http://schemas.android.com/apk/res/android"
       android:shape="rectangle">
  <gradient
      android:angle="0"
      android:centerColor="#81d4fa"
      android:endColor="#b3e5fc"
      android:startColor="#4fc3f7" />
</shape>
```

activity_authenticate.xml

https://raw.githubusercontent.com/textbrowser/smokestack/master/SmokeStack/app/src/main/res/layout/activity_authenticate.xml

```xml
<?xml version="1.0" encoding="utf-8"?>
<android.support.design.widget.CoordinatorLayout
xmlns:android="http://schemas.android.com/apk/res/android"
    android:layout_width="match_parent"
    android:layout_height="match_parent"
    android:layout_marginStart="10dp"
    android:layout_marginEnd="10dp">

    <android.support.design.widget.AppBarLayout
        android:layout_width="match_parent"
        android:layout_height="wrap_content">

        <android.support.v7.widget.Toolbar
            android:layout_width="match_parent"
            android:layout_height="0dp"
            android:background="?attr/colorPrimary"
            android:theme="?attr/actionBarTheme" />
```

```xml
        </android.support.design.widget.AppBarLayout>

    <RelativeLayout
        android:layout_width="match_parent"
        android:layout_height="match_parent">

        <EditText
            android:id="@+id/password"
            android:layout_width="wrap_content"
            android:layout_height="wrap_content"
            android:layout_alignParentStart="true"
            android:layout_alignParentEnd="true"
            android:ems="10"
            android:hint="@string/authenticate_password"
            android:inputType="textPassword"
            android:selectAllOnFocus="true" />

        <Button
            android:id="@+id/authenticate"
            android:layout_width="wrap_content"
            android:layout_height="wrap_content"
            android:layout_below="@+id/password"
            android:layout_alignParentStart="true"
            android:text="@string/authenticate_authenticate"
            android:textAllCaps="false" />

        <Button
            android:id="@+id/reset"
            style="@style/Widget.AppCompat.Button.Colored"
            android:layout_width="wrap_content"
            android:layout_height="wrap_content"
            android:layout_alignBottom="@+id/authenticate"
            android:layout_toEndOf="@+id/authenticate"
            android:text="@string/reset_smokestack"
            android:textAllCaps="false" />
    </RelativeLayout>

</android.support.design.widget.CoordinatorLayout>
```

activity_settings.xml

https://github.com/textbrowser/smokestack/blob/master/SmokeStack/app/src/main/res/layout/activity_settings.xml

```xml
<?xml version="1.0" encoding="utf-8"?>
<android.support.design.widget.CoordinatorLayout
xmlns:android="http://schemas.android.com/apk/res/android"
    xmlns:tools="http://schemas.android.com/tools"
    android:layout_width="match_parent"
    android:layout_height="match_parent"
    android:layout_marginStart="10dp"
    android:layout_marginEnd="10dp"
    android:fadeScrollbars="false">

    <android.support.design.widget.AppBarLayout
        android:layout_width="match_parent"
        android:layout_height="wrap_content">

        <android.support.v7.widget.Toolbar
            android:layout_width="match_parent"
            android:layout_height="0dp"
            android:background="?attr/colorPrimary"
```

```xml
            android:minHeight="?attr/actionBarSize"
            android:theme="?attr/actionBarTheme" />

    </android.support.design.widget.AppBarLayout>

    <RelativeLayout
        android:layout_width="match_parent"
        android:layout_height="match_parent"
        android:background="@android:color/transparent"
        android:fadeScrollbars="false"
        tools:context="org.purple.smokestack.Settings">

        <ScrollView
            android:layout_width="match_parent"
            android:layout_height="match_parent"
            android:background="@android:color/transparent"
            android:fadeScrollbars="false">

            <LinearLayout
                android:layout_width="match_parent"
                android:layout_height="wrap_content"
                android:orientation="vertical">

                <TextView
                    android:layout_width="match_parent"
                    android:layout_height="wrap_content"
                    android:layout_marginEnd="5dp"
                    android:background="@drawable/sectiongradient"
                    android:paddingStart="5dp"
                    android:paddingEnd="5dp"
                    android:text="@string/about"
                    android:textColor="@android:color/white"
                    android:textSize="18sp"
                    android:textStyle="normal|bold" />

                <TextView
                    android:id="@+id/about"
                    android:layout_width="match_parent"
                    android:layout_height="wrap_content"
                    android:layout_marginEnd="5dp"
                    android:textIsSelectable="true" />

                <TextView
                    android:id="@+id/database_cursors_closed"
                    android:layout_width="match_parent"
                    android:layout_height="wrap_content"
                    android:layout_marginEnd="5dp" />

                <TextView
                    android:id="@+id/database_cursors_opened"
                    android:layout_width="match_parent"
                    android:layout_height="wrap_content"
                    android:layout_marginEnd="5dp" />

                <TextView
                    android:id="@+id/memory"
                    android:layout_width="match_parent"
                    android:layout_height="wrap_content"
                    android:layout_marginEnd="5dp" />

                <LinearLayout
                    android:layout_width="match_parent"
                    android:layout_height="match_parent"
```

```xml
        android:orientation="horizontal">

        <Button
            android:id="@+id/clear_log"
            style="@style/Widget.AppCompat.Button"
            android:layout_width="wrap_content"
            android:layout_height="wrap_content"
            android:text="@string/clear_log"
            android:textAllCaps="false" />

        <Button
            android:id="@+id/gc"
            style="@style/Widget.AppCompat.Button"
            android:layout_width="wrap_content"
            android:layout_height="wrap_content"
            android:text="@string/recycle_memory"
            android:textAllCaps="false" />
    </LinearLayout>

    <TextView
        android:layout_width="match_parent"
        android:layout_height="wrap_content"
        android:layout_marginEnd="5dp"
        android:background="@drawable/sectiongradient"
        android:paddingStart="5dp"
        android:paddingEnd="5dp"
        android:text="@string/listeners"
        android:textColor="@android:color/white"
        android:textSize="18sp"
        android:textStyle="normal|bold" />

    <TextView
        android:id="@+id/internal_listeners"
        android:layout_width="match_parent"
        android:layout_height="wrap_content"
        android:layout_marginEnd="5dp" />

    <TextView
        android:layout_width="match_parent"
        android:layout_height="wrap_content"
        android:layout_marginEnd="5dp"
        android:text="@string/remote_clients" />

    <android.support.v7.widget.RecyclerView
        android:id="@+id/listeners_clients_recycler_view"
        android:layout_width="match_parent"
        android:layout_height="100dp"
        android:layout_marginEnd="5dp"
        android:scrollbars="vertical" />

    <android.support.v4.widget.NestedScrollView
        android:layout_width="match_parent"
        android:layout_height="200dp"
        android:layout_marginEnd="5dp"
        android:fadeScrollbars="false"
        android:scrollbarAlwaysDrawVerticalTrack="true"
        android:scrollbars="vertical">

        <TableLayout
            android:id="@+id/listeners"
            android:layout_width="match_parent"
            android:layout_height="match_parent"
            android:layout_marginEnd="5dp"
```

```xml
                    android:scrollbars="horizontal|vertical">

            </TableLayout>
        </android.support.v4.widget.NestedScrollView>

        <CheckBox
            android:id="@+id/automatic_refresh_listeners"
            android:layout_width="wrap_content"
            android:layout_height="wrap_content"
            android:text="@string/automatic_refresh" />

        <Button
            android:id="@+id/refresh_listeners"
            style="@style/Widget.AppCompat.Button"
            android:layout_width="wrap_content"
            android:layout_height="wrap_content"
            android:text="@string/refresh"
            android:textAllCaps="false" />

        <EditText
            android:id="@+id/listeners_ip_address"
            android:layout_width="match_parent"
            android:layout_height="wrap_content"
            android:layout_marginEnd="5dp"
            android:ems="10"
            android:hint="@string/ip_address"
            android:inputType="textPersonName"
            android:nextFocusDown="@+id/listeners_port" />

        <LinearLayout
            android:layout_width="match_parent"
            android:layout_height="match_parent"
            android:orientation="horizontal">

            <EditText
                android:id="@+id/listeners_port"
                android:layout_width="0dp"
                android:layout_height="wrap_content"
                android:layout_weight="1"
                android:ems="10"
                android:hint="@string/port"
                android:inputType="number"
                android:nextFocusDown="@+id/listeners_scope_id" />

            <CheckBox
                android:id="@+id/private_server"
                android:layout_width="0dp"
                android:layout_height="match_parent"
                android:layout_weight="1"
                android:text="@string/private_server" />

            <EditText
                android:id="@+id/listeners_scope_id"
                android:layout_width="0dp"
                android:layout_height="wrap_content"
                android:layout_marginEnd="5dp"
                android:layout_weight="1"
                android:ems="10"
                android:hint="@string/scope_id"
                android:inputType="textPersonName"
                android:nextFocusDown="@+id/neighbors_ip_address" />
        </LinearLayout>
```

```xml
<RadioGroup
    android:id="@+id/listeners_ipv_radio_group"
    android:layout_width="match_parent"
    android:layout_height="0dp"
    android:layout_weight="1"
    android:checkedButton="@+id/listeners_ipv4"
    android:orientation="horizontal">

    <RadioButton
        android:id="@+id/listeners_ipv4"
        android:layout_width="wrap_content"
        android:layout_height="wrap_content"
        android:layout_weight="1"
        android:text="@string/ipv4" />

    <RadioButton
        android:id="@+id/listeners_ipv6"
        android:layout_width="wrap_content"
        android:layout_height="wrap_content"
        android:layout_marginEnd="5dp"
        android:layout_weight="1"
        android:text="@string/ipv6" />

</RadioGroup>

<LinearLayout
    android:layout_width="match_parent"
    android:layout_height="match_parent"
    android:layout_weight="0.01"
    android:orientation="horizontal">

    <Button
        android:id="@+id/add_listener"
        style="@style/Widget.AppCompat.Button"
        android:layout_width="wrap_content"
        android:layout_height="wrap_content"
        android:text="@string/add"
        android:textAllCaps="false" />

    <Button
        android:id="@+id/reset_listener_fields"
        style="@style/Widget.AppCompat.Button"
        android:layout_width="wrap_content"
        android:layout_height="wrap_content"
        android:text="@string/reset_fields"
        android:textAllCaps="false" />
</LinearLayout>

<TextView
    android:layout_width="match_parent"
    android:layout_height="wrap_content"
    android:layout_marginEnd="5dp"
    android:background="@drawable/sectiongradient"
    android:paddingStart="5dp"
    android:paddingEnd="5dp"
    android:text="@string/neighbors"
    android:textColor="@android:color/white"
    android:textSize="18sp"
    android:textStyle="normal|bold" />

<TextView
    android:id="@+id/internal_neighbors"
    android:layout_width="wrap_content"
```

```
            android:layout_height="wrap_content"
            android:layout_marginEnd="5dp" />

        <LinearLayout
            android:layout_width="match_parent"
            android:layout_height="match_parent"
            android:orientation="horizontal">

            <TextView
                android:layout_width="0dp"
                android:layout_height="wrap_content"
                android:layout_weight="0.31"
                android:text="@string/control" />

            <TextView
                android:layout_width="0dp"
                android:layout_height="wrap_content"
                android:layout_marginEnd="5dp"
                android:layout_weight="0.31"
                android:text="@string/remote" />
        </LinearLayout>

        <android.support.v4.widget.NestedScrollView
            android:layout_width="match_parent"
            android:layout_height="200dp"
            android:layout_marginEnd="5dp"
            android:background="#00ffffff"
            android:fadeScrollbars="false"
            android:scrollbars="vertical">

            <TableLayout
                android:id="@+id/neighbors"
                android:layout_width="match_parent"
                android:layout_height="match_parent"
                android:layout_marginEnd="5dp"
                android:scrollbars="horizontal|vertical">

            </TableLayout>
        </android.support.v4.widget.NestedScrollView>

        <LinearLayout
            android:layout_width="match_parent"
            android:layout_height="match_parent"
            android:orientation="horizontal"
            android:weightSum="1">

            <CheckBox
                android:id="@+id/automatic_refresh_neighbors"
                android:layout_width="wrap_content"
                android:layout_height="match_parent"
                android:text="@string/automatic_refresh" />

            <CheckBox
                android:id="@+id/neighbor_details"
                android:layout_width="wrap_content"
                android:layout_height="match_parent"
                android:layout_marginEnd="5dp"
                android:text="@string/details" />

        </LinearLayout>

        <LinearLayout
            android:layout_width="match_parent"
```

```xml
        android:layout_height="match_parent"
        android:orientation="horizontal">

        <Button
            android:id="@+id/refresh_neighbors"
            style="@style/Widget.AppCompat.Button"
            android:layout_width="wrap_content"
            android:layout_height="wrap_content"
            android:text="@string/refresh_neighbors"
            android:textAllCaps="false" />

    </LinearLayout>

    <EditText
        android:id="@+id/neighbors_ip_address"
        android:layout_width="match_parent"
        android:layout_height="wrap_content"
        android:layout_marginEnd="5dp"
        android:ems="10"
        android:hint="@string/ip_address"
        android:inputType="textPersonName"
        android:nextFocusDown="@+id/neighbors_port" />

    <LinearLayout
        android:layout_width="match_parent"
        android:layout_height="match_parent"
        android:orientation="horizontal">

        <EditText
            android:id="@+id/neighbors_port"
            android:layout_width="0dp"
            android:layout_height="wrap_content"
            android:layout_weight="1"
            android:ems="10"
            android:hint="@string/port"
            android:inputType="number" />

        <EditText
            android:id="@+id/neighbors_scope_id"
            android:layout_width="0dp"
            android:layout_height="wrap_content"
            android:layout_marginEnd="5dp"
            android:layout_weight="1"
            android:ems="10"
            android:hint="@string/scope_id"
            android:inputType="textPersonName"
            android:nextFocusDown="@+id/proxy_ip_address" />
    </LinearLayout>

    <RadioGroup
        android:id="@+id/neighbors_ipv_radio_group"
        android:layout_width="match_parent"
        android:layout_height="0dp"
        android:layout_weight="1"
        android:checkedButton="@+id/neighbors_ipv4"
        android:orientation="horizontal">

        <RadioButton
            android:id="@+id/neighbors_ipv4"
            android:layout_width="match_parent"
            android:layout_height="wrap_content"
            android:layout_weight="1"
            android:checked="true"
```

```xml
                    android:text="@string/ipv4" />

            <RadioButton
                android:id="@+id/neighbors_ipv6"
                android:layout_width="match_parent"
                android:layout_height="wrap_content"
                android:layout_weight="1"
                android:text="@string/ipv6" />

            <Spinner
                android:id="@+id/neighbors_transport"
                android:layout_width="match_parent"
                android:layout_height="wrap_content"
                android:layout_marginEnd="5dp"
                android:layout_weight="1" />

        </RadioGroup>

        <EditText
            android:id="@+id/proxy_ip_address"
            android:layout_width="match_parent"
            android:layout_height="wrap_content"
            android:layout_marginEnd="5dp"
            android:ems="10"
            android:hint="@string/proxy_ip_address"
            android:inputType="textPersonName"
            android:nextFocusDown="@+id/proxy_port" />

        <LinearLayout
            android:layout_width="match_parent"
            android:layout_height="match_parent"
            android:orientation="horizontal">

            <EditText
                android:id="@+id/proxy_port"
                android:layout_width="0dp"
                android:layout_height="wrap_content"
                android:layout_weight="1"
                android:ems="10"
                android:hint="@string/proxy_port"
                android:inputType="number"
                android:nextFocusDown="@+id/ozone" />

            <Spinner
                android:id="@+id/proxy_type"
                android:layout_width="0dp"
                android:layout_height="wrap_content"
                android:layout_marginEnd="5dp"
                android:layout_weight="1" />
        </LinearLayout>

        <LinearLayout
            android:layout_width="match_parent"
            android:layout_height="match_parent"
            android:orientation="horizontal">

            <Button
                android:id="@+id/add_neighbor"
                style="@style/Widget.AppCompat.Button"
                android:layout_width="wrap_content"
                android:layout_height="wrap_content"
                android:text="@string/add"
                android:textAllCaps="false" />
```

```xml
                <Button
                    android:id="@+id/reset_neighbor_fields"
                    style="@style/Widget.AppCompat.Button"
                    android:layout_width="wrap_content"
                    android:layout_height="wrap_content"
                    android:text="@string/reset_fields"
                    android:textAllCaps="false" />
            </LinearLayout>

            <TextView
                android:layout_width="match_parent"
                android:layout_height="wrap_content"
                android:layout_marginEnd="5dp"
                android:background="@drawable/sectiongradient"
                android:paddingStart="5dp"
                android:paddingEnd="5dp"
                android:text="@string/ozones"
                android:textColor="@android:color/white"
                android:textSize="18sp"
                android:textStyle="normal|bold" />

            <android.support.v4.widget.NestedScrollView
                android:layout_width="match_parent"
                android:layout_height="200dp"
                android:layout_marginEnd="5dp"
                android:fadeScrollbars="false"
                android:scrollbars="vertical">

                <TableLayout
                    android:id="@+id/ozones"
                    android:layout_width="match_parent"
                    android:layout_height="wrap_content"
                    android:layout_marginEnd="5dp"
                    android:scrollbars="horizontal|vertical">

                </TableLayout>
            </android.support.v4.widget.NestedScrollView>

            <LinearLayout
                android:layout_width="match_parent"
                android:layout_height="match_parent"
                android:orientation="horizontal">

                <Button
                    android:id="@+id/refresh_ozones"
                    android:layout_width="wrap_content"
                    android:layout_height="wrap_content"
                    android:text="@string/refresh"
                    android:textAllCaps="false" />
            </LinearLayout>

            <LinearLayout
                android:layout_width="match_parent"
                android:layout_height="match_parent"
                android:orientation="horizontal">

                <EditText
                    android:id="@+id/ozone"
                    android:layout_width="0dp"
                    android:layout_height="wrap_content"
                    android:layout_weight="1"
                    android:ems="10"
```

```xml
                        android:hint="@string/address"
                        android:inputType="textPersonName" />

                    <Button
                        android:id="@+id/save_ozone"
                        style="@style/Widget.AppCompat.Button"
                        android:layout_width="wrap_content"
                        android:layout_height="wrap_content"
                        android:layout_marginEnd="5dp"
                        android:text="@string/save"
                        android:textAllCaps="false" />
                </LinearLayout>

                <TextView
                    android:layout_width="match_parent"
                    android:layout_height="wrap_content"
                    android:layout_marginEnd="5dp"
                    android:background="@drawable/sectiongradient"
                    android:paddingStart="5dp"
                    android:paddingEnd="5dp"
                    android:text="@string/participants"
                    android:textColor="@android:color/white"
                    android:textSize="18sp"
                    android:textStyle="normal|bold" />

                <TextView
                    android:layout_width="match_parent"
                    android:layout_height="wrap_content"
                    android:layout_marginEnd="5dp"

android:text="@string/retrieved_content_will_be_stored_for_approximately_one_w
eek" />

                <LinearLayout
                    android:layout_width="match_parent"
                    android:layout_height="match_parent"
                    android:orientation="horizontal">

                    <TextView
                        android:layout_width="0dp"
                        android:layout_height="wrap_content"
                        android:layout_weight="0.23"
                        android:text="@string/name" />

                    <TextView
                        android:layout_width="0dp"
                        android:layout_height="wrap_content"
                        android:layout_weight="0.3"
                        android:text="@string/smoke_id" />

                    <TextView
                        android:layout_width="0dp"
                        android:layout_height="wrap_content"
                        android:layout_weight="0.23"
                        android:text="@string/out_in_total" />

                    <TextView
                        android:layout_width="0dp"
                        android:layout_height="wrap_content"
                        android:layout_marginEnd="5dp"
                        android:layout_weight="0.23"
                        android:text="@string/last_activity" />
```

```xml
        </LinearLayout>

        <android.support.v4.widget.NestedScrollView
            android:layout_width="match_parent"
            android:layout_height="200dp"
            android:layout_marginEnd="5dp"
            android:fadeScrollbars="false"
            android:scrollbars="vertical">

            <TableLayout
                android:id="@+id/participants"
                android:layout_width="match_parent"
                android:layout_height="wrap_content"
                android:layout_marginEnd="5dp">

            </TableLayout>
        </android.support.v4.widget.NestedScrollView>

        <LinearLayout
            android:layout_width="match_parent"
            android:layout_height="match_parent"
            android:orientation="horizontal">

            <Button
                android:id="@+id/refresh_participants"
                style="@style/Widget.AppCompat.Button"
                android:layout_width="wrap_content"
                android:layout_height="wrap_content"
                android:text="@string/refresh_participants"
                android:textAllCaps="false" />
        </LinearLayout>

        <LinearLayout
            android:layout_width="match_parent"
            android:layout_height="match_parent"
            android:orientation="horizontal">

            <EditText
                android:id="@+id/participant_name"
                android:layout_width="0dp"
                android:layout_height="wrap_content"
                android:layout_weight="1"
                android:ems="10"
                android:hint="@string/name"
                android:inputType="textPersonName"
                android:nextFocusDown="@+id/participant_siphash_id" />

            <EditText
                android:id="@+id/participant_siphash_id"
                android:layout_width="0dp"
                android:layout_height="wrap_content"
                android:layout_marginEnd="5dp"
                android:layout_weight="1"
                android:ems="10"
                android:hint="@string/smoke_id"
                android:inputType="textPersonName" />

            <Button
                android:id="@+id/siphash_help"
                android:layout_width="32dp"
                android:layout_height="wrap_content"
                android:layout_marginEnd="5dp"
                android:layout_weight="0"
```

```xml
            android:background="@android:color/transparent"
            android:textAllCaps="false" />

    </LinearLayout>

    <CheckBox
        android:id="@+id/accept_without_signatures"
        android:layout_width="wrap_content"
        android:layout_height="wrap_content"
        android:text="@string/accept_without_signatures" />

    <LinearLayout
        android:layout_width="match_parent"
        android:layout_height="match_parent"
        android:orientation="horizontal">

        <Button
            android:id="@+id/add_participant"
            style="@style/Widget.AppCompat.Button"
            android:layout_width="wrap_content"
            android:layout_height="wrap_content"
            android:text="@string/add"
            android:textAllCaps="false" />

        <Button
            android:id="@+id/reset_participants_fields"
            style="@style/Widget.AppCompat.Button"
            android:layout_width="wrap_content"
            android:layout_height="wrap_content"
            android:text="@string/reset_fields"
            android:textAllCaps="false" />
    </LinearLayout>

    <TextView
        android:layout_width="match_parent"
        android:layout_height="wrap_content"
        android:layout_marginEnd="5dp"
        android:background="@drawable/sectiongradient"
        android:paddingStart="5dp"
        android:paddingEnd="5dp"
        android:text="@string/password"
        android:textColor="@android:color/white"
        android:textSize="18sp"
        android:textStyle="normal|bold" />

    <LinearLayout
        android:layout_width="match_parent"
        android:layout_height="match_parent"
        android:orientation="horizontal">

        <TextView
            android:layout_width="179dp"
            android:layout_height="wrap_content"
            android:text="@string/iteration_count"
            android:textSize="14sp" />

        <Spinner
            android:id="@+id/iteration_count"
            android:layout_width="0dp"
            android:layout_height="wrap_content"
            android:layout_marginEnd="5dp"
            android:layout_weight="1" />
```

```xml
        </LinearLayout>

        <EditText
            android:id="@+id/password1"
            android:layout_width="match_parent"
            android:layout_height="wrap_content"
            android:layout_marginEnd="5dp"
            android:ems="10"
            android:hint="@string/password"
            android:inputType="textPassword" />

        <EditText
            android:id="@+id/password2"
            android:layout_width="match_parent"
            android:layout_height="wrap_content"
            android:layout_marginEnd="5dp"
            android:ems="10"
            android:hint="@string/password_confirmation"
            android:inputType="textPassword" />

        <LinearLayout
            android:layout_width="match_parent"
            android:layout_height="match_parent"
            android:orientation="horizontal">

            <CheckBox
                android:id="@+id/overwrite"
                android:layout_width="wrap_content"
                android:layout_height="wrap_content" />

            <Button
                android:id="@+id/set_password"
                android:layout_width="wrap_content"
                android:layout_height="wrap_content"
                android:text="@string/set_password"
                android:textAllCaps="false" />
        </LinearLayout>

        <LinearLayout
            android:layout_width="match_parent"
            android:layout_height="match_parent"
            android:orientation="horizontal">

            <Button
                android:id="@+id/reset"
                style="@style/Widget.AppCompat.Button.Colored"
                android:layout_width="wrap_content"
                android:layout_height="wrap_content"
                android:text="@string/reset_smokestack"
                android:textAllCaps="false" />

        </LinearLayout>

            </LinearLayout>
        </ScrollView>
    </RelativeLayout>

</android.support.design.widget.CoordinatorLayout>
```

client_bubble.xml

https://raw.githubusercontent.com/textbrowser/smokestack/master/SmokeStack/app
/src/main/res/layout/client_bubble.xml

```xml
<RelativeLayout xmlns:android="http://schemas.android.com/apk/res/android"
    xmlns:app="http://schemas.android.com/apk/res-auto"
    xmlns:tools="http://schemas.android.com/tools"
    android:layout_width="match_parent"
    android:layout_height="wrap_content">

    <TextView
        android:id="@+id/address"
        android:layout_width="match_parent"
        android:layout_height="wrap_content" />

</RelativeLayout>
```


authenticate_menu.xml

https://raw.githubusercontent.com/textbrowser/smokestack/master/SmokeStack/app
/src/main/res/menu/authenticate_menu.xml

```xml
<menu xmlns:android="http://schemas.android.com/apk/res/android">
    <item
        android:id="@+id/action_exit"
        android:orderInCategory="100"
        android:title="@string/exit" />
    <item
        android:id="@+id/action_settings"
        android:orderInCategory="200"
        android:title="@string/action_settings" />
</menu>
```


settings_menu.xml

https://raw.githubusercontent.com/textbrowser/smokestack/master/SmokeStack/app
/src/main/res/menu/settings_menu.xml

```xml
<menu xmlns:android="http://schemas.android.com/apk/res/android">
    <item
        android:id="@+id/action_authenticate"
        android:orderInCategory="100"
        android:title="@string/authenticate" />
    <item
        android:id="@+id/action_exit"
        android:orderInCategory="200"
        android:title="@string/exit" />
</menu>
```


colors.xml

https://raw.githubusercontent.com/textbrowser/smokestack/master/SmokeStack/app
/src/main/res/values/colors.xml

```xml
<?xml version="1.0" encoding="utf-8"?>
<resources>
    <color name="colorGray">#2B292E</color>
    <color name="colorPrimaryDark">#303F9F</color>
    <color name="colorAccent">#FF4081</color>
</resources>
```

dimens.xml

https://raw.githubusercontent.com/textbrowser/smokestack/master/SmokeStack/app/src/main/res/values/dimens.xml

```xml
<resources>
    <!-- Default screen margins, per the Android Design guidelines. -->
    <dimen name="activity_horizontal_margin">16dp</dimen>
    <dimen name="activity_vertical_margin">16dp</dimen>
</resources>
```

strings.xml

https://raw.githubusercontent.com/textbrowser/smokestack/master/SmokeStack/app/src/main/res/values/strings.xml

```xml
<resources>
    <string name="about">About</string>
    <string name="accept_without_signatures">Accept Without
Signatures</string>
    <string name="action_settings">Settings</string>
    <string name="add">Add</string>
    <string name="address">Address</string>
    <string name="app_name">SmokeStack</string>
    <string name="authenticate">Authenticate</string>
    <string name="authenticate_authenticate">Authenticate</string>
    <string name="authenticate_password">Password</string>
    <string name="automatic_refresh">Automatic Refresh</string>
    <string name="clear_log">Clear Log</string>
    <string name="control">Control</string>
    <string name="details">Details</string>
    <string name="ip_address">IP Address</string>
    <string name="ipv4">IPv4</string>
    <string name="ipv6">IPv6</string>
    <string name="iteration_count">Iteration Count</string>
    <string name="last_activity">Last Activity</string>
    <string name="listeners">Listeners</string>
    <string name="remote_clients">Remote Clients</string>
    <string name="name">Name</string>
    <string name="neighbors">Neighbors</string>
    <string name="out_in_total">Out / In / Total</string>
    <string name="ozones">Ozones</string>
    <string name="participants">Participants</string>
    <string name="password">Password</string>
    <string name="password_confirmation">Password Confirmation</string>
    <string name="port">Port</string>
    <string name="private_server">Private Server</string>
    <string name="proxy_ip_address">Proxy IP Address</string>
    <string name="proxy_port">Proxy Port</string>
    <string name="refresh">Refresh</string>
    <string name="refresh_neighbors">Refresh</string>
    <string name="refresh_participants">Refresh</string>
    <string name="remote">Remote</string>
    <string name="reset_fields">Reset Fields</string>
    <string name="reset_smokestack">Reset SmokeStack</string>
    <string
name="retrieved_content_will_be_stored_for_approximately_one_week">Retrieved
content will be stored for approximately one week.</string>
    <string name="save">Save</string>
    <string name="scope_id">Scope ID</string>
    <string name="set_password">Set Password</string>
    <string name="settings">Settings</string>
    <string name="smoke_id">Smoke ID</string>
```

```
    <string name="steam">Steam</string>
    <string name="exit">Exit</string>
    <string name="recycle_memory">Recycle Memory</string>
</resources>
```

styles.xml

https://raw.githubusercontent.com/textbrowser/smokestack/master/SmokeStack/app
/src/main/res/values/styles.xml

```
<resources>

    <!-- Base application theme. -->
    <style name="AppTheme" parent="Theme.AppCompat.Light.DarkActionBar">
        <!-- Customize your theme here. -->
        <item name="colorPrimary">@color/colorGray</item>
        <item name="colorPrimaryDark">@color/colorPrimaryDark</item>
        <item name="colorAccent">@color/colorAccent</item>
    </style>

</resources>
```

References:

Ackermann, Evelyn & Klein, Michael (2020): Caesura in Cryptography: My first Workshop about Encryption - An Introduction with Teaching and Learning Material for School, University and Leisure, 2020, PDF-E-Book ISBN 978-3752676921.

Nomenclatura (2019): Encyclopedia of modern Cryptography and Internet Security: From AutoCrypt and Exponential Encryption to Zero-Knowledge-Proof Keys, ISBN: 978-3748191513 & ISBN: 978-3746066684.

Smoke (2017): Documentation of the Android Messenger Application Smoke, URL: https://github.com/textbrowser/smoke/raw/master/Documentation/Smoke.pdf, 2017.

SmokeStack (2017): Server Software for Echo Messaging, URL: https://github.com/textbrowser/smokestack.

Spot-On Suite: Handbook and User Manual as practical software guide, ISBN: 978-3749435067.

Wake, Mancy A. / Hibernack, Dorothy / Lullaby, Lucas (2020): Echo on a Chip (EoC) – A New Perception for the Next Generation of Micro-Controllers handling Encryption for Mobile Messaging: From Secure Embedded Systems to Separated Secure Embedded Systems (SSES) in Cryptography. Hardware supported Trusted Execution Environments (TEE) for Encryption / Decryption Processes separated from Transport-Processes and Server-Processes respective even other Operational Processes, ISBN 9783751916448.